History and the Texture of Modern Life

History and the Texture of Modern Life

Selected Essays

Lucy Maynard Salmon

Edited by
NICHOLAS ADAMS and BONNIE G. SMITH

PENN

University of Pennsylvania Press

Philadelphia

Copyright © 2001 University of Pennsylvania Press
Printed in the United States of America on acid-free paper

10 9 8 7 6 5 4 3 2 1

Published by
University of Pennsylvania Press
Philadelphia, Pennsylvania 19104-4011

Library of Congress Cataloging-in-Publication Data
Salmon, Lucy Maynard, 1853–1927.
    [Essays. Selections]
    History and the texture of modern life: Selected essays / Lucy Maynard Salmon ; edited by
Nicholas Adams and Bonnie G. Smith.
        p. cm.
    Includes bibliographical references (p.   ) and index.
    ISBN 0-8122-3587-8 (cloth : alk. paper)
    1. Salmon, Lucy Maynard, 1853–1927.   2. Histories — United States — Biography.
3. Women historians — United States — Biography.   4. Historians — Untied States — History —
20th century.   I. Adams, Nicholas.   II. Smith, Bonnie G., 1940–   III. Title.
D15.S35   A25   2001
973 — dc21   00-062863

Contents

Introduction

Lucy Maynard Salmon and the Texture of Modern Life

NICHOLAS ADAMS AND BONNIE G. SMITH

A little more than a century ago, Lucy Maynard Salmon started down an intellectual path that made her one of the most innovative historians of all time. Among the first and most distinguished professional women scholars, Salmon developed novel forms of historical analysis and a strikingly original modernist writing style. Her topics included education, newspapers, the household, and municipal life, but increasingly her career centered on questions of historical writing: the collection, organization, evaluation, and presentation of the past. Born in upstate New York in 1853 — in the same generation as the celebrated modernists Friedrich Nietzsche and Sigmund Freud — Salmon wrote presciently about topics in history that have become major academic subjects only in the past few decades: the historical museum, the cookbook, the vernacular landscape, train schedules and clocks, the mass media, and consumption. Although James Harvey Robinson would lay claim to beginning this kind of "New History" in 1912, by that time Salmon had already written on the kitchen, the backyard, and many other subjects. While others continued the professional historian's mission to delve into the intricacies of politics, Salmon forged an avant-garde approach with an object-based historical epistemology and pedagogy.

Displaying a broad, integrated vision of history, Salmon was lionized wherever she traveled by the late 1890s, receiving warm welcomes from such foreign celebrities as actress Sarah Bernhardt, historian Charles Seignobos, and archaeologist Sir Arthur Evans. One might accurately call her the most famous woman historian from the English-speaking world, someone who bucked the trend to Balkanize historical research and teaching. A force to be reckoned with in the American Historical Association for her dedication to advancing pedagogy and scholarship, she nonetheless was shy and serious, prone to bouts of depression after stretches of hard work. Critics found her final publications far richer than those of the young Alan Nevins, but they also disparaged her because her historical vision was so broad and new. Salmon was the typical woman professional of these early years, earnest and sober minded: "I was surprised at such an outburst of humor of the genuine sort," one of her relatives exclaimed about a piece of her writing, "from so sedate a person as yourself."[1] In terms of intellect, however, she was far from sedate, spinning out wild historical ideas and advocating a new role for the historian from within the confines of Vassar College.

Fig. 1. Lucy Maynard Salmon, ca. 1905. Courtesy of Vassar College, Special Collections.

Who would suspect this rebelliousness from a daughter of upstate New York? Her father, George Salmon, owned a tannery—George Salmon and Son Manufacturer of Hemlock Sole and Rough Leather—and engaged in vigorous good works, while her mother, Maria Maynard Salmon, pioneered new methods of teaching after attending Mary Lyons's Ipswich Academy.[2] Both mother and father were deeply religious, and George frequently asked his daughter about the state of her religious belief. Though Maria died when Lucy was seven, the Salmon family's daily reading of newspapers set the agenda for dinner conversations, and busy-ness was a family creed, too. As a teenager Salmon went to boarding school followed by four years at the University of Michigan starting in 1872, where she studied with Charles Kendall Adams, a student of Andrew Dickson White. Adams's teaching of history depended on the new "seminar" method, which he had just introduced at Michigan. Adams claimed that women were not "suitable for seminar work," but Salmon flourished in his seminar and maintained contact with her teacher. At every point in her academic career, Salmon was an eager student, despite her father's death while she was in college. She overcame bouts of depression with work and kept in touch with her remaining family members, including her stepmother.

Salmon's early intellectual horizons at Michigan are also suggested by her membership in the women-only "Q.C." group at which members introduced themselves at roll call with quotations from "Whittier, Lowell, Bret Harte, Macaulay, Bacon, Ruskin," a notable list of progressive and naturalistic authors.[3] She graduated in 1876 and taught at the high school in McGregor, Iowa, for six years before returning to the University of Michigan for her master's degree, which she received in 1883. She described her decision to take up graduate study as resulting from a conversation with her brother, who had seen her looking haggard and drawn at the prospect of returning to teaching: "Before the day was over I had planned for graduate work at Ann Arbor."[4]

From 1883 until 1886, she was an admired and innovative teacher at the Normal School in Terre Haute, Indiana. Yet Salmon wanted more education herself, and when she was offered a fellowship to pursue her research at Bryn Mawr, she left secondary teaching for good, though she would become one of the most influential forces in developing the high school history curriculum across the United States. Woodrow Wilson, then a professor of political science and history at Bryn Mawr, oversaw Salmon's research, which she pursued by commuting to libraries in Philadelphia several times a week. Charles Kendall Adams had warned her, however, of Wilson's shortcomings, especially that he would know far less history than she did. Just remember, Adams consoled her, "it is better to give than to receive." In the 1920s, looking back at Wilson for his biographer, Ray Stannard Baker, Salmon offered a devastating comment on his character and intellectual cast of mind. It was clear from the beginning, she remembered, that he had no interest in her mental development, though he met with her faithfully three times a week for two hours. In less than an hour she reported on her studies and findings. Then, instead of pursuing issues raised by her work in the time remaining, he mainly talked about himself. Salmon's assessment was that Wilson had only one topic of conversation — his personal advancement. He had become a college professor not out of interest, as he admitted, but because there was no palatable route to political power as in England. Owing to his inability to discuss contemporary issues or politics, try as she might to direct the conversation away from rehearsals of his disillusionments, Salmon saw Wilson as intellectually deficient and unsuitable for the civic leadership he eventually attained.[5]

Once she had completed her M.A. thesis, acclaim came quickly, for her subsequent publication on the appointive powers of the president was a masterwork that gained fame among historians, winning a prize from the recently founded American Historical Association. It appeared in the first volume of the AHA *Papers* in 1886, the only article by a woman in the *Papers* and a much-admired piece of scholarship.[6] Senator George Franklin Edmunds of Vermont described it as "the best thing that had ever been written on the subject," and it was favorably reviewed in *Harper's*.[7] Salmon was rewarded with a position on the executive council of the American Historical Association, though she was often unable to join her fellow council members for dinner after their meetings, which were held in clubs that excluded women.

"History of the Appointing Power of the President" showcased the virtues of the new scientific history. As in much of her early work, historical sections preceded the analysis of current problems and recommendations for reform. In her thesis Salmon described the efforts of the new republic to strike a balance between the absolute right of the president to make appointments and the congressional need for oversight. Reform legislation passed in 1820, for example, limited tax collectors to four-year terms, but the result was not reform. Instead, it became the source of rewards for political cronyism rather than payment for honorable service. In a satirical passage that foreshadows the range of her interests and her mature style of expression, Salmon contrasted current governmental practices with those of society at large.

No man refused to accept his morning mail from a postman who did not agree with him, in regard to internal improvements made at government expense, nor did he welcome the tax-gatherer more cordially because a believer in his favorite hobby of free trade, nor think twice before sending for a fire company, every member of which disagreed with him in regard to a national bank, nor hesitate to summon a policeman who was a Know-Nothing, though himself a bitter enemy of the organization. No one organized a raid on the business of a successful grocer, on the pleas that he had enjoyed the emoluments of trade long enough, and someone else needed the store. No company of "workers" demanded that a leading banker should dismiss a teller of ten years' experience in order to employ someone who had voted the straight ticket. No railroad president was urged to dismiss a hundred conductors and employ instead a disbanded company of Mexican soldiers. No proprietor of the Fifth Avenue Hotel was threatened with loss of patronage in case he refused to discharge his waiters in favor of one-armed soldiers whose terms had expired. No man was recommended as a college president because he had been successful as an internal-revenue inspector. Yet practically the same absurdities were committed day after day in local, State, and Government service.[8]

In short, Salmon used the results of her analysis to show how history and the historian's critical insight were potential agents for change, and she looked forward to a truly reformed period "when the chief Executive can boast like the great Premier that his sole patronage is the appointment of his private secretary; when every legislator can say, with a leading member of the House of Commons, that he is without power to influence in the smallest degree the appointment of a customhouse officer or an exciseman."[9] Scientific history would prepare the way for that improved future.

In 1887 Salmon accepted a post at Vassar College in Poughkeepsie, New York, and began as the sole instructor of economics, political science, and history there. None of these was a regular part of the curriculum at the time, though Salmon developed the Vassar history department as a lively, integrated teaching corps within little more than a decade. She introduced the seminar method there, taught students to use the library and do research, and encouraged them to found historical associations, libraries, and archives after they graduated and entered community life. While recognizing her talent, Vassar's administration resisted the changes she introduced. In steadfastly breaking with traditions of rote learning, however, Salmon transformed Vassar. She took seriously the young institution's goal of educating women, but she pushed its mission harder than its founders had perhaps intended, and Vassar College became renowned for its history department and its graduates.

By the end of her first decade at Vassar, Salmon was deeply involved in her teaching, but she ventured further, organizing a range of professional initiatives and pursuing a crushing research agenda. She helped found groups that would evolve into the American Association of University Women (AAUW) for women graduates of universities and the College Board for the development of standardized university entrance exams. She chaired the first committee for the history examination. Simultaneously, she threw herself into the work of the American Historical Association and was one of the first women to have any influence in that organization. Given her experience as a secondary and normal school teacher, Salmon became a member of the Committee of Seven, whose mission was to expand and guide the teaching of history in the schools. At the time, history was a fledgling member of the curriculum, if it was included at all. Moreover, few of the professional standards then taking shape in newly modernized curricula and manuals of scientific historical method had trickled down to secondary and grammar schools.[10] Traveling around the eastern United States, Salmon advocated a history program suitable for every level of intellectual development: from vivid stories for the very young to unifying themes and critical thinking for the more advanced to a more sophisticated level of actual historical production by those in colleges and universities. The very existence of these levels meant that all teachers had to be aware of history's complexity, especially its multiple guises, its array of primary material, and the constant need for revision.

Salmon's energetic travels on behalf of educational reform were congruent with the reform spirit of suffragists and Progressive women. Abundant in the early twentieth century, women's efforts emerged from a belief that society could be changed for the better with study and hard work. Reformers worked to relieve bad treatment of children, to reform delinquents, to improve the lot of immigrants, and to break barriers to women's economic and political equality. Jane Addams's Hull House in Chicago, for example, was one of the institutions resulting from this progressive confidence. Consumer leagues aimed to improve the conditions of workers by boycotting manufacturers who employed exploitative labor practices. Social work developed as a major component of civic life. Salmon, amid nagging bouts of depression, shared the faith that study, dissemination of social scientific findings, and commitment to civic virtue would benefit almost every branch of the social order. In Salmon's view, knowledge existed to be used, former student Caroline Ware reported.[11]

Such a set of beliefs was unusual among historians, many of whom were conservative, but even those who could be labeled Progressive hardly deployed their beliefs in the original way Salmon did. In the 1880s, just as she arrived at Vassar, she began an investigation into the history, economics, and contemporary conditions of domestic labor. The topic was bizarre for a historian, and her methods were equally innovative. Influenced by techniques used in the fledgling social sciences, and with the help of her first classes at Vassar, Salmon mailed thousands of questionnaires (she called them "schedules") on the conditions of household service to women's exchanges, clubs, agencies, groups of Vassar alumnae, and other organizations to distribute to individuals in their purview. She tapped relatives and old friends and their relatives and friends—anyone her fertile mind designated a likely source. It was the first statistical survey of domestic work undertaken in the United States, and its findings would engage a broad public.

The survey, unusual indeed as the tool of the historian in those days, asked for a range of quantifiable data, including age, length of service, and category of service. It also posed more qualitative questions about reasons both for choosing service over other types of employment and for remaining on the job. Salmon ultimately used a local consulting firm and the Massachusetts Bureau of Statistics of Labor to help compile the data, laying out hundreds of dollars of her own. The result was her second monograph, *Domestic Service* (1897), a work that received hundreds of reviews. The verdict was mixed. The professional and literary worlds were shocked that an honored historian should produce a work on so degraded a topic, "unworthy of her talents," the *Nation* decried.[12] Other groups outside the academy, especially those wedded to rational social change, hailed the book and recognized the value of Salmon's message that the one place in the U.S. polity immune from equality, democratic civic values, and rational organization was the household. Still another round of speaking obligations ensued.

The first part of the book consisted of a discussion of household work in the colonies and the changing role of the servant in American life. It quoted extensively from early diaries and legal documents. In the second section Salmon reported on the questionnaire, and by placing the statistical survey in a historical context she could evaluate the nature of the proposals that had been made for the improvement of conditions for domestic service. In these chapters, dealing with "doubtful" and "possible" remedies, Salmon demonstrated the value of scientific history applied to contemporary problems. "It is the opinion of a very large class that all difficulties can be removed by the application of the golden rule," she wrote.[13] And she proceeded to show how economic competition from other industries "where the golden rule may be observed with equal conscientiousness" would still have the effect of draining the potential labor pool.[14] The evidence of the survey also convinced her that cooperative housekeeping, despite its many advantages, would also fail because "the majority of persons do not wish it."[15] As Marion Talbot noted in her review in the *Journal of Political Economy*: "Domestic service is everywhere made a topic of conversation of gossip. The value of Miss Salmon's work lies largely in showing that it should rather be a subject for scientific investigation and study."[16]

The book was an extraordinary success among the reform public at large. The issue of household work was much on people's minds, as it had been since the Civil War.[17] The freeing of the slaves had raised moral issues about service, and the rise of an industrial infrastructure keen to employ young women in assembly-line manufacturing had created a dearth of workers to sustain bourgeois society's abhorrence of household work for middle- and upper-class women. In addition, new technologies made special demands on domestic workers, freeing them from certain kinds of labor but creating the need for new skills. Scientific history thus brought welcome order to the debate.[18] There were reviews in all the major newspapers in the United States and Great Britain. As the reviewer for the Boston *Evening Transcript* wrote: "*Domestic Service* should have a place on the table in every home, and should be read by every housekeeper and by anyone who is in any way interested in the subject of economics."[19] Salmon also received personal testimonials and was, ever after, in demand as a speaker on the theme at women's clubs and exchanges. A typical letter came from a certain Harriet M. Scott in Pasadena following the publication of the second edition in 1901. Scott was interested in setting up a school for domestic science, and she had read Salmon's book in the Los Angeles Public Library "with as great delight as many women read the latest novel."[20]

Nonetheless, the end of this effort dragged Salmon down another level in the cycle of depression, and she applied for a sabbatical. One could see this as the not unusual aftermath of releasing a book to the publisher. But in Salmon's case, overwork and historians' ambivalent reception of *Domestic Service*, in which she had invested so much money, time, and original thought, may have also contributed. Not only was Salmon fulfilling many obligations in the professional world; at Vassar she lived in a dormitory and continued pedagogical innovation. The seminar method, for instance, meant that instead of meeting with a single group she met with several smaller ones, doubling and tripling the time spent in the classroom. Teaching in her own room, she gave unstintingly to students and alumni, encouraging the latter in their civic and scholarly pursuits. Most of all, the regimentation of college life weighed on her: "I sigh for a quiet corner where I shall not have to get up by a bell, eat by a bell, talk by priority of appointment and dress according to other people's standard of propriety."[21] She longed to live like a normal member of a community.

With many of these concerns uppermost, Salmon set out for Europe in the summer of 1898. Her agenda was full, for she aimed to report on innovations in pedagogy, brush up her several languages, visit historic sites, buy books for the Vassar library, and do original research. From sordid scenes of urban growth in England to the social exhilaration of Paris where she threw herself into investigating schools and doing research, Salmon worked every terrain. She bought as many books of primary materials for the library as Vassar would allow and lamented the college's accusation that she was making personal purchases. Wherever she went, she questioned leading scholars for the latest trends in research. The privileges men received made her jealous. For example, she wished that Vassar's women students could enjoy the same facilities as the young men at the Ecole Normale Supérieure. Society opened up to her, allowing inspections of lycées and gymnasia and attendance at lectures on the latest in colonial ventures. And European politics — the Dreyfus affair and the Boer War, most notably — provided the subjects for her developing political acuity.[22]

As her return to Vassar loomed at the end of a year, Salmon begged for and received another year off, during which she traveled to Italy and Greece and hoped to go to Istanbul. The payoff was large. She was open, energized, ripe for new ventures, and full of ideas: she labeled the experience "her belated girlhood."[23] Free from the constraints of Vassar's propriety, her mind was galvanized by contemporary politics, and she produced a book arguing against the imperial fever that had gripped Europe and the United States. The manuscript went against the current of public opinion and as importantly against the gender order, as prospective publishers bluntly told her: "Nobody cares a straw what a woman has to say on a public question (unless she writes to the newspapers on the horrors of war and signs the letter 'A Mother')," she wrote bitterly to former pupil and Vassar librarian Adelaide Underhill. Some editors suggested anonymous publication; others, a pseudonym. Salmon went on to propose that the manuscript receive a new title page and acknowledgments, the first with the author listed as L. M.

H. Salmon, with the latter thanking "a friend" (instead of Underhill) as proofreader and indexer. "It is the conventional phrase a man always uses when he means his wife."[24]

"Imperialism" was never published, but, still in Europe, Salmon was developing another major strand in her life's work — that on historical source material. She envisioned that her new methodological approach would have the working title *History*, and its universality suggested the range of vision Salmon had achieved. To Underhill she proposed using all the varied sources available to historians to write their narratives. The historical museum appeared to her at this time as a topic ripe for study and interpretation, and so did monuments: "My material has been absolutely lacking on the side of the relation of monumental and literary historical evidence."[25] She had also studied numismatics and other sources during these intense two years. Of all her many European experiences the most powerful was the visit to Corfú, where she was shown around the excavations by Arthur Evans and had firsthand experience of a history without written texts in company with a knowledgeable guide.[26] Walking the streets of fast-paced European cities had revealed layers of history, the stark contrast between former times and a burgeoning modernity as the late 1890s saw a building boom replete with Art Nouveau style and the first glimpses of buildings influenced by the clean lines of Japanese buildings. She was starting to direct her eyes differently, training them on novel historical sources.

Simply put, in the years up to and including World War I, Salmon developed an object-based epistemology that anticipates many of the ideas that James Harvey Robinson was to group under the heading of New History.[27] At the opening of the twentieth century, she was casting a far wider net than anyone else, one woven certainly from her travels and experiences of European monuments but ironically stretched to include the objects of everyday life. In 1901 Salmon and Adelaide Underhill set up housekeeping outside the Vassar walls in downtown Poughkeepsie. They became a team, intertwining their lives and concerns. When either was traveling, they wrote daily letters. From Europe Salmon chronicled her intellectual breakthroughs and even when apart briefly in the United States conveyed her passionate feelings of absence and longing: "This is the last day of the very happiest year I have ever known because the only year in which I could claim you every day," she wrote at the end of 1902. She closed her letters with "Love, — inexhaustible, unending, for you alone" and "How I wish it were possible to tell you even half my love."[28] It was a partnership of intimates.

Details of their housekeeping also appeared in their correspondence. The house was decorated with some Victorian furniture combined with a dining set from United Crafts of Eastwood, New York, and other modern pieces from Gustav Stickley, the Arts and Crafts furniture maker. The gradual introduction of electrical appliances testified to Salmon's general love of the modern, which also included photography, bicycling, and regular use of

Fig. 2. Lucy Maynard Salmon and Adelaide Underhill occupied the right-hand house at 263 Mill Street in Poughkeepsie, New York.

the typewriter for her correspondence. They received many guests, who admired the home's modern kitchen, arranged for efficient, rational house-work, and the execution of one of Salmon's major themes: that the private sphere should enjoy the same modern sense of civility and democracy as the public world. Thus, a succession of household helpers were addressed by their surnames and the courtesy titles of Mr., Miss, or Mrs.; they also partici-pated in household governance and received other public sphere consider-ations: The house and its small staff became another of Salmon's preoccupa-tions, absorbing both attention and money.

The experience proved as liberating as the sojourn in Europe, opening a world of observation unfamiliar to someone who had boarded for her entire adult life. In 1901 Salmon began a short essay, "Housekeeping," in which she denounced a world ruled by bells that dealt out ignominy, including cold meals or none at all, for those who ran late. Turned out of the dorms in the summer, the author described herself willingly heading for Europe. But then the incivility and tyranny of it all pushed her into setting up her own household, replete with its new sights and routines. The first day yielded a trip to the market, but the take was greater than that, for the novice house-keeper discovered the streets and backyards of Poughkeepsie: "As one may find a world of new interests in the backyard of a New York City home, so the boarder by taking unto himself a house and shifting the scenes of his daily work may find undreamed of pleasures." The move to housekeeping fur-ther exposed the view of the everyday landscape that formed the foundation of Salmon's work over the next decade.

> It is impossible to describe our sense of importance as we started out the first morning with basket and fillet to do errands. We had always secretly scorned our city friends who apparently spent their lives shopping and doing errands, but now we realized that they were pursuits always to be followed, never to be completed. The morning errands were succeeded by the noon errands as these were in turn by those of the afternoon. And evening found us making out the list of errands to be done the next day. We felt a sort of community of interest with the whole world when we discovered that doing errands rose to the dignity of paid occupation in the person of the professional errand man who went daily into the nearest metropolis and for a small charge did the errands that could not be done in the smaller city.[29]

What had been an academic study of housekeeping in *Domestic Service* became personal experience, as an essay about her kitchen also revealed.[30] A renovation, the kitchen had been "planned by the landlord and carpenter for unknown tenants, and the general arrangement had conformed to the plan of a house built many years before." Despite the thoughtless nature of the original work, she shows how it has been possible to arrange the func-tional elements of the room for maximum efficiency. The three significant walls of the room have been divided by the women into a "cooking side," a "baking side," and a "cleaning side." Traditional elements of the kitchen — pots, pans, sinks, and the like — are mixed with newer devices, including an electric fan, a gas range, and an instantaneous water heater. The kitchen, she argues, requires its own "unity of plan," and she goes on, expressing the connection between society and object through a language of functionalism that recalls Frank Lloyd Wright's contemporaneous formulation of an or-ganic "art and craft of the machine."[31]

During these years Salmon churned out dozens of articles, many of them published later as collections that worked two domestic themes: that the household should be rational and civil and that the world of ordinary peo-ple was dense with historical evidence. Technically, none of this was new, for amateur women historians had gained enormous popularity in the nine-teenth century writing on the details of social and cultural life, their work claiming the immanence of history in objects. At the turn of the century Alice Morse Earle was but one of those earning a living from histories of furniture, kitchens, and domestic customs. Whereas Earle easily found publishers, however, Salmon did not. Earle's work drew in the casual reader, aroused historical nostalgia, focused in large part on the rich historical context for objects, and attracted a growing pool of connoisseurs and collectors. In contrast, Salmon aimed for a scientific audience, primarily of professional scholars but also of well-educated citizens. She tried mightily to place the many articles of these years in broadly marketed elite journals like the *Nation* or the more scholarly *Yale Review*; even such luminous pieces as "History in a Back Yard" were rejected. "Ode to a Kitchen Sink," "The Family Cook-Book," and "Our Kitchen" spilled from her pen, and most found their audience in the *Vassar Miscellany*, *Vassar Quarterly*, and *Good Housekeeping*.

In the early twentieth century, Salmon was more successful in publishing works espousing democracy and the rational operation of daily life. While continuing her activities for educational reform, both at Vassar and in school curricula, she produced many an essay outlining the shortfalls in the realization of full civic participation. Vassar College was her prime example during the prewar period. Its president, James Monroe Taylor, thwarted Salmon at almost every turn — from her purchase of library books to her ideas about history. Indeed, Taylor's opposition sharpened Salmon's wits, for he was an adversary against whose theories she pitted her own. With ultimate authority in a board of trustees drawn from outside education, Vassar exemplified ill-informed and tyrannical rule. Salmon produced essays on these matters, claiming that the faculty-run universities of imperial Germany were democratic while the trustee-governed institutions of the supposedly democratic United States were dictatorial. She also wrote on behalf of "progress" in the household, and many of these works appeared in the *Educational Review* and then *Progress in the Household* in 1906. She bucked conventional wisdom in many arenas and was not a conventional member of Progressive Era society. Urged to read a popular book written by Madison Grant on eugenics and the perils of miscegenation, she rebutted a Vassar alumna's endorsement of the work: "I have always felt that our great strength as a nation has come from the mingling of the many races in it and never feared the 'racial abyss' that Mr. Grant thinks confronts us."[32]

Salmon put many of her beliefs into action. A committed suffragist, she nonetheless debated suffragists who did not know their history or law. She herself tried out dress reform, although such attire was forbidden by Vassar officials, who found it unladylike. In Poughkeepsie, she agitated for good government, urban improvements like playgrounds and parks, and rational urban planning. She brought the planning expert John Nolen to Vassar and sought his advice concerning improvements in Poughkeepsie. At Vassar she fought against an honors program because it undemocratically promoted a quest for marks of distinction rather than a love of learning, and she declined membership in the University of Michigan's Phi Beta Kappa society for the same reason. Her campaign for democracy at Vassar went further, however, as by the 1920s she had successfully achieved a measure of faculty rule in matters of curriculum and staffing. She championed free speech and self-rule for students, vigorously objecting to the system of hall wardens and the censorship of student meetings.

Although her relationship with the Vassar College administration was rarely steady, Salmon's dedication to Vassar as an institution suggests that, whatever its flaws, she saw it as her crucible for women's education, the place where she could bring to bear her learning and experience. Thus she analyzed its political structure, aiming to show the relation between normal practices in society at large and practices within the institution. In a way, she started asking low and ordinary questions about an institution that was supposed to be exclusively high and ideal. What, she asked, explains "the spirit of carping criticism that prevails on all sides" at Vassar?[33] Her analysis concerned the confusion between the activities of Vassar College as a residential living unit and Vassar College as an educational institution, a confusion exacerbated because not all institutions of higher education had residential facilities and the relation between residential and educational institutions was not articulated under the law of the state or under the laws of the institution. Practically speaking, she concluded, the residents of the college were disenfranchised. Her opinions on faculty governance were a continual thorn in the administration's side. She also rewrote the canonical scholarly historical narrative of the college. One essay discusses the role of Lydia Booth (1803–54), a niece of Matthew Vassar, in the founding of the college. Booth ran a school for girls in Poughkeepsie, and it was she who encouraged Matthew Vassar to found a college for women. "It is a fact that every student and every graduate of Vassar College should know and keep in mind, and every year as the memory of Matthew Vassar is honored on Founder's Day there should be united with it the name and memory of Lydia Booth. Without the fortune contributed by Mr. Vassar the college could not have been founded, but without the idea given by Miss Booth that fortune would have been given to another object."[34]

Drawing on an increasingly vast array of intellectual and activist ingredients, Salmon's teaching also grew more complex in her fifties and sixties. She lobbied to reduce class size across the college so that students might concentrate on developing their powers of observation — whatever the field. It was this modern skill that Salmon promoted above all others and for an ever-widening range of materials and venues. She stumped her junior colleagues with her proposals that they accompany her class on walking historical excursions. President Taylor saw such exercises as wastes of time: "I am wondering sometimes whether, in some of our departments, we are not tending too much to pictorial illustration, and whether it is not better in the main to hold students to the more strenuous use of their minds."[35] Salmon, however, by 1907 had published an article containing photographs of rocks as evidence of the history of New York.[36] The bewilderment was general:

"Your suggestion of 'an historical garden' puzzles me," assistant professor Violet Barbour wrote. "You will have to explain it in full to me when I am back in Poughkeepsie so that I may help in any way I can. There is a painful lack of constructive imagination in my make-up as a teacher."[37] For most novices, trained in the new scientific history (as Salmon herself had been), excursions, gardens, museums, and monuments seemed to have only slight connection if any to their metier.

It becomes apparent that Salmon's historical innovations were operating on two fronts. To accompany an object-based epistemology she was initiating an object-based pedagogy, as she devised a curriculum using an array of items from material culture. Even the history books themselves were to be the object of study. In a lecture delivered in New Orleans in December 1903 she announced:

> To the average freshman entering college, the history he used in the high school was large or small and had a red cover over a green back. Ask him why the history he studies has a preface, why it has a table of contents, what the difference is between the table of contents and the index, why the book is divided into chapters, why the page has a margin, what matter goes into the body of the page, what into the footnotes, and what into the appendices, why the book has illustrations, why different kinds of type are used, in a word, the explanation of the external difference between his history and his algebra, and he confesses that he has never noticed any special difference: to the average boy, a book is a book. . . . The child clamors for "true stories." Ask the boy how he knows the history he studies is true, and he cannot tell. Ask him where he can find the letter of recommendation which the book should carry with it, and he does not know. Ask him whether the name, by which he calls the book, is that of the author or that of the publishing house, willing to assume the responsibility for authorship, shirked by the author himself, and again he does not know. The history, as regards its external form and its internal character, is to him a chemical unknown, but it does not always occur either to him or to his instructor to treat it as such.[38]

From the examination of the book she turned to examination of the world around the student, such as the names of towns and other evidence of the successive waves of migration. Domestic and civil architecture offered "another opportunity for training the observation," and she showed how the forms of architecture reflected the societies from which they derived and how they were transformed by the societies that took them up. Thus, in this period following her return from Europe Salmon sketched in a new role for the historian as interpreter of the way history is refracted in its many representations: in language, myth, legend, and tradition, to be sure, but as she would demonstrate in the newspaper, in art and architecture, and most surprisingly in the vernacular landscape and cityscape, in the fences along the backyard, in the desks and chairs in classrooms, even in the laundry lists provided by commercial laundries and the celebratory pennants pinned to the walls of student rooms in college dormitories. Salmon was demanding an increased range of activity, even for the most scientifically trained historian. As was clear in her essay "On the College Professor," she was also expanding the spectrum through which one viewed and taught history.

By professional standards Salmon grew more eccentric and modern as a teacher and scholar. She actually collected the laundry lists, railway schedules, fans, and newspaper clippings about domestic topics that she was putting at the center of history.[39] These were historical materials or sources that students received as the raw material from which they were to do history. Believing in sequential teaching, Salmon had written of the imaginative lessons the very young should receive so as to stimulate their interest; that was followed ultimately by teaching general themes and critical evaluation with the endeavor crowned for the very few by the ability to write history itself. By the time Vassar students reached her seminar, she expected them to handle these sources, drawing from her teaching an ability to answer more sophisticated questions than simply what happened when and where. Her teaching was a revelation, opening new worlds, as Beatrice Berle and countless other alumnae testified.[40]

Examination questions in Salmon's courses generally did not ask for the traditional summaries of events or even for exercises in comparison but turned the students' attention to the methodological issues underpinning the study of history. In January 1914, for example, she asked students to evaluate the textbook they were using:

1. Give in bibliographical form the name of the textbook used.
2. State what principles can be applied to test the authoritativeness of any textbook.
3. Apply these tests to the textbook used.
4. Why is the study of the textbook the first step in the study of any period of history?
5. What classes of material are needed to supplement the textbook in the study of (a) frontier life (b) the Stamp Act (c) the Philadelphia Convention.

In February 1918, she asked them to "make out a set of ten questions that will best illustrate the work of the semester. The questions should have logical sequence and express one central idea; they may be framed as single or as group questions; it is not necessary to consider the length of time or the preparation required to answer them; the textbook may be consulted in preparing the questions." There were two additional parts: "Why is this an examination?" And "What proportion of your questions could you answer?" She also asked students to discuss the Vassar College catalog as a historical document (June 1918) and to find what historical records could be found in the student's backyard or the house in which she lived (May 1911). Her course on municipal government culminated with an examination that asked students to identify the chief defects in the plan of Poughkeepsie and how they could be remedied (May 1910). And in another examination dealing with the Vassar College campus (January 1915) she asked students to "apply to the re-planning of the Vassar College campus the principles

From *The Vassar Miscellany News,*
March 21, 1925.

"COLLECT LAUNDRY LISTS

For some time Miss Salmon has been making a collection of laundry lists, both American and foreign. Laundry lists, being closely and continuously connected with daily life, reflect custom and change in social conditions, industry, or in language, with a detail and rapidity with which other sources seldom do. The collection numbers now about 60 lists,* and Miss Salmon and members of her class in historical material will gladly receive additional lists gathered by members of the College during vacation, either this spring or this summer. Each list should be accompanied by the date, the name of the locality where it has been found, and the concern which issued it.

E. M. V. H., '25."
(E. M. Van Houten)
* 200, December, 1925.

To you personally,—
A Merry Christmas,
A Happy New Year,
And many of them.

To the collection of laundry lists,—
Many additions
domestic and foreign,
from every section,
in any language.

To all friends,—
Much appreciation and
many thanks for gifts,
from

THE COLLECTION
AND
LUCY M. SALMON

3. This appeal for laundry lists was distributed to students on brightly colored cards to encourage them to enrich Salmon's collection. Courtesy of Vassar College, Special Collections.

deduced from a study of city planning."[41] As her reputation spread, Henry Morse Stephens called her "the greatest teacher of history in the world."[42]

In 1911 and 1914, Salmon published privately two masterly articles, culminating two decades of this dramatic refocusing of scholarship and pedagogy to center history in objects. These two short texts, "History in a Back Yard" and "Main Street," are her manifestos for this new form of history.[43] They are disarmingly simple, seemingly even simpleminded. "History in a Back Yard" began with a brief lament about the inability to travel to Europe in the coming summer and the anxiety provoked by absence from archives and historic sites. The writer—a historian—then turned to study her own property. The fence, for example, that divided her lot from that of her neighbor signified property values, the need for privacy, and the need to separate the animals from the garden. It also brought to mind the traditions of property boundaries. "The fence in its turn may be a record of pioneer days when the first settlers cleared the forest and the stump fence became a by-product;

the zig-zag rail fence is a later development of pioneer life, while the plain board fence and the picket fence were the plebeian and the patrician divisions between village lots." This rumination led to consideration of the surveyor and the legal system that enforced boundary laws, and to the "elaborate legal system that has been developed for the purpose of establishing and maintaining the claims of rightful ownership." From there she then turned to the garden, with its few spring bulbs and other plants and shrubs.

It all seems very simple and commonplace and there is nothing that at first indicates its cosmopolitan character. But a study of genealogy reveals many surprising and interesting family relationships. The crocus comes from the Levant, the hyacinth and the narcissus bear Greek names, the daffodil is a native of England, the tulip in its name is allied with Turkey and in its history with Holland, the fleur-de-lis is the insignia of France and also of Florence, our lilac is Persian, the wisteria is Japanese, the aster Chinese, the rose of Sharon suggests Palestine, the ubiquitous thistle is Scotch, while cosmos in its name connects us with the order and harmony of the whole created universe.

She examined the garden bench, the hammock, and the little summer house, all part of society's growing love of fresh air, and she showed how industrial changes had affected the house. "Once the weekly laundry was displayed on lines strung between posts, then came the clothes reel, and now both have disappeared since the laundry is done out of the house." She also noted the presence of electricity, modern sanitation, and municipal water and their effect on the appearance of the yard.

So our back yard has the records of all the ages within its narrow enclosure. Prehistoric questions of the ownership of land lie in our fences, classical mythology blooms in our bulbs, the discovery of a new world rises in our Norway maple, affection for mother country blooms in daffodil and thistle, the Dutch West India Company lives in our mulberry tree, new trade routes are opened up in our lilies, commercial treaties are signed in our shrubs, Italian independence shimmers in our Lombardy poplar, political liberty and the downfall of tyrants climb over our grape trellis, and international peace is proclaimed in all that grows within our domain.

She concluded: "If work presses, or the bank fails, or a sprained ankle comes, or unexpected demands on time arise, — seek the records of history in the back yard."[44]

In "Main Street" Salmon turned her attention to Poughkeepsie (disguised under the name of "Apokeepsing" to divert attention from any specific town and toward her general interpretation) and its key commercial street. Here, too, a historian found the ubiquity of history. The names of businesses, the architectural orders on many of the buildings, and many customs recalled the classical world: sundials in the gardens, inscriptions on buildings, urns for flowers in the cemetery. The medieval world was invoked in the many shop signs and through the fraternal societies (the Knights of Columbus, the Knights of Pythias), who called to mind the guilds of the past. History was thus construed broadly, as what is there, as well as what is not there. "The external records show an excess of individualism, — streets have been laid out without plan, there is no common architectural or civic center and no town hall and these negative records indicate the lack of a common civic purpose." Seen historically, the vernacular could even unseat old aesthetic hierarchies. "Main Street may not rival in beauty Unter den Linden or the Champs-Elysées, but it is possible that it surpasses them in inherent interest. If beauty is an undefined, even an undefinable, term, may not beauty be interpreted as including interest, and thus in a very true sense may not the main street of Apokeepsing really be 'the most beautiful city in the world'?"

Hyperbole? Perhaps. Yet it is an exaggeration designed to show the merits of a local vision — though not an antiquarian one — for the understanding of history. Indeed, one of the distinctive features of these histories is that they are seen at eye level by one person in one place: one ordinary town, one ordinary garden seen from sidewalk and back porch. By contrast, contemporary observers of anonymous urban life in the nineteenth and early twentieth centuries often required the fiction of an aerial voyage to take in the city. John Ruskin described a fictional flight over Europe to verify the difference between the Mediterranean and northern regions; Victor Hugo flew over Paris, and Frank Lloyd Wright over Chicago.[45] Even Patrick Geddes's idealized vision of city development was a biological process as seen from an observatory. The history of Main Street cannot be reconstructed in its entirety, Salmon wrote, "if by history is meant a chronological account of what the corporate city has done, but we can reconstruct its changing and successive interests, the different problems with which it has had to deal, and it is possible thus to know the mind and spirit of Main Street more perfectly than we can know it through formal history." History was conceived of without a goal, based in methodology, apparatus, and object and seen through the eyes of one historian. The vision prefigured that of Freud's mental wandering through the layered ruins of Rome and Foucault's subsequent advocacy of "archeologies" and "genealogies" of knowledge.[46] Moreover, this history took up subjects like the vernacular landscape that it would take decades for historians to discover.[47]

What were her models for this new form of history? Salmon's historical vision was derived from eclectic sources. Her intellectual mentors at the University of Michigan, notably Charles Kendall Adams, provided training in the modern scientific manner of history writing, and that was clearly sufficient for her first works. From Adams, she also learned techniques and methods of nineteenth-century history that would lead her to an object-based epistemology in which objects held history and objects told stories. Adams most likely pointed to the work being done with classical inscriptions to reconstruct history, and in a letter, probably written in 1874, Salmon remarked that he had brought to class "a manuscript 900 years old of a part of Genesis and an old book printed only a few years after printing was invented."[48] All of these "sources" Salmon ultimately came to construe doubly — as themselves objects. This notion came to her through John Ruskin as well, whose writings she had known since she was an undergraduate. From Ruskin, William Morris, and other Arts and Crafts writers she learned a sensuous apprehension of art and architecture and how to read history through their form. Gothic architecture, wrote Ruskin, was the product of the gothic mind: "the habit of hard and rapid working; the industry of the tribes of the North, quickened by the coldness of the climate, and giving an expression of sharp energy to all they do."[49] Objects were the physical manifestation of society's values, and history inhabited them. In "History in a Back Yard" and "Main Street" she also found a way to represent objects in a novel way. In "Main Street," the ordinary commodities of the commercial street became fragmented and refracted, like the disembodied signs of cubist painting.

Main Street in its numerous rebus signs records a mediaeval period when illiteracy prevailed and education was the prerogative of the Church. The barber pole, tea-kettle, fish, watch, key, boot, shoe, last, foot, pair of glasses, large eye, horseshoe, head of a horse, wooden horse, wooden hat, shears, three balls, red flag, saw, anvil, chair, wooden Indian, large awl, and other emblems all record a mediaeval period when it was necessary to identify every trade and occupation, not by the name of the proprietor of the place which could not have been read, but by the symbol of the trade

Lists tumbling assemblies of object-signs became Salmon's way of representing the reality of the world and the ever-presentness of history. Only by wrenching the objects from their quotidian context, piling them up like a series of photographic details, could she reassemble a larger, more trustworthy historical image.

Our back yard has nothing that even by courtesy could be called a garden, — a few spring bulbs blossom in the lawn, a row of rosebushes reminds us when June comes, bunches of old-fashioned artemesias announce the arrival of autumn, a trumpet vine all but conceals a rustic summer house, honeysuckles cover the lower branches of a mulberry tree, berry bushes and morning glories conceal in summer the long dividing fence, a high trellis for grapevines is at the lower end of the yard, immediately in front of the high division fence covered with woodbine.

These lists became layered incantations that alternately held the attention and yet left one free to forge linked associations. Not only was everything in this world evidence of history, in ways that later historians of material culture like Marc Bloch would understand, but Salmon used the commonplace, as Gaston Bachelard has suggested, to provoke evocations, reverberations, and stream-of-consciousness echoes rather than to generate discussion of cause and effect.[50] Although Salmon sought to uncover the world of the everyday as a place for scientific historical treatment, the list moved in the opposite direction toward poetry. Description creates impressions to resonate in the reader's psyche. The description of Main Street provokes one of the longest and most sustained lists, one that evokes the staccato visual effects of modern street advertising and comes closest to the flickering street signs of the first painters and photographers of American modernism or the poetic effects of a Walt Whitman.[51]

The bargain-hunters are earliest on the street and for them are offered the advantages of seasonable sales described in all the terms of the calendar months, and also as "mid-winter," "spring," "Easter," "mid-summer," "harvest," "harvest home," "autumn," and "fall" sales. Special day sales appear for every day in the week from Monday to Saturday and the special day expands in Hallow'en sales, Thanksgiving sales, Christmas sales, and holiday sales. Time sales are devised and "ten days' sales," "six days' sales," "morning sales," "one hour sales," "five minute sales," and "as-long-as-they-last sales" greet the early shopper. . . . According to size and characteristics, Main Street describes its sales as "big," "great," "gigantic," "mammoth," "mammoth publicity," "record-breaking," "sales of sales," "clean sweep," and "stirring." . . . Sales are announced as "bankrupt," "sacrifice," "money-getting," "reorganization," "expiration of lease," "dissolution," "inventory," "removal," "auction," "closing out," "cost," "below cost," "fire," "flood," "insurance," "damaged goods," "reduction," "what's left," "shovel 'em out," "liquidation," "salvage," "eviction," "evacuation," "receivers," "forced," "cut price," "last call." . . . Colors are pressed into service and sales announced as "red tag," "yellow tag," "green tag," and "white." Amid all this bewildering variety of sales, Main Street occasionally offers a plain, humble "sale."

Could these lists also be the realization of William James's challenge to philosophy in his lectures (1907) on pragmatism? Salmon's account is not the "simple, clean, and noble" world of the old philosophy or, for that matter, the old history. "The world of concrete personal experiences to which the street belongs," James writes, "is multitudinous beyond imagination, tangled muddy, painful and perplexed."[52] Salmon's lists suggest the pluralistic experience of street life, descriptions that require the abandonment of any effort at neutral observation — the simple, clean, and noble — in favor of a world that is fully experienced and recorded, that seems to try to duplicate the effects of the street.

In staking out our claims for the novelty of Salmon's historical approach with its seemingly contradictory affinities to the Arts and Crafts movement and modernism, we should note that many of her concerns overlapped with those of other historians.[53] The advanced history of her youth, the popular eight-volume history of the United States by John Bach McMaster, promised a history of the American presidents as well as a description of "the dress, the occupations, the amusements . . . [and] the rise and progress of a long series of mechanical inventions and discoveries."[54] And in *The New History*, James Harvey Robinson could call on historians to refocus on "the normal and generally prevalent conditions."[55] Robinson looked to "the new allies of history" — anthropology, archaeology, social psychology, and biology — for models, and he advocated a "history for the common man" that would describe "what men knew of the world, or what they believed to be their duty, or what they made with their hands, or the nature and style of their buildings."[56] Yet even this coincidence of interests reveals more clearly Salmon's distinctive focus. For Robinson the objective was to tame the chaotic world of things and to reestablish the authority of orthodox history over those comparative amateurs, like Henry Chapman Mercer, Julia Cartwright, and Alice Morse Earle, who had already proved that history could indeed be written about "the small, the common, and the obscure."[57]

Robinson's goal, at least until around 1914, was to include more history and to improve the scientific objectivity of one's account—and in that respect his aims were positivistic—whereas for Salmon the values of the new scientific objectivity were entwined with a recognition that historical truths were inevitably relative. Salmon was always self-conscious about the historians' role in the construction of history. As she explored her yard or walked on Main Street or, later still, examined the "colored prisms," not the "white light of truth," of the newspaper, she could affirm that the historian's knowledge was relative, whereas Robinson (at least until World War I) thought the new history was something that would reinforce its value as a science and further support the position of the dispassionate observer.[58]

To the question of why "history must from time to time be rewritten," Robinson in *The New History* answered that "more and more is being learned about the past as time goes on."[59] In answer to the same question, posed a little later, Salmon recognized that no definitive answer was ever possible: "While thought is cumulative, history is always contemporaneous, and therefore again is always new."[60] Or, as she noted in an undated aphorism typed on a sheet of paper: "Needed: Connection between past and present constructive imagination to make past live again."[61] Among the photographs in the Salmon Collection at Vassar College are two taken by Salmon of York & Sawyer's Rockefeller Hall on the Vassar campus. One shows the exterior of the south façade. The interior seems, at first, to be rather poorly framed. It shows a lecture room with a blackboard and lectern at the head of the room, but the bottom part of the picture is framed by the back of a wooden desk. On closer inspection it is clear that the photograph is designed to show the view of the lecturer that a student would have.

Few were in a position to understand this new form of history writing— methodologically so new and yet stylistically so mellifluous—and both "History in a Back Yard" and "Main Street" were privately printed. Henry S. Canby, secretary to the editors of the *Yale Review*, to whom "History in a Back Yard" was sent in early 1912, wrote back with bad news: "We do not feel that your 'History in a Back Yard' has quite enough specific gravity for the *Yale Review*, although we do not wish to indicate that we want something heavy." It was not a text that was easy to understand. Hope Traver, a former student, informed Salmon that she thought it a "veritable gospel for the disappointed," since it demonstrated how to turn "a hopeless snarl into a

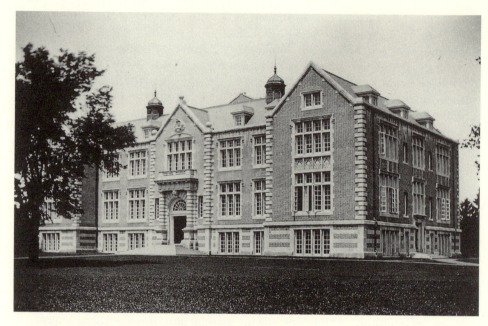

Fig. 4. Rockefeller Hall at Vassar College. Photograph attributed to Lucy Maynard Salmon. Courtesy of Vassar College, Special Collections.

thing of beauty." Another former student, Alice Lathrop, wrote Salmon: "I would like to see your backyard." But others seemed to understand. Francis P. Donnelly S.J. (1869–1959), a young classicist and historian at St. Andrew-on-Hudson, observed: "I have never forgotten what you said the first time I met you about the history around us in every object," and Carl Becker described it as "so compounded of philosophy and history," which suggests that he fully understood that the backyard was really a cipher for a way of thinking about history.[62]

In 1923, Salmon's civic interests, her modern concern for the low and ordinary, and her ongoing scholarly survey of historical sources and their uses merged in the monumental two-volume study of newspapers — *The Newspaper and Authority* and the *Newspaper and the Historian*. These hyper-sophisticated studies drew on her seminar teaching based in primary materials as well as on the deep family traditions of discussing current events. Salmon herself alluded to the freshness of this work. She pointed to the use of newspapers as sources as only a few decades old and to many a problematic undertaking. She walked her readers through every detail of newspaper composition and publication, teaching them how to read and analyze everything from an advertisement to a feature. For the historian, however, the books worked the complex terrain of truth, historical atmosphere and

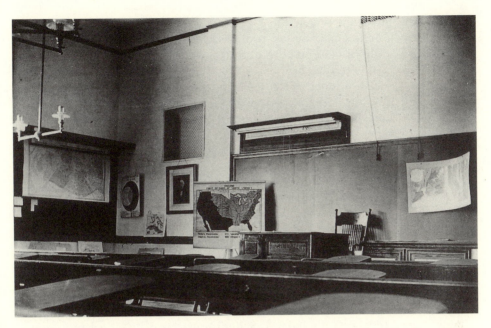

Fig. 5. A classroom in Vassar's Rockefeller Hall. Photograph attributed to Lucy Maynard Salmon. Courtesy of Vassar College, Special Collections.

values, and the historical importance of addressing everyday life with the same scrupulousness applied to high politics.

The newspaper was a crucial centerpiece to her new way of seeing the world. Newspapers interested her precisely because they did not leave a unified impression; her books chronicled the way newspapers gather information and then retransmit it. It was not her object to write a "history, even a fragmentary one, either of the newspaper or of journalism."[63] Rather, her goal was "to discover, if possible, how far the restrictions placed on the newspaper press by external authority have limited its serviceableness for the historian in his attempt to reconstruct the past." How did censorship, press regulation, and advertising affect the newspaper's serviceableness for the historian? Thus, she could say that her book did not "concern itself at all with the press, since the person ultimately in mind has been the student of history" rather than the student of journalism.[64] Indeed, the value of the newspaper as a source of history was not so much its reports, she concluded, which can only aspire to be authoritative (rather than literally accurate). It served as a record of "all contemporaneous human interests, activities, and conditions."[65] For Salmon, therefore, the main parts of the newspaper that could serve the historian in reconstructing the past were the editorial, the illustration, and the advertisement.[66]

Salmon's life as she reached her seventies abounded with duties and the task of maintaining her myriad professional and personal relationships. Happy in her life as a citizen beyond the reach of Vassar officials, she nonetheless had taken on a tyrannical alcoholic named William to cook and do household help. For much of her later life, Salmon spent time finding him clinics and other forms of medical treatment. The struggle with William was but one of the complexities that made her aware of the increasing responsibilities of someone in her position, especially if one had intellectual ambition and a tireless imagination.[67] Nonetheless, Salmon collected clippings on the pros and cons of retirement, and she clearly opposed the growing trend toward a fixed retirement age. To her this was another antidemocratic feature of modern life. It went against the notion of progress, and she resisted it, accepting an official exemption to the mandatory retirement age of seventy granted by the college.

Her mind brimming, Salmon turned to putting together her ideas on history and historiography, conceiving of two books — one on source material and one on the nature of history itself. She brought to fruition instincts and research on some of the topics she had studied almost three decades earlier: institutions such as museums and monuments, then proceeding to beds, sinks, and large appliances. Salmon's work on historical museums reached both Vassar and the public beyond. In March 1900, she had written to Underhill about her interest in writing about museums as a historical source and historical institution and pursued her hunch in the summer of 1907 when she visited more than two dozen Scandinavian ones. Subsequently she proposed the foundation of a historical museum of Vassar College. Inspired in part by Artur Hazelius's development of the ethnographic Nordiska Museum in Stockholm, which she visited in 1907, she suggested a museum to collect and display the range of historical evidence provided by Vassar: "records of the meetings of trustees, presidents' reports, catalogues, alumni registers, student publications and 'letters home' would all give a fairly complete idea of the individual forms of activity that make up a college." But to these she wished to add "classes of record that have for the most part been neglected." These are the material records of architecture, furniture, costume, and all those that concern the communal and private daily life both on its material and on its intellectual side. The ground plan of the main college building as it was originally constructed shows, for example, a radically different conception of community life from the one that prevails today, and the series of plans showing the changes through which the building has passed are invaluable records of the development of educational ideas and ideals. Salmon's museum would show "original plans of the individual rooms" and "indicate the change from the first rooms built without closets to those furnished with heavy wardrobes, and to the latter ample closets with special facilities for keeping the different articles of costume." In addition, this museum would house examples of dorm room furniture, pictures found on student dormitory walls at different times, and clothing. "A collection of the clothing worn by students at different periods would at least raise, if it did not answer, the question of how far dress has been influenced by education."[68]

Salmon would have found welcome support for her ideas in the plans for a museum of tools undertaken by Henry Chapman Mercer in Doylestown, Pennsylvania, which opened in 1916 but on which he had been working since 1897, or in the new museological displays of James Cotton Dana at the Newark Museum. Mercer, like Salmon, was nominally a follower of the Arts and Crafts movement, and like Salmon he had trained as a historian but had begun his professional career as an archaeologist working on American Indian sites. He described his museum, dedicated to the tools used by early Americans (pre-1820), as archaeology "turned upside down, reversed, revolutionized."[69] Dana, by contrast, was at least nominally a librarian although he had arranged remarkable exhibitions, including one on the colonial kitchen (1917) and another, in St. Louis, of a little red schoolhouse (1917).[70]

Along with museums, Salmon wrote on many other topics, like cookbooks, and these would find their way into her work on historical sources. As she taught, she expanded her sense of historical material to include games, toys, children's books, words, and ordinary objects found in everyday life such as pins and tools. Her newer insights, however, concerned the most mundane of objects, those most easily overlooked or disdained by historians of the day despite the advances of consumer society in the 1920s. As a historian, Salmon was weaving everyday life into her scholarship, modernizing the latter as it became more and more devoted to material culture. As everyday life changed, her historical interests became ever more modern right along with it by focusing on the lower and more ordinary in the vernacular landscape. On the eve of her death, Salmon's modernism was more pronounced than ever.[71]

Salmon never completed these two volumes on sources and the nature of history, for she died suddenly in January 1927. Students and friends marked her passing with a vast outpouring of tributes including a resolve to finance the publication of the two volumes, *Historical Material* and *Why History Is Rewritten*, by Oxford University Press. The foundation for these had been built in Greece late in 1900: "My material has been absolutely lacking on the side of the relation of monumental and literary historical evidence and I am finding everything at hand here and have quite changed the plan of one part of the book-to-be. I want to work up as completely as possible the whole subject of the relation of 'source' to historical teaching."[72] Edward Cheyney, reviewing the books for the press, found them exciting as well as the work of a mature scholar, and later reviewers praised their originality. Even then, Salmon's literary executor, Adelaide Underhill, had to insist on maintaining Salmon's original vision, including her titles, in the face of opposition from editors with their own ideas.[73] This posthumous publication of two major books symbolized Salmon's entire career, which never ceased to reverberate and expand. In 1985, at the conference in honor of Vassar College history professor Evalyn A. Clark, the great presence who loomed over several generations of women historians trained by Vassar professors was Lucy Maynard Salmon — vivid despite her death almost sixty years earlier.[74]

The essays that follow are a sampling of Salmon's often visionary writing. In presenting a representative selection, we have omitted rich sources such as her study of the Dutch East India Company, "On Spending," and her detailed statistical material on domestic service. Nor in drawing this sketch of Salmon have we had space to trace in detail the dense network of intellectual influences in which she flourished. Instead, certain themes have seemed central to her teaching and writing, especially her commitment to modernization, modernity, and the democratization of American society at all levels. Developing an object-based epistemology and pedagogy, Salmon charted pathways that would be rediscovered only several generations later, while her own modernist style offered the possibility — mostly ignored at the time — that historical writing might take other directions. We would situate Salmon with the likes of Freud, Dewey, Proust, and Stein — a lofty and often intellectually unruly cast of characters. In 1910 Salmon received one of her predictable scoldings from the president of Vassar, James Monroe Taylor: this time it was for bringing in too many outside lecturers. There had been many others: for excessive use of lantern slides, for making her students walk too much, and for too much looking and not enough memorization. He charged that she willfully flouted regulations and traditional ways of doing things. Avant-garde and democratic, Salmon responded that such "irregularity" and innovation were, in fact, "the essence of life."[75]

Domestic Space

Two events determined the range of Lucy Salmon's interests in domestic life. The first was her appointment to Vassar College in 1887 as professor of history, economics, and political science. Would she have taken up the subject of domestic life had a position been possible, say, at one of the men's colleges? Or would the topic have presented itself had she stayed at Bryn Mawr under the aristocratic eye of Woodrow Wilson? It seems unlikely. At Vassar she joined a significant tradition of domestic reformers, including Ellen Swallow Richards, who had received their training there. In retrospect, it is hard to imagine a scholarly research topic more appropriate than domestic service to someone at Vassar College with what we would now call her "interdisciplinary" teaching responsibilities. *Domestic Service*, published in 1897, was the fruit of this period. The second event, coinciding with the publication of the second edition of *Domestic Service* in 1901, was her decision to move off campus into her first independent home along with her companion, Adelaide Underhill. Ironically, at the time of the research and writing of *Domestic Service*, its author had never kept house for herself. She had never directed her own maid or kitchen help, and she had little experience in household management except what she learned as a girl in Fulton, New York. The initial elation provoked by the move was electric, expressed in essays on kitchen organization and tools ("Philosophy, Art, and Sense for the Kitchen," 1906, republished as "Our Kitchen"), beds and bedding (published in *Good Housekeeping*, June 1911), and household labor. Salmon rejected Ellen Swallow Richards's interests in cooperative kitchens and the collective life for solving the problems of women's work. Having experienced boardinghouse and dormitory life for twenty years, she believed in the virtues of independent living. Unlike Richards, she did not believe that women were unfit for labor. Her efforts, therefore, focused on the possibilities of the home as an economic enterprise.

Salmon herself viewed the subject of domestic life ambiguously. In a letter of June 1906 to a much-favored former student and later a distinguished professor of literature, Edith Rickert (class of 1891), she writes, "It seems an irony of my life that the greater part of what I have had in print concerns my diversion, not my real business in life," and in a letter three months later to another former student she refers to the essays as "slight sketches written for the most part on railway journeys and steamer." And yet regardless of her own uncertainty about the difficulty of the subject, a value much prized in the male-dominated world of historical studies, her experience in domestic life had a direct impact on Salmon's subsequent choice of subject matter and method. Without her experience as a householder the messy world of things could never have intruded so forcibly or demanded incorporation so insistently into the historian's vision.

Domestic Service Since the Colonial Period

It has been said that domestic service in America has passed through three distinct phases. The second phase began about the time of the Revolution, when at the North the indentured servants as a class were gradually supplanted by free laborers, and at the South by negro slaves who inherited with large interest the reproach attached to the redemptioners. The social chasm that had existed at the North between employer and employee, under the system of bonded servants, disappeared. The free laborers, whether employed in domestic service or otherwise, were socially the equal of their employers, especially in New England and in the smaller towns. They belonged by birth to the same section of the country, probably to the same community; they had the same religious belief, attended the same church, sat at the same fireside, ate at the same table, had the same associates; they were often married from the homes[1] and buried in the family lots of their employers.[2] They were in every sense of the word "help."[3] A survival of this condition is seen to-day in farming communities, especially at the West. In the South, on the contrary, the social chasm became impassable as negro slavery entirely displaced white labor.

This democratic condition at the North seemed especially noteworthy to European travellers,[4] and it was one to which they apparently never became accustomed. Harriet Martineau, in planning for her American journey, was perplexed by the difficulty of securing a travelling companion. "It would never do," she says, "as I was aware, to take a servant, to suffer from the proud Yankees on the one hand and the debased slaves on the other."[5] On arriving here, she found "the study of domestic service a continual amusement," and what she saw "would fill a volume."[6] "Boarding-house life," she says, "has been rendered compulsory by the scarcity of labour — the difficulty of obtaining domestic service."[7] But she was quick to appreciate the difference between the spirit of service she found in America and that with which she was familiar in the old world. She writes:

I had rather suffer any inconvenience from having to work occasionally in chambers and kitchen, and from having little hospitable designs frustrated, than witness the subservience in which the menial class is held in Europe. In England, servants have been so long accustomed to this subservience; it is so completely the established custom for the mistress to regulate their manners, their clothes, their intercourse with friends, and many other things which they ought to manage for themselves, that it has become difficult to treat them any better. Mistresses who abstain from such regulation find that they are spoiling their servants; and heads of families who would make friends of their domestics find them little fitted to reciprocate the duty. In

Domestic Service (New York: Macmillan, 1897), 54–73.

America it is otherwise: and may it ever be so! . . . One of the pleasures of travelling though a democratic country is the seeing no liveries. No such badge of menial service is to be met with throughout the States, except in the houses of the foreign ambassadors at Washington.

She then gives illustrations to show "of how much higher a character American domestic service is than any which would endure to be distinguished by a badge."[8]

De Tocqueville, also, found that "the condition of domestic service does not degrade the character of those who enter upon it, because it is freely chosen, and adopted for a time only; because it is not stigmatized by public opinion and creates no permanent inequality between the servant and the master."[9]

Francis J. Grund was also able to appreciate the difference between external servility and true self-respect, for he writes in 1837: "There are but few native Americans who would submit to the degradation of wearing a livery, or any other badge of servitude. This they would call becoming a man's man. But, on the other hand, there are also but few American gentlemen who would feel any happier for their servants wearing coats of more than one color. The inhabitants of New England are quite as willing to call their servants 'helps,' or 'domestics,' as the latter repudiate the title of 'master' in their employers." And he adds, "Neither is an American servant that same indolent, careless, besotted being as an European." He has another word of praise too for the American servants, "who work harder, and *quicker* than even in England."[10]

The absence of livery was a subject of constant comment. William Cobbett, in 1828, asserts that "the man (servant) will not wear a *livery*, any more than he will wear a halter round his neck. . . . Neither men nor women will allow you to call them *servants*, and they will take especial care not to call themselves by that name." He explains the avoidance of the term "servant" by the fact that slaves were called servants by the English, who having fled from tyranny at home were shy of calling others slaves; free men therefore would not be called servants.[11]

But while the democratic spirit that prevailed during this period found commendation in the eyes of those of similar tendencies, it often evoked only mild surprise or a half sneer. Mrs. Trollope found that "the greatest difficulty in organizing a family established in Ohio, is getting servants, or, as it is there called, 'getting help,' for it is more than a petty treason to the Republic to call a free citizen a *servant*."[12] Chevalier asserted that "on Sunday an American would not venture to receive his friends; his servants would not consent to it, and he can hardly secure their services for himself, at their own hour, on that day."[13] Samuel Breck considers that "in these United States nothing would be wanting to make life perfectly happy (humanly speaking) had we good servants."[14] Isabella Bird wrote of Canada in 1854,

"The great annoyance of which people complain in this pleasant land is the difficulty of obtaining domestic servants, and the extraordinary specimens of humanity who go out in this capacity." "The difficulty of procuring servants is one of the great objections to this colony. The few there are know nothing of any individual department of work—for instance, there are neither cooks nor housemaids, they are strictly '*helps*'—the mistress being expected to take more than her fair share of the work."[15] The conditions she found there were the same as in the United States.

Thomas Grattan wrote of the condition:

One of the subjects on which the minds of men and women in the United States seem to be unanimously made up, is the admitted deficiency of *help*. . . . Disguise it as we may, under all the specious forms of reasoning, there is something in the mind of every man which tells him he is humiliated in doing personal service to another. . . . The servile nature of domestic duties in Europe, and more particularly in England, is much more likely to make servants liable to the discontent which mars their merits, than the common understanding in America, which makes the compact between "employer" and "help" a mere matter of business, entailing no mean submission on the one hand, and giving no right to any undue assumption of power on the other. . . . Domestic service is not considered so disgraceful in the United States, as it is felt to be in the United Kingdom.[16]

Grattan's observations lead him to believe that the democratic spirit is not always to be deplored.

An American youth or "young lady" will go to service willingly, if they can be better paid for it than for teaching in a village school, or working on a farm or in a factory. . . . They satisfy themselves that they are *helps*, not servants,—that they are going to work with (not for) Mr. so and so, not going to service,—they call him and his wife their *employers*, not their master and mistress.[17]

But like all Europeans, he never ceases to be surprised by this spirit, particularly by those manifestations of it that led to active work on the part of the mistress of a home and to the use of the word "help." "There are no housekeepers," he writes, "or ladies' maids. The lady herself does all the duties of the former. . . . Servants are thus really justified in giving to themselves the favorite designation of 'helps.' "[18] But he closes a long and interesting chapter on the subject with the prophecy, "They (employers) will, by degrees, give up the employment of native servants who will be in future less likely than even now to submit to their pretensions, and confine themselves to the fast increasing tribes of Irish immigrants."[19]

Curiously enough nearly forty years earlier Madame d'Arusmont had written of friends who thought of coming to America and urged, "Let them by all means be advised against bringing servants with them. Foreign servants are here, without doubt, the worst; they neither understand the work which the climate renders necessary, nor are willing to do the work which they did elsewhere."[20] She, like all travellers, found that however subservient domestic servants might be when they left Europe, the first contact with the democratic atmosphere of America wrought a sudden change; subserviency disappeared, and the servant boasted of his equality with all. She explains that those educated in America perceive the difference placed between the gentleman and the laborer by education and conditions, but the foreigner taking a superficial view of the matter sees no difference.[21]

This second period in the history of domestic service continued from about the time of the Revolution until 1850. It was the product of the rapid growth of democratic ideas fostered by the Revolution and the widespread influence of the French philosophical ideas of the latter part of the eighteenth century. It was a period chiefly characterized by social and industrial democracy, as the political system was also in its spirit democratic. This democratic industrial spirit showed itself in the universal use at the North of the term "help," in the absence of liveries and all distinguishing marks of service, in the intolerance on the part of both employer and employee of servility and subserviency of manner, in the bridging of the social chasm between master and servant as long as the free employment of native born Americans continued, and in the hearty spirit of willingness with which service was performed. The results of this democratic régime were the difficulty of securing help, since new avenues of independent work were opening out to women and the class of indentured servants had disappeared; the lack of all differentiation in household work, since the servant conferred a favor in "going out to work" and did what she knew how to do without troubling to learn new kinds of work; and, most important, the subtle change that the democratic atmosphere everywhere wrought in the servants who came from Europe.

This condition of free, democratic, native born white service at the North and compulsory slave service at the South continued practically unchanged until about the middle of the century. Between 1850 and 1870 four important political changes occurred which revolutionized the personnel in domestic service and consequently its character. These changes brought about the third period in the history of the subject.

The first of these changes was due to the Irish famine of 1846. Previous to this time the immigration to this country from Ireland had been small, averaging not more than twenty thousand annually between 1820 and 1846. In the decade preceding the famine the average number of arrivals had been less than thirty-five thousand annually. In 1846 the number was 51,752, and this was more than doubled the following year, the report showing 105,536 arrivals in 1847. In 1851 the number of arrivals from Ireland had risen to 221,253. Since that time the number has fluctuated, but between fifty and seventy-five thousand annually come to this country from Ireland.[22] A large proportion of these immigrants — forty-nine per cent during the decade from 1870 to 1880 — have been women who were classed as "unskilled laborers." Two occupations were open to them. One was work in factories where as manufacturing processes became more simple unskilled labor could be utilized. The Irish immigrants, therefore, soon displaced in factories the New England women who had found, as has been seen,[23] new opportunities for work of a higher grade. The second occupation open to the Irish immigrants was household service. Here physical strength formed a partial compensation for lack of skill and ignorance of American ways, and the Irish soon came to form a most numerous and important class engaged in domestic employment.[24]

A second important European change, influencing the condition of domestic service, was the German Revolution of 1848 with the events preceding and resulting from it. Before this period the emigration from Germany had been insignificant, fewer than fifteen thousand having come to this country annually between 1830 and 1840. In 1840, owing to political reasons, the number had risen to 29,704. It soon became evident that the hopes raised by the accession of the new monarch were without foundation, and emigration rapidly increased until the number of emigrants coming to America reached 74,281 in 1847. During the year of the Revolution the number decreased, but the failure of the cause of the revolutionary party and the political apathy that followed again increased the movement towards America. This reached its climax in 1854, when the sympathies of the Court had been openly expressed during the Crimean War in favor of Russian despotism. During this year the number of Germans arriving in this country was 215,009 — a number equalled but once since that time, although the number has averaged nearly a hundred and fifty thousand annually during the last decade.[25] A large number of these immigrants have been women, the proportion of women emigrating from Germany being greater than from any other foreign country except Ireland.[26] The ranks of domestic service have been recruited from their number also, the Germans being second only to the Irish as regards the number and proportion engaged in this occupation.[27]

A third political influence affecting the question was the establishment of treaty relations between the United States and China in 1844. This fact and the discovery of gold in California in 1848, together with the building of the Union Pacific railroad in 1867–1869, opened the doors to the immigration of considerable numbers of Chinese. Many of these found their way into domestic service, and on the Pacific coast they became formidable competitors of household servants of other nationalities.[28]

The political and economic conditions in Europe and the breaking down of long-established customs in Asia have thus since 1850 brought to this country large numbers of men and women who have performed the household service previously done by native born Americans. The presence of the Irish in the East, of the Germans in the West, of the Scandinavians in the Northwest, and of the Chinese on the Pacific coast has thus introduced a new social, as well as a new economic, element at the North. It has led to a change in the relation of employer and employee; the class line which was only faintly drawn in the early part of the century between employer and "help" has been changed into a caste line which many employers believe it to their interest to preserve. The native born American fears to lose social position by entering into competition with foreign labor.

While this change, owing to political conditions in the Old World, was taking place at the North in the character of the service, a similar change was taking place at the South growing out of the abolition of slavery in 1863. The negroes who had previously performed all domestic service for their personal expenses have since then received for the same service a small remuneration in money. This fact prevents now as effectually as during the slavery period any competition in domestic service on the part of native born white employees. It does not prevent all competition on the part of foreign born white employees, since prejudice against the negro does not exist in Europe owing to the fact that negro slavery has not prevailed there. The effects of these great movements upon the nature and personnel of domestic service will be discussed later in considering its present condition. They have had a direct and conspicuous influence on the condition of domestic service and even in the use of the term applied to those who engage in it.

But other political influences more subtle and possibly more far-reaching in their effect have been at work. Our loose naturalization laws, and the determining of the qualifications for the right of suffrage by as many standards as there are states, have made the enormous number of men coming to this country annually an easy prey to scheming politicians and demagogues. The labor vote, the Irish vote, the German vote, have been flattered and sought by party managers until the wage-earning man feels that "like Atlas of old he carries the world on his shoulders." If the laboring man feels the weight of the world, his wife and daughter believe that some share of the burden rests on them. The democratic tendencies of the country, the political practices of the day, have everywhere broken down the high wall of separation between employer and employee. They are subversive even in the household of that patriarchal relationship that has been driven from every stronghold but this.

While the political movements of the century have thus changed the personnel of domestic service in America, the development of the material resources of the country has affected its status. Before the present century employees of every kind were in a sense stationary. This was due partly to the influence of the English poor laws; partly to the system of indenture which bound a servant for seven, five, or four years, and to the system of slavery which bound the servant for life; partly to the system of apprenticeship which made the servant a member of the family of his master; partly to the custom prevailing in the country districts and small towns for unmarried workmen in all industries to board with their employers; and partly to the lack of facilities for cheap and easy means of communication between different sections of the country. There was no mobility of labor as regards either employment or place of employment—a fact true alike of domestic service and of other occupations. But this condition of affairs gradually changed. As has been seen, indentured servants disappeared and every employee was free to break as well as to make an engagement for service. The establishment of the factory system of manufactures and the consequent substitution of mechanical for skilled processes of labor broke down the system of apprenticeship, and workmen of every occupation, except domestic service, ceased to be members of the families of their employers. A mobility of labor was made possible such as could not have been secured under the old system. At a later time the great era of railroad development and similar enterprises gave opportunity for a certain mobility as regards place of employment. The tide of western emigration due to the discovery of gold and the cheapness of western land caused much shifting of labor among the non-capitalist class, and this was increased as means of communication were rendered more easy. The establishment of companies to encourage foreign immigration with the object of developing the material resources of the country was another weight in the scale in favor of greater mobility of labor as regards both place and employment. The abolition of slavery removed the last important legal barrier against perfect mobility.

All of these industrial movements have been important factors in changing the condition and character of domestic service. It is true, in a general sense, that every great change in economic conditions affects all occupations. But domestic service has through these causes been affected in certain specific ways. The employee who disliked housework, but to whom no other occupation had been open, could go into a factory or a mill, since no time was consumed in learning the simple processes of mechanical work. Every invention formed the basis for a new occupation. Domestic service had a hundred competitors in a field where before the era of inventions it had stood alone. Moreover, these new occupations required little skill, no preparation, and possessed the charm of novelty. Again, the rapid development of railroad interests, with the increase of competition and consequent lowering of passenger rates, often influenced families emigrating to the West to take with them their trusted employees. The same fact made it possible for women seeking new employments to go from place to place in ways unthought of in the early part of the century.

In view of these changed and changing economic conditions it may be said that the immobility of labor, which has seemed to some economists so great an obstacle to the industrial advancement of women,[29] has practically ceased to exist in the case of domestic service. In fact, industrial development has so far changed conditions that the problem has now come to be how to make this form of labor not more mobile, but more stable. One illustration of this is found in the fact that when seven hundred domestic employees represented on the schedules were asked how many of them had ever been engaged in any other occupation, twenty-seven per cent replied that they had. The mobility as to the place of labor was found to be even greater. Twenty-seven per cent of the native born employees did not reside in the same state in which they were born, and adding to these the number of foreign born, it was found that sixty-eight per cent did not reside in their native country or state. Moreover, this statement is below the truth as it does not take into account the number of changes made within a single year and refers to only one change from place of birth to present residence.[30]

An indication of these various changes in the condition of domestic service during these different periods is seen in the history of the word "servant." As used in England and in law at the time of the settlement of the American colonies it signified any employee, and no odium was in any way attached to the word.[31] But five things led to its temporary disuse: first, the reproach connected with the word through the character and social rank of the redemptioners; second, the fact that when the redemptioners gave place at the South to negro slaves the word "servant" was transferred to this class,[32] and this alone was sufficient to prevent its application to whites;[33] third, the levelling tendencies that always prevail in a new country; fourth, the literal interpretation of the preamble of the Declaration of Independence; and fifth, the new social and political theories resulting from the introduction of French philosophical ideas. At the North the word "help" as applied especially to women superseded the word "servant," while at the South the term "servant" was applied only to the negro. From the time of the Revolution, therefore, until about 1850 the word "servant" does not seem to have been generally applied in either section to white persons of American birth.[34]

Since the introduction of foreign labor at the middle of the century, the word "servant" has again come into general use as applied to white employees, not, however, as a survival of the old colonial word, but as a reintroduction from Europe of a term signifying one who performs so-called menial labor, and it is restricted in its use, except in a legal sense, to persons who perform domestic service. The present use of the word has come not only from the almost exclusive employment of foreigners in domestic service, but also because of the increase of wealth and consequent luxury in this country, the growing class divisions, and the adoption of many European habits of living and thinking and speaking.[35]

These simple historical facts are one explanation of the unwillingness of American women to engage in work stigmatized by an offensive term applied to no other class of laborers.

In studying the question of domestic service, therefore, the fact cannot be overlooked that certain historical influences have affected its conditions; that political revolutions have changed its personnel, and industrial development its mobility. It is as impossible to dream of restoring the former condition of household service as it is of restoring former household employments, and neither is to be desired. In each case the question is one of preparing for the next step in the process of evolution, not of retrograding toward a condition impossible to restore. Any attempt to secure a change for the better in the present condition of domestic service must be ineffective if it does not take into consideration these historic aspects of the subject.

Possible Remedies: Specialization of Household Employments

The efforts to remove the social stigma that now brands domestic service will not alone accomplish the desired result. Another means of lessening the difficulties in the modern household is to put all household employments on the same business basis as are all employments outside of the household. The principles which lie at the foundation of modern business activities are division of labor and unconscious co-operation. This statement does not mean that both of these principles are carried out perfectly, but that industrial progress has been made and is being made along these lines, that the advance already made by household employments has been in the same direction, and that the reforms proposed for the household that diverge from these lines, however wise in themselves, cannot lead to the best results because they are out of the current of general progress.

In considering the historical phase of the subject, a long list of articles was suggested[1] which were formerly made within the household, but are now made out of the house both better and more cheaply than they could be made at home.

A list can be drawn up of other articles made out of the house, which if made in factories are inferior, and if purchased through the woman's exchanges, though as well or even better prepared, are more expensive because the demand for such articles made in the homes of others has up to this time been limited. The articles in this transitional state are vegetable and fruit canning, the making of jellies, pickles, and preserves, the baking of bread, cake, and pastry, the preparation of soups, pressed meats, cold meats, ice-cream, and confectionary, condensed, sterilized, and evaporated milk, and the making of butter not yet abandoned in all rural homes. The transitional list also includes the making of underclothes for women and children, which can be made more cheaply out of the house but not always so well; and millinery and dressmaking, which can be done better but at greater expense. There is every indication that all the articles in this transitional state must soon be enumerated among those articles made both better and more cheaply out of the house than within.

A third list can be made of articles that are now seldom if ever manufactured out of the house but which can be made elsewhere. This list includes in the first place bread and cake of every description; it is possible by taking all of this work out of the house to save, considered in the aggregate both as regards the individual and the community, an enormous waste of time and

Domestic Service (New York: Macmillan, 1897), 212–34.

fuel, and at the same time to secure through the application of scientific principles articles often more uniform and superior in quality to what can be produced in the home.[2] A second class includes the preparation of all vegetables for cooking. It is not sentiment but economic principle that should release the human hand from performing this part of housework, more purely mechanical and more justly entitled to be called drudgery than any other work carried on in the house. A few years since coffee was roasted in every kitchen. If it has been found that an article requiring such delicate treatment as this can be prepared by business firms better than it can be in the household oven, there can be no serious obstacle in the way of delivering at the door all vegetables ready for cooking.[3] Compensation for the additional cost at first incurred would be found in the hygienic advantage of removing from many cellars the supply of winter vegetables. A third class of articles includes the preparation of all cold meats, half-cooked meats, as croquettes, all stuffed meats, as fowl and game, all "made" dishes, as salads and cold desserts, and the cooking of all articles which need only heating to make ready for use. The careful study of a large number of elaborate menus as well as of more simple bills of fare shows a very small proportion of articles which could not be made out of the house and sent in ready for use or requiring only the application of heat. The Aladdin oven constructed on scientific principles renders the cooking and heating of food a most simple matter. The sending of hot food to individual homes has in no case as far as can be learned proved a success, but the delivery of all articles ready for the final application of heat is possible through business enterprise and scientific experiment.

This partial, although not entire, solution of the problem of domestic service, by taking a large number of servants out of the house and by having a large part of the work now done by them in the house done elsewhere, is in direct line with the progress made in other occupations.

It was estimated by Mr. Gallatin in 1810[4] that two-thirds of the clothing worn in the United States was the product of family manufacturing — then in a flourishing state. During the twenty years following, a part of this family weaving and spinning was transferred to factories, and this transfer created the great factory industry. Its rapid growth was due to the fact that the power loom and the factory took the place of the hand loom and of home manufacturing. A similar change has taken place in the manufacture of cheese. Until about 1830 all cheese was made at home, and in 1860 not more than twenty cheese factories had been built.[5] After that time factories multiplied rapidly, until now practically all cheese is factory made. The demand for ready-made clothing for men was a generation ago very small. It grew out of a demand on the part of sailors, and was increased in large proportions at the time of the Civil War; the manufacture of such articles is now so firmly established in our industrial system that a return to the home system of manufacturing, even in the most isolated and primitive communities, would be as impossible as the revival of the spinning wheel. The demand for ready-made clothing for women is nearly as great and is annually increasing through the facilities offered by all large retail houses for shopping by mail. The tailoress and the maker of shirts have disappeared from the homes of their employers and have set up establishments of their own, or have become responsible to large business houses; the dressmaker and the seamstress are fast following in their footsteps, and the cook must set her face in the same direction.

The trend in this direction can be seen in many ways. The growing prevalence of camping has increased the demand for articles of food ready for use, and even tea, coffee, and soups are delivered hot for the benefit of pleasure seekers.[6] The development of Western resources by Eastern capitalists has also increased the demand for such articles, and at least one housekeeper among the Black Hills of South Dakota, one hundred miles from a railroad station, speaks casually of doing her marketing in Chicago, and a housekeeper in North Carolina gives frequent and elaborate lunches through caterers in Philadelphia. The tendency even among persons of moderate means is more and more towards the employment of caterers for special afternoon and evening entertainments, although in villages and small towns this course as yet involves the employment of persons from large cities. The practice is not uncommon for the women connected with church organizations to hold every Saturday afternoon sales for the benefit of the society, of all articles of food that can be prepared the previous day for Sunday dinners and teas.[7]

The most important medium for the sale of such commodities is the Woman's Exchange.[8] It has already become an economic factor of some little importance, and it will become of still greater importance when it is taken out of the domain of charity and sentiment and becomes self-supporting on a business basis. One of its most valuable results is that it has set a high standard for work and has insisted that this standard be reached by every consignor, not only once or generally, but invariably. It has maintained this standard in the face of hostile criticism and the feeling that a charitable organization ought to accept poor work if those presenting it are in need of money. It has shown that success in work cannot be attained by a simple desire for it or need of it pecuniarily. It has taught that accuracy, scientific knowledge, artistic training, habits of observation, good judgment, courage, and perseverance are better staffs in reaching success than reliance upon haphazard methods and the compliments of flattering friends. It has raised the standard of decorative and artistic needle work by incorporating into its rules a refusal to accept calico patchwork, wax, leather, hair, feather, rice, splatter, splinter, and card-board work. It has taught many women that a model recipe for cake is not "A few eggs, a little milk, a lump of butter, a pinch of salt, sweetening to taste, flour enough to thicken; give a good beating and bake according to judgment."

But still more it has opened up to women what has been practically a new occupation. Domestic work within the house performed by members of the family without fixed compensation and by those not members of the family with compensation had been the previous rule. The Exchange has shown that it is possible for the women of a family to prepare within the house for sale outside many articles for table consumption, both those of necessity and luxury. Innumerable instances are on record of women who within the past fifteen years have supported themselves wholly or in part by making for general sale or on orders different articles for the table.[9]

It seems inevitable that eventually all articles of food will be prepared out of the house except those requiring the last application of heat, and that scientific skill will reduce to a minimum the labor and expense of this final stage of preparation. This change is in direct line with the tendency toward specialization everywhere else found in that it thus becomes possible for every person to do exclusively that thing which he or she can do best; it allows the concentration of labor and capital and thus by economizing both secures the largest results; it permits many women to retain their home life and at the same time engage in remunerative business; it improves the quality of all articles consumed, since they are produced under the most favorable conditions; it brings the work of every cook into competition with the work of every other cook by providing a standard of measurement now lacking and thus inciting improvement; it is the application of the principle of unconscious co-operation and therefore in harmony with other business activities. More definitely, as one illustration, it permits all fruits to be canned, pickled, and preserved in every way in the locality where they are produced at a cost ultimately less than can now be done when fruit is shipped to cities and there sold at prices including high rents; it prevents a glut in the market of such perishable articles by providing for their preservation on farms and in villages and subsequent transportation to cities at leisure; it makes it possible to utilize many abandoned farms in the East which could be used as fruit farms but are too remote from shipping centres to permit the transportation of ripe fruit; it ultimately lightens the labors of many women on farms by enabling them to purchase in cities many articles now produced by them at a disadvantage. The canning in cities, by individual families, of fruits, often in an over-ripe condition, is as anomalous as would be today the making of dairy products in city homes. The preservation of fruit is but one example of articles that could be prepared better and more cheaply in the country than in the city. Miscellaneous articles of every description, as plum-pudding, boned turkey, chicken broth, jelly, croquettes and salad, minced meat, pressed veal, bouillon, calf's-foot jelly, pure fruit juices, blackberry cordial, and a score of other articles, could be added to the list.

It is sometimes objected that this plan of taking out of the house to as great an extent as possible all forms of cooking lessens the individuality of the home by requiring all persons to have the same articles of food. But the objection presupposes a limited variety of articles, while the method suggested must result in an unlimited variety, as has been the case in regard to articles used for wearing apparel since the custom has been established of having so many made out of the house. It presupposes also that individuality depends on externals. The gentleman who wishes to preserve his individuality through his cook could also preserve it through employing a private tailor, but he gladly sacrifices it in the latter case for the better work of one who serves a hundred other customers as well. Individuality is preserved when a person builds his own house, but the doubtful benefit of the result is suggested by Oliver Wendell Holmes when he says, "Probably it is better to be built in that way than not to be built at all." The individuality of the present generation is certainly not less than that of the preceding one when all clothing worn by a family was made up in the house, or of an earlier one when all cloth was spun and woven, as well as made up, in the house, or of a still more remote one when our ancestors troubled themselves comparatively little about either the weaving or the making. The very perfection of the principle of the division of labor makes possible the expression of the greatest individuality in that it offers the possibility of selection from a hundred varieties whereas before no choice was given. The ability to choose between the work of a hundred cooks permits a truer individuality than does the command of the services of but one. Whims, caprices, and eccentricities sometimes masquerade as individuality and are not always entitled to respect.

Another form of work now done in the house that could be done outside is laundry work. The inconveniences resulting from the derangement of the household machinery according to the present method have formed the theme of many jests; a serious consideration of the subject must lead to the conclusion that this system results in great waste as well as in unnecessary wear and tear of the household machinery. An objection on hygienic grounds is sometimes made to the proposal to have articles of clothing laundered out of the house together with articles sent by other families. But science has already accomplished much at the bidding of business enterprise, and this objection can be overcome. Even as it is, the question may well be asked whether the price paid is not a heavy one for individual laundresses. The vast army of persons who board are compelled to send out articles to be laundered, and this is apparently done without serious results. A beginning has been made in many families where a competent laundress cannot be secured by sending to public laundries all starched clothing, especially all collars and cuffs. The laundries of Troy, New York, have branches for the reception and delivery of goods in all parts of the country, and launder many articles better and more cheaply than can be done at home. The amount of space now occupied in cities for laundering purposes that could be used for business or for homes is far from inconsiderable. It seems not altogether unreasonable to believe that if the space now occupied by laundries in individual homes could be used for other purposes rents would be perceptibly lower. On economic grounds alone this generation should relegate the washing machine and the wringer to the attic or the front parlor, where it has already placed the spinning wheel of its ancestors.

Still another field is open for business enterprise in connection with the household. A very large part of the work connected with it concerns the care of the house and grounds. This includes the semi-annual house-cleaning and the cleaning of windows, floors, brass, silver, and lamps; the sweeping, dusting, and general care of rooms, including the special attention that must be given to books, pictures, and bric-a-brac; the care of lawns, walks, porches, and furnaces; the repairing of articles of clothing and furniture; table service and chamber service. Here again economic tendencies are showing themselves. Much if not all of this work can be done by the piece or by the hour, and men and women are everywhere taking advantage of the fact.[10] A very large part of the work of the household can be thus done, especially if housekeepers are willing to waive the tradition that silver must be cleaned on Thursdays, sweeping done on Fridays, and all sleeping-rooms put in order before nine o'clock in the morning.

One other measure of relief concerns the purchase of supplies. Marketing is a science and might be made a profession. At present it is usually done in a haphazard, makeshift fashion. It is done by the head of the household on his way to business and thus done in haste; or orders are given through a clerk who goes from house to house and thus serves primarily the firm he represents, while at the same time the purchaser loses the benefit of competition in the markets; or commissions are given by telephone and the customer has no opportunity of inspecting the goods before purchase; or marketing is done by the mistress of the household, who is unable to reach the markets in time to make her purchases with the care that should be given; or it is done by the cook, who may know the best articles to purchase but is ignorant of their money value. It requires time, skill, and experience to purchase judiciously the supplies for a household, and in many households time, skill, and experience are lacking. It would seem possible for one person to do the marketing for fifteen or twenty families, taking the orders at night and executing them in the morning. Supplies could then be purchased in quantity, this gain would pay the commission of the purchaser, and marketing would be done in a much more satisfactory manner than it is at the present time. At the same time such a plan would relieve the members of individual households of the burden and care of a difficult part of household management.

All of these measures suggested must tend ultimately to take as far as possible the domestic employee out of the house, letting her perform her work through the operation of unconscious business co-operation. This method would enable a large number of women to go into household employments who have ability in this direction but who now drift into other occupations which permit them to maintain their own home life. It is generally assumed that an unmarried woman has no desire for a home and no need of a place that she can call her own. When she goes into domestic employment, therefore, she must merge her individual life into that of her employer and relinquish all the social instincts, although as strong in her as in another. But this is what many are not willing to do. If the opportunity were presented of performing housework and remaining at home, large numbers would in time enter the work. Many who have no homes would still be glad to share the home of an employer, but where no alternative is presented, as under the present system, except where negroes are employed, the requirement of residence becomes irksome and is a hindrance in this as it would be in any other industry. It is also true that many employees particularly dislike to live in flats. The sleeping accommodations are generally poor, with little light or ventilation, and all parts of the household are cramped and crowded. To take the employee out of the modern flat and let her go to her own home or lodging place would be a boon to both employer and employee. The plan proposed also lessens materially the amount of care and responsibility now incurred by the employer, since it decreases the number of personal employees. The presence of the employee in the family is a disadvantage to the household of the employer as well as to the employee. Again, it enables large numbers of women who have only a few hours each day or week to give to outside work to do it in their own houses or in the houses of others without neglect of their own households. Moreover, it lessens much of the difficulty that now exists owing to the migratory habits of the modern family. The question of what shall be done with the employees of a household during the summer and how new ones shall be secured in the autumn is answered in a measure if the work performed by them can be done by the piece, hour, or season and a large part of the family supplies can be purchased ready for use. Then, too, it renders both employer and employee more independent. Whether the desire for independence is right or wrong is not the question — it is a condition and must be met.

It has often been pointed out that the aristocracy of the Church broke down at the time of the Reformation, that the aristocracy of the State was overthrown by the Bastille mob, that aristocracy in education is yielding to the democratic influences of university extension, and that aristocratic economics are disappearing in the light of the industrial discussions of the day. The aristocracy of the household must succumb to this universal desire for personal independence on the part of employees.

The plan suggested of specializing household industries to as great an extent as possible and encouraging the domestic employee to live in her own home has much in its favor. It substitutes for the responsibility to an individual employer, so irritating to many and so contrary to the industrial spirit of the age, the responsibility to a business firm. It throws the responsibility for success on the individual employees by bringing them into more immediate competition with other workers in the same field. It provides a channel through which advance becomes possible and also independent business life if executive ability is present. It reduces house rent in proportion as the number of employees is lessened, or it places at the disposal of the family a larger portion of the house than is now available for their personal uses. It simplifies the problem in all families where there is more work than can be done by one employee but not enough for two. It makes possible such a division of labor in the household as will discriminate between skilled and unskilled labor. Under the present system the employer expects to find in one individual for $3 per week and expenses, a French chef, an Irish laundress, a discreet waitress, a Yankee maid-of-all-work, a parlor maid a Quaker in neatness, all this, "with the temper of a saint and the constitution of a cowboy thrown in." Expectations are often disappointed and the blame is thrown, not on a bad system, but on the individual forced to carry it out. The separation of skilled and unskilled labor permits each one to do a few things well and prevents the friction inevitable when the skilled workman is called upon to do unskilled work, or the unskilled laborer to perform tasks requiring the ability of an expert. It is a more flexible system of co-operation than the one technically known as such, since all articles are purchased, not of a certain manufacturer or dealer whom it has been agreed upon by contract to patronize, but whenever it is most convenient. It is easily adapted to the present system of living in flats and apartment houses rendered almost necessary in some places by high rents; this way of living makes it difficult to employ a large number of domestics, but on the other hand it makes it possible to do without them. It enables the domestic employee to have the daily change in going back and forth from her work which the shop-girl and the factory-girl now have. The domestic employee now has out-of-door exercise not oftener than once or twice a week, and the effect is as deleterious physically, mentally, and morally as a similar course would be in other walks of life. It must decrease that pernicious habit, so degrading to the occupation as well as to the individual, of discussing the personal characteristics of both employers and employees, since the relationship between the two is changed from the personal to the business one. It elevates to the rank of distinct occupations many classes of housework now considered drudgery because done at odd moments by overworked employees. It must in time result in many economic gains, one illustration of which is the fact that the kitchen could be heated by the furnace and all cooking done by kerosene, gas, or electricity; on the other hand, the necessities of employers would cease to be the gauge for measuring the minimum of work that could be done by employees without losing their places.

Two objections are sometimes raised to this plan. The first is that the cost of living would be increased. This would undoubtedly be the effect at first, but it is not a valid objection to this mode of housekeeping. The list of articles now made out of the house shows that every article of men's dress is made more cheaply and better than formerly when made at home. This is due to the fact that in the transitional period men of means were willing to pay a higher price for goods made out of the house for the sake of obtaining a superior article. Competition subsequently made it possible for men of moderate means to share in the same benefit. The same tendency is seen among wage-earning women. They could make their own dresses at less expense than they can hire them made, but it would be done at a loss of time and strength taken from their own work, and they prefer to employ others. Moreover, cost of living is a relative term — an increase in the family income makes it possible to employ more service and therefore to live better than before. Families of wealth now have two alternatives, either to employ more domestics within the home, or to purchase more ready-made supplies. The alternative usually chosen is the former, but if such families would choose the second and instead of employing additional domestics would, as far as practicable, purchase ready-made supplies for the table and have more work done by the hour, day, or piece, as great ease of living would be secured as through the employment of additional service within the house under the present system. Though the cost of living might be increased, it is a price many would be glad to pay for a release from the friction of a retinue of domestics in the home. When it has become the custom for families of wealth to have few or no domestics under their own roofs, the great problem of how people of limited incomes can have comfortable homes will be solved.

The second objection is the fact that it would take from the women of the household much of their work. The problem, however, has not been to provide a means of excusing from their legitimate share in the work of the world one half of its population, but to use that labor at the least cost of time and strength. The argument that would maintain the present system because it provides women with work is the same as that which destroyed the machines of Arkwright and Crompton; it is the argument that keeps convicts in idleness lest their work should come into competition with the work of others; it is the opposition always shown to every change whereby the number of workers in any field is at first lessened. But the plan proposed does not contemplate abolishing household work for women, but changing its direction so that it may be more productive with less expenditure than at present. It calls for specialization of work on a business basis, rather than idleness or charity. It asks that the woman who can bake bread better than she can sweep a room should, through unconscious co-operation, bake bread for several families and hire her sweeping done for her by one who can do it better than she. It asks that the woman who likes to make cake and fancy desserts but dislikes table service should dispose of the products of her labor to several employers, rather than give her time to one employer and do in addition other kinds of work in which she does not excel. It asks that the woman who cannot afford to buy her preserves and jellies at the Woman's Exchange but crochets for church fairs slippers that are sold at a dollar a pair shall dispose of the products of her industry at a remunerative rate and buy her jellies put up in a superior manner. The plan allows the person who has skill in arranging tables and likes dining-room work, but dislikes cooking, to do this special kind of work, when otherwise she would drift into some other light employment. It provides that women in their own homes who are now dependent for support on the labors of others shall have opened to them some remunerative occupation. The preparation of food in small quantities always secures more satisfactory results than when it is prepared in larger amounts. Women in their own homes can give foods the delicate handling necessary for the best results and at the same time use the spare hours that are now given to unprofitable tasks. It makes every member of the family a co-operator in some form in the general family life. What is needed indeed in the household is more co-operation among the different members of it rather than conscious co-operation with different families. It has been recently pointed out that the carrying of electricity as a motive power to individual houses may cause a partial return to the domestic system of manufacturing which will be carried on under more favorable conditions than was the old domestic system.[11] This is in the future — its possibility is only hinted at. But the domestic system of housework, if that expression may be used to distinguish it from the present individual system, and the proposed system of unconscious co-operation, enables women to work in their own homes and, by exchange of such commodities and services as each can best dispose of, to contribute to the general welfare.

The plan of specialization of household employments has already been put into partial operation by many housekeepers and its success attested by those who have tried it.[12] Conscious co-operative housekeeping has in nearly every case proved a practical failure, but the unconscious co-operation that comes through business enterprise has brought relief to the household in many directions and it is one of the lines along which progress in the future must be made.

Economics and Ethics in Domestic Service

The cynic observed yesterday that the interests of womankind were confined to the three D's — Dress, Disease, and Domestics. To-day the bicycle
has become a formidable competitor of dress and promises to do its part
toward settling some of the disputed questions in regard to the rival it has
partially supplanted. Biology is wrestling with disease, and bids fair to be the
victor. Domestics still hold the field, but if business methods are introduced
into the household, as it seems inevitable will be the case, the interests of
women will have passed on and upward from the three D's to the three B's,
and the cynic will be forced to turn his attention from woman to a more
fruitful field.

It is not indeed strange that the old conception of household service
should have yielded so slowly its place in the thoughts of women. The whole
subject of economic theory of which it is but a part is itself a recent comer in
the field of discussion; it was scarcely more than a century and a quarter ago
that Adam Smith wrote his "Wealth of Nations" and gave a new direction to
economic thought.

As a result of these economic studies of the present century, something
has already been done to improve industrial conditions outside of the
household. They have led to improved factory legislation, to better relations
between employer and employee, to wide discussion of the principles on
which business is conducted, but what has been accomplished has been
brought about through an unrest and an agitation that have often brought
disaster in their train.

From this general economic discussion the household has been in the
main cut off, largely because it has been considered as belonging to the
domain of sentiment rather than of business, because the household has
shrunk from all agitation and discussion of the questions with which it is
immediately concerned, because it has refused to see that progress is condi-
tioned on this agitation and discussion, because it has cried "Peace, peace,"
when there was no peace. It is this very aloofness that constitutes to-day the
most serious obstacle in the way of any improvement in domestic service —
the failure on the part of men and women everywhere to recognize that the
occupation is governed by economic law, that it is bound up inextricably
with every other phase of the labor question, and that the initial step toward
improvement must be the recognition of this fact. Housekeepers everywhere resent what they deem interference with their personal affairs; they
betray an ill-concealed irritation when the economic side of the question is
presented to them, and they believe, if their own household machinery runs

Progress in the Household (Boston: Houghton Mifflin, 1906), 95–120.

smoothly, that no friction exists anywhere and that their own responsibility has ceased. Nothing today is so characteristic of women as a class as their inability to assume an impersonal attitude toward any subject under discussion, while in methods of work they are prone to work from day to day and seldom plan for results to be reached years after a project has been set on foot.

This means that before any improvement in household affairs can come, the attitude of mind with which they are approached must undergo a radical change; both men and women must recognize the analogy between domestic service and other forms of labor, and must work, not for more competent cooks and parlor-maids in their individual households, not for any specific change for the better tomorrow, but for improvements in the system — improvements, the benefits of which will be reaped not by this but by subsequent generations. It is a fact from which we cannot escape that domestic service has been affected by historical and economic development, that it is today affected by economic conditions, that it must in the future be in like manner affected by them. That we do not all see these facts does not in the least alter their existence. Nothing is so inexorable as law. Law works itself out whether recognized or not. If we accept the workings of the law and aid in its natural development, peace and harmony result; if we resist the action of law and struggle against it, we do not stay its progress, but we injure ourselves as the bird that beats its wings against prison-bars. "Delhi is far," said the old king of Delhi when told that an enemy had crossed his border. "Delhi is far," he answered when told that the enemy was in sight. "Delhi is far," he repeated when the enemy was at the gate. "Delhi is far," he still repeated when the sword of the enemy was at his throat.

Yet certainly we may hope that another view is coming to prevail, and that housekeepers will not shrink from the storm and stress period that is the inevitable accompaniment of discussion of household affairs, but will bring the courage of their convictions to bear on the discussion of the problem. It is indeed encouraging to find so many of them beginning their studies of household affairs, not with a proposal of remedies that may chance to meet the disease, but with a recognition of the existence of a great question to be investigated, with a determination to understand the problem.

What is the problem that is presented to the housekeeper? To have a healthy, happy, virtuous, and useful household. What are some of the external conditions necessary to such a household? Palatable, nourishing food, regularity of meals, prompt and efficient service. With what tools has the young housekeeper heretofore been expected to grapple with the problem in her own home? Instinct, intuition, love of home, the cardinal virtues, especially meekness and humility, orthodox views in regard to the relation of the housekeeper to her home, and a belief that personal experience, however restricted, is an infallible guide.

What has been the result? Often disastrous failure, sometimes a measurable degree of success, always an unnecessary expenditure of time, money, and mental, physical, and spiritual energy. That most pathetic story in "Pratt Portraits," "A New England Quack," has had more than one counterpart in the household. The results of innocent quackery there may not always be so consciously pathetic, the effects may be more subtle, but they are none the less fatal. Dora Copperfield has been, unhappily for the race, no mere picture of the imagination.

The problem should not in itself be an insoluble one; a happy, well-ordered household ought to be the normal condition of every home. But to expect to secure this end with the means given a young housekeeper is often to expect the impossible. Behind the housekeeper is not only personal ignorance but all the force of tradition; she must face difficulties so deep-seated as to seem almost inherent and ineradicable.

One of the greatest of these difficulties is the belief that the subject is not worthy of consideration and that time and strength are wasted in discussing it. This attitude of mind is well illustrated by Lord Orrery's "Remarks on the Life and Writings of Swift," apropos of Swift's "General Instructions to Servants."[1] Lord Orrery may not indeed have been altogether free from malice and jealousy in penning these words, and he certainly showed himself deficient in a sense of humor, but whatever his motive, his comments on Swift's work illustrate fairly well a belief still prevalent. "How much time," Lord Orrery comments, "must have been employed in putting together such a work! What an intenseness of thought must have been bestowed upon the lowest and most slavish scenes of life! . . . A man of Swift's genius ought constantly to have soared into higher regions. He ought to have looked upon persons of inferior abilities as children, whom nature had appointed him to instruct, encourage, and improve. Superior talents seem to have been intended by Providence as public benefits; and the person who possesses such blessings is certainly answerable to heaven for those endowments which he enjoys above the rest of mankind. Let him jest with dignity, and let him be ironical upon useful subjects; leaving poor slaves to heat their porridge, or drink their small beer, in such vessels as they shall find proper."[2]

Another great difficulty is the persistent refusal to consider domestic service as a question of general interest and a part of the labor question of the day. "What is needed," an English critic remarks, "is an infallible recipe for securing a good £16 girl and for keeping her when secured." But alas, who shall give an infallible recipe for accomplishing the impossible? Who shall lay down the principle that will make coal-miners contented with low wages and long hours, that will make the employers of masons satisfied with bungling work that threatens life and limb, that will lull into ease a conscience aroused by the iniquities of the sweating system? Nothing can be more chimerical than to expect a perfect automatic adjustment of the household machinery while other parts of the industrial world are not in harmonious relation to each other.

A third obstacle is the persistent belief that nothing can be done until this magic recipe has been discovered. If it is suggested that one measure of alleviation is to take a part of the work out of the household, it is answered that it is useless to propose it because all work cannot be taken out of the household, because the plan would not work in the rural districts, because it would not meet the case in England, because it is expensive. Certainly all these are valid objections to considering the plan a sovereign remedy. But to refuse to try a remedy that may prove of benefit in some households because it will not work in all is quite the same as to refuse to administer a medicine in case of fever because it will not also cure consumption.

The preceding is illustrative of another difficulty that is implied in it — a fundamental ignorance on the part of many housekeepers of the processes of reasoning. This is illustrated by the reasoning that many go through with in discussing the question:

"Public laundries are in the hands of men whose standard of perfection in laundry-work is a smooth shirt-front and a stiff collar and cuff. This standard of perfection cannot be applied to the laundering of linen and children's clothing. Therefore, table-linen and children's clothing must be laundered in the house."

"My mother's cook received a part of her wages in lodging and board. My cook receives a part of her wages in lodging and board. Therefore, my daughter's cook will receive a part of her wages in lodging and board."

"Negro employees lodge out of the house at the South. White employees do not lodge out of the house in England. Therefore employees cannot lodge out of the house at the North."

"Employees should be treated with consideration. My employees are treated with consideration. Therefore all employees are treated with consideration."

"Some employees are incompetent. Good results cannot be secured with incompetent employees. Therefore good service is impossible."

The only way of meeting this difficulty is found in the slow process of careful, systematic education. What many housekeepers need is not so much instruction in cooking or domestic sanitation as training in calculus and quaternions, Herodotus and Livy, logic and geology.

Still another hindrance is the tone of certainty and finality that characterizes all discussions concerning the household. It is a part of the religious belief of many persons that every woman has been foreordained by Providence to be a wife, mother, and housekeeper, and that any deviation from this fundamental law is an infringement on the designs of Providence. But some of us remember that scarcely more than fifty years ago Daniel Webster said in the United States Senate that slavery had been excluded from California and New Mexico by the law of nature, of physical geography, the law of the formation of the earth, and that he would not through the Wilmot Proviso take pains uselessly to reaffirm an ordinance of nature or to reenact the will of God. Many apparently believe, through the same specious reasoning, that to provide instruction in household affairs would be in a similar way to reaffirm an ordinance of nature.

Not only does this tone of finality characterize the household when it is assumed that because the majority of women will always choose to be housekeepers, therefore all woman must be housekeepers, but the same tone of finality also characterizes methods in the household. It is interesting to read to-day the objections raised fifty years ago to the use of anesthetics in surgery; it was argued that since pain was sent by heaven, it was sacrilegious to use any means of alleviating it. It may be of equal interest fifty years hence to read the protests of our contemporaries against the present effort to combat instinct with science.

Another difficulty is the inherent proneness of Americans to look for results before establishing the conditions on which alone results are to be based. The nervous haste that characterizes us physically as a nation also characterizes us mentally. We seize eagerly suggestions and scorn the slow processes through which alone suggestions can be made realities; then comes the inevitable reaction and we drift into the fatalistic tendency to put up with evils rather than fight against them.

One other general difficulty is the assumption that any improvement in domestic service must mean putting the domestic employee on a plane of absolute equality with the employer. Yet nothing could be farther from the truth than this. It is doubtful whether equality ever meant either in America or in France what the rhetorical phrases of the Declaration of Independence and the Declaration of the Rights of Man would on the surface seem to imply. Certainly to-day we interpret equality to mean that all persons should have the opportunity of making of themselves all that is possible; to jump at the conclusion that reform in domestic service means subscription to the literal interpretation of the preamble of the Declaration of Independence is to make an unwarranted assumption. If, however, we were to accept the doctrine of equality, it would be with an appreciation of what it involves. The establishment of social equality would sometimes mean the elevation of the employer to the natural social and moral position of the employee. Our present social status is well characterized by the late Lawrence Oliphant in "The Tender Recollections of Irene Macgillicuddy," where the heroine describes her mother, suddenly elevated in the social scale, as being very democratic toward all those who were socially above her and very aristocratic toward all those who were socially below her. It is specious, not genuine, democracy that to-day blocks the progress of improvement in domestic service.

These are general conditions that confront any and all attempts to put the household on a more reasonable basis. Not less serious are the specific economic conditions existing in the household. One of these is the truck system of wages.

In every other occupation the truck system has disappeared; formerly the teacher boarded around, the minister received an annual donation party, and the tailor and the carpenter shared the home of the master workman. The more recent attempt to pay employees in part in orders for household supplies on an establishment kept by the head of a factory or a mill has met with the most bitter protest. The truck system of payment in general industry is antiquated and disadvantageous to both parties of the labor contract. But in the household it is accepted as one of the foreordained provisions of the household, and meets with neither protest nor objection.

That the difficulties in the way of substituting another method of payment are very great must be accepted by all, but to say that it is impossible to bring about a change before any attempt has been made is idle. Wherever negroes are employed, the custom is almost universal for them to live in their own homes. In many families the experiment among white employees has been made successfully. It has been made on a somewhat extensive scale at the hotel at Saranac Inn, New York, where the employees lodge in a large house fitted up attractively with a dining-room that is used for dancing, while a billiard-room and smoking-room are provided for the married men who board in the house with their wives. So far these experiments are only variations of the truck system; the negro employees sleep at home, but have their meals in the families of their employers; in Saranac Inn the boarding-house for employees is owned and managed by the proprietor of the hotel. But they are illustrations of the fact that in limited areas it has been found possible to take the employee out of the house of the employer as far as lodging is concerned. To accomplish this must be the first step toward any modification of the truck system. Fifty years ago the teacher who "boarded 'round" probably looked on the truck system as an inevitable accompaniment of the occupation. Teaching is being raised from an occupation to a profession and one of the elements in the change is the fact that wages have been put on a different plane.

Another economic difficulty that some persons have found lies in the fact that, as has been said, the substitution of contract for status is at once the object and the method of modern civilization, and that domestic service owes nearly all of its difficulties to the fact that it is based on status. The reason why it has not been transferred to contract is because it is part of family life and no one has as yet shown how the family can be preserved as an institution if its members rest their relations on contract and not on status.

This may be true if the domestic employee is to be considered a part of the family. Yet just here is the anomaly and the fallacy of the objection. The domestic employee is not, and cannot be, a part of the family; she never in all her history has had more than a semblance of such a relationship and even that semblance has long since disappeared. The presence of the domestic employee in the family is not essential to the existence of the family; the domestic employee comes and goes, but the family remains. More than this, it must be said that the presence of the domestic employee does something to destroy the integrity of the family life. Family life presupposes the existence of congenial tastes and sympathetic relationships. It argues nothing against domestic service as an occupation that those engaged in it are rarely those who would be chosen as life companions or even as temporary companions by those with whom the accident of occupation has thrown them.

Yet more than this must be said. The statement that family life cannot be preserved if its members rest their relations on contract ignores the fact that the tendency in family life is precisely in this direction. The wife has her allowance, sons and daughters are given their allowances, financial dealings between members of the same family are becoming more definite and even legal in their character, and the result is not the disintegration of the family as it passes from status to contract, but a greater freedom of the individual members and therefore a more complex and perfect organization of the family relationships.

Another economic difficulty lies in the fact that so much of the service is largely personal in character, and that, therefore, payments are regulated by personal feelings and not by a recognized standard of payment. The result of this is the obnoxious system of fees — a system difficult to be done away with as long as employees expect to receive them. Fees could be abolished by the action of the employers, but as long as they prefer to have their employees paid by other persons — a practice that would be tolerated by no other class of employers — the initiative will not come from them. Fees could be abolished by the action of the individuals disposed to give them, but so long as men selfishly believe that money ought to purchase privileges that are not rights, the initiative will not come from them. Fees could be abolished by the concerted action of employees, but so long as they are ignorant of economic principles and indifferent to the social results of the system, the initiative will not come from them. But one of the hopeful signs of the times is the recent statement that in Paris waiters are coming to appreciate the fact that fees ultimately must mean smaller wages, since employers not only refuse to pay their employees but demand a certain percentage of the fees received. The movement among the waiters to refuse fees and to insist on wages paid by employers is full of promise.

What, then, are the conditions under which improvement in domestic service is possible?

First of all must come that attitude of mind that is willing to recognize not only the impossibility of separating domestic service from other parts of the household life, but still more the impossibility of separating the economic conditions within the household from the economic conditions without, a willingness to give up *a priori* reasoning in regard to domestic employments and to study the historical and economic development of the household. All superficial treatment of the question must fail of securing the desired results, and all treatment must be superficial that does not rest on the solid basis of economic history and theory.

Granted, then, the existence of economic conditions in the household, the method of procedure is the same as in all other fields of action. In medicine the first step is to diagnose the case; in law, to take evidence; in mathematics, to state the problem; in science, to marshal the facts. No set of *a priori* principles can be assumed in the household with the expectation that the household will conform to them. Investigation to-day stands at the door of every entrance into a new field and bars the way to any attempt to force a passage without its aid. The household has been slow to accept the inexorable fact that it must demolish its Chinese wall of exclusion and throw open its facts to investigation, but this is the inevitable end.

Next to the household, the most conservative element in society is the school. Yet the school is already yielding to the spirit of the times. It has been pointed out in a recent number of the *Atlantic Monthly*[3] that the profession of teaching, starting with a definite and final code of principles of education, has clung tenaciously to it, and it is but to-day that the occupation is realizing that it can make progress only as progress is made in other fields, and that is through scientific investigation; only to-day is it coming to appreciate that all conclusions to be valid must be based on facts. Every occupation has passed through the same experience and the law of progress that governs all development will work itself out in the household. Minds open to conviction and trained to scientific investigation are the prerequisites for an improved condition in domestic service.

Is it said that this discussion of the subject has dealt only with its economic phases and has ignored the ethical side? Alas, life is everywhere one long protest against a varying standard of ethics. Shall we separate the ethics of household service from the ethics of the shop, the ethics of the factory, the ethics of the professions? Shall we be governed by one code in the family, by another code in the church, by a third code in the school, and a fourth code in the state? Is the subject of ethics to be divided and pigeon-holed in compartments labeled "ethics for domestic service," "ethics for skilled labor," "ethics for unskilled labor," "ethics for employers," and "ethics for employees"? Who shall separate any question in economics, nay more, any question in life from its ethical phases? Who shall declare that the ethical code for one is not the ethical code for all?

It is said that every book is but the elaboration of a single idea. In a similar way all discussion of domestic service must have its beginning and its end with the idea that no improvement is possible that is not inaugurated by that class in society that sees most clearly the economic as well as the ethical elements involved in it, and that work by the slow methods of careful, patient investigation is the only way by which its difficulties, all too evident, may be lessened, not for ourselves but for those who shall come after us.

Our Kitchen

Our kitchen is not that of a millionaire; it has not a tiled floor, enameled brick walls or glass shelves; it is not fitted with appliances for cooking by electricity or with automatic arrangements for bringing up coal and sending down ashes. It is a plain, ordinary kitchen, built new six years ago, and attached to an old house to take the place of the former basement kitchen. It was planned by the landlord and the carpenter for unknown tenants, and the general arrangement had to conform to the plan of a house built many years before. If, then, it has been possible, with these usual, everyday conditions to develop a kitchen that possesses convenience of arrangement and unity of purpose, it would seem that similar ends might be obtained in any kitchen, anywhere, by any person, through use of the same means — careful thought.

We are busy women who have learned, in other lines of work outside the household, the value of order and system, and when we began housekeeping we saw no reason why the application to the kitchen of the same principles that were used in arranging a study or a library should not produce the same ease and joy in the work of the household. If a library, to be of service to those who work in it, must have its books classified according to some clearly recognized principle, would not a kitchen gain in usefulness if some principles of classifying its utensils were employed? If a study-table demands every convenience for work, ought not a kitchen-table to be equally well equipped? If the student can work more effectively in a cool room than in one that is stifling hot, will not a cook produce better results if working in a well-ventilated room? If the librarian needs special equipment, does not the butler need appliances adapted for his work? If the instructor needs the materials for investigation if his work is not to perish of dry rot, should not the houseworker have at hand all the materials needed if her work is to represent progress? If the parlor gains in attractiveness if its colors are harmonious, will not the kitchen gain if thought is given to appropriate decoration?

It was the affirmative answer to these and similar questions that led to the evolution of our kitchen from a state of unadorned newness to its present condition. An indulgent landlord provided a model range, a copper boiler, a porcelain-lined sink, and a double shelf; we have added the gas stove, the instantaneous water heater, the electric fan, two double shelves and all the utensils. Thus equipped, what does our kitchen represent?

To answer this question it is necessary to consider its general arrangement. The north side is filled by a window, the range, and the outside door.

Progress in the Household (Boston: Houghton Mifflin, 1906), 135–44.

Fig. 6. The "baking side" and the "cooking side" of Salmon's kitchen on Mill Street, ca. 1905. Courtesy of Vassar College, Special Collections.

This with the adjacent east side, we call "the cooking side." Here are arranged boilers, sauce-pans, broilers, and all implements large or small needed for cooking.

The south side is filled by the door leading into the refrigerator-closet, the baking-table, and the door leading into the butler's pantry. This we call the "baking side," for here is the baking-table with its bins for flour and meal, its drawers for baking-spoons, knives and forks, and sliding shelves for baking and for bread-cutting. Above it are various small utensils needed in baking, together with spices, essences, and various condiments. A "kitchen indicator" showing articles needed from the grocer's hangs at the left of the shelf, a peg at the end holds the household bills, and pegs at the right are for shears, scissors, a pin-cushion, and a cushion for needles used in preparing roasts.

The west side is the "cleaning side." This side is our special pride and delight, for here on a corner shelf is our electric fan, the drop-leaf table for drying dishes, the porcelain sink with its shining brass faucets, the nickel instantaneous water heater, and our fine forty-gallon copper boiler. Here above the sink are collected the cleaning brushes of various kinds, ammonia, borax, scouring-sand, and all cleaning preparations. The sink is set about three inches too low for comfortable use, a fault in sinks almost universal, and to remedy this defect a rack was evolved from four nickel towel-bars joined by connecting metal plates. Lack of wall space required that the shelf on this side of the room should be shared equally between the preparations for cleaning and the kitchen library, while the basket for news-papers and magazines occupies the end of the cleaning-table. But does not cleanliness of mind accompany cleanliness of material equipment?

The outside entry to the kitchen serves, in default of other place, as a cleaning-closet. Here are kept brooms, dusters, scrubbing brushes, polish-ing brushes, dusting mops and cleaning mops. Here also, easy of access, is kept the garbage pail, — three times each week emptied by the city garbage collector and three times each week scrubbed with hot soapsuds.

This is our kitchen as regards its ground plan and its exterior aspect. But the student of history always looks behind the external surface and studies the record; hence our kitchen records a belief in a few principles that seem fundamental in a household.

The first principle is that a kitchen should be absolutely sanitary in all its appointments. This means not only filtered cistern water, a still for distilling water, a porcelain-lined sink, and an abundance of hot water, but it means an absence of cubby-holes and cupboards where articles may be tucked away and accumulate dirt. Everything is in the open, every part of the kitchen is kept spotlessly clean, and we have never seen a rat or a water-bug about the house.

A second belief recorded by our kitchen is that of unity of plan. If the artist places before all else in importance the composition of his picture, if the author believes that his book should be the elaboration of a single idea, if the engineer knows that every part of his engine fits by design into every other part, it would seem clear that the application of the same principle is essential in the household. If the kitchen is to sustain an organic relation-ship to the other parts of the house it must represent in the arrangement of all its details the same idea of unity of composition that is expressed in a painting, a unity of development that gives life to a book, of unity of design that makes the perfect engine.

A third idea represented in our kitchen is that it must be equipped with every labor-saving device and with every convenience for work, if satisfactory results are to be secured. The first thought of the manufacturer is for the equipment of his manufacturing plant with every modern appliance. Can a perfect product come from imperfect, inadequate means of work in the household? The application of this principle has of necessity involved many experiments, — inventions will not work, or good ones are superseded by better ones, or a new need arises and must be met. Every week sees some article discarded because an improvement on it has been found. In the city of twenty-two thousand inhabitants in which we live, automobiles have been

Figs. 7 and 8. The "cleaning side" of the "philosophical kitchen" on Mill Street, before and after its remodeling about 1905. Courtesy of Vassar College, Special Collections.

Fig. 9. The "storage side" of Salmon and Underhill's kitchen. Courtesy of Vassar College, Special Collections.

used six years and approximately three hundred are now owned there and in the vicinity, but not one can be found of a pattern prior to that of three years ago. If an automobile must be disposed of because it is not of the most recent model, does it seem unreasonable to cast aside a twenty-five cent eggbeater that chafes the hands, a pineapple-snipper that wastes the fruit, an unsightly broken sauce-pan, and a patent water-cooler that will not cool the water?

But man does not live by bread alone, and a kitchen may be sanitary in all its arrangements, it may represent unity of plan, it may have every modern convenience, and yet it may lack the essential of attractiveness. The arts and crafts movement has not yet reached the kitchen, and it is thus almost impossible to secure cooking-utensils of good artistic design and color. But the second-hand store will often furnish a piece of good pottery, brass, or copper that may be utilized in the kitchen and serve the added purpose of increasing its attractiveness.

Yet a kitchen may illustrate all of these principles and still lack those subtle features that establish, unconsciously, some connection between it and its predecessors in other times and in other places. If the theory of evolution has taught us not only in science but in art and in politics and in everything connected with our daily life to look behind the surface and to seek the origins of things, if it has taught us ever to look for the relationship between the present and the past, surely the kitchen must not be excluded from this process of thought. Apparently the work performed there each day has neither connection with the past nor outlook into the future, yet this is but a superficial aspect of the situation. The kitchen of to-day with gas-range and instantaneous water-heater is the direct heir of the kitchen of yesterday with coal-range and copper boiler, and of that of the day-before-yesterday, with open fire and cauldron. An attempt to maintain this connection with the past is sought through the photographs on the walls. Two views of early colonial kitchens gave historic continuity with the past, a photograph of the interior of a Dutch kitchen gives a touch of that cosmopolitanism that makes the whole world akin, while that of a famous hotel in New York City places us by prophetic fiction in the class of millionaires.

Such is our kitchen. "Does it pay?" It has paid us.

The Family Cook-Book

The family cook-book seems destined to disappear as one of the pillars in the domestic fabric. The grandfather's clock has already been translated to the museum of relics. The spinning wheel has a corner reserved to it in such parlors as have not already passed. The copper kettle of many homely back-yard uses has been transferred to the front yard where it becomes a gipsy kettle and holds the sturdy geranium. The warming-pan finds a resting-place in the living-room or in the dining-room. All the once useful domestic articles, in their transmigration to other worlds, have apparently entered one socially more exalted, and such as survive utter annihilation may look forward to finding their ultimate and final abode in the historical museum.

But the family cook-book can anticipate no such honored end. Covered with protecting oil cloth, its binding broken, its leaves thumbed, dog-eared, torn, and smeared, it offers no attractions to the collectors of domestic "antiques." As a book it has no temptations for the collector even of first editions of modern authors who may be forgotten to-morrow; much less is it an object of pursuit comparable with the search for first folios of Shake-speare or Gutenberg Bibles.[1] The aristocratic cook-books of the seventeenth and eighteenth centuries, or even those of later date printed in unfamiliar languages, may become desiderata of collectors, but such objects of desire have little in common with the family cook-book of our grandmothers. That once-prized occupant of the kitchen shelf, where it stood in honored rela-tionship to *The Family Doctor*—was their proximity significant?—has like its twin companion found its last home with the junkman.

The family cook-book has been pushed into oblivion by different, some-what conflicting forces. One force that has destroyed it has been busy, bus-tling business efficiency that has substituted for it the next index card that is hung on a shelf-hook facing the worker, and then returned to its proper place in its polished wooden box. The worker incidentally saves the eye-strain involved in looking down at the cook-book on the kitchen table. She tosses off the simple articles called for by the cards in a tithe of the time demanded by the elaborate recipes of the cook-book, and she then goes cheerfully to her regular business.

Another business influence that has been the undoing of the family cook-book has been the delicatessen shop around the corner or on the way home. This can only be thought of as the degenerate offspring of the women's exchange that once seemed about to develop into a genuine co-operative business but was killed by charity, philanthropy, and the apotheosis of the sheltered life. The small shiplike kitchen, the kitchenette, the dining-room alcove included in the kitchen that goes with the apartment of four rooms and a bath; prepared foods, the thermos bottle, the chafiing dish, the gas plate, the fireless cooker, and the multifarious electric domestic contrivances have smothered the portly family cook-book. Domestic life *in petto* has everywhere in ordinary circles been substituted for the spacious life of our ancestors.

But the old law that action is equal to reaction finds an illustration in domestic life. The contracting walls of the material home have seemed to some to be symbolized by the iron maiden that held its victim in unescapable death-grasp. But as the home shrinks in size, its spirit, no longer self-contained, flies through the window and seeks new and broader contacts without itself. The college and the university do not teach cooking, but in every field of knowledge entered by them through research they promote a method of work that cultivates accuracy, observation, exactness, and all the mental traits that connote intelligence and independence of thought and action. This mental equipment transforms the happy-go-lucky ways of the old kitchen into a workroom where tools of precision take command. Chemistry, biology, physiology, and the various sciences that deal with the natural world are all enlarging the kitchen on the fact side, as they are cooperating with all other branches of human knowledge in enlarging it in acquaintance with more basic methods of work.

The recipes drawn from the family cook-book are no longer passed around among friends, neighbors and relatives; it is now the state and the federal government that gather up the work and the workers of the smaller units and then redistribute them over wide-spread areas. The family cook-book presumably had but a limited circulation in the immediate family of the owner. But government bulletins are distributed far and wide and the results of experiments made in the federal capital may redound to the benefit of a housekeeper in an Alaskan village. Reports on the use of the fireless cooker made in Wisconsin may give aid and comfort the unknown housewives in Atlantic coast fishing villages.

Thus one of the interesting records of the entrance of the government into the domestic circle is that of the different point of view it presents. The ultimate aim of the family cook-book was to give the members of the household everything "good to eat." In this it must have been successful beyond all cavil of a doubt. But at what an expenditure of human life! It must have been the housewife of a former day who gave the idea — she had no time to give the idea literary form — that heaven was a place of eternal rest, as recorded in the old hymnals. The variety and the quantity of the food placed on the family board three times a day is staggering to those who to-day live a more abstemious and simple life. To the housewife who ordered her table by the family cook-book, the balanced ration was unknown. Calories, proteins, carbohydrates, vitamins were terms not to be found in any dictionary her husband may have owned. Life extension institutes did not exist. Insurance companies did not calculate the probable duration of human life. The substitute, *not* "so good," for all the great health-saving organizations was found in the cook-book itself. An early cook-book might have as a sub-title *Incomparable secrets in physick, chirugery, Preserving, Candying, and Cookery*; or it might be called *A Collection of three hundred Receipts in Cookery, Physic, and Surgery*; or it might be *The Lady's Companion: Or, an infallible Guide to the Fair Sex. Containing Rules, Directions, and Observations, for their Conduct and Behaviour through all Ages and Circumstances of Life, as Virgins, Wives, or Widows . . . and above one thousand Receipts in every Kind of Cookery, etc., etc., etc.* A typical cook-book was, like all Gaul, divided into three parts, — one for recipes, one for cosmetics, and one for medicines. The antidote for the victim of defective or of too excellent cooking was always at hand, and the inroads on beauty made by a too assiduous devotion to domesticity could be concealed, it was hoped, by the application of cosmetics.

But the point of view of the Government is not concrete but abstract and impersonal. It does not have to meet the frowns that accompany sour bread, heavy cake, or burnt vegetables, and its objects are far-reaching in time and in space. It seeks to preserve life, to avoid unnecessary expenditure of time and effort, to apply within the home the principles that have been deduced from an extended and thorough study of all conditions affecting domestic life. The family cook-book is thus being superseded by government leaflets, by the instructions sent out from state experiment stations, by directions prepared by colleges of agriculture or of fisheries, by information circulated by experts attached to government bureaus — by every instrumentality at the service of the State. Socialism as a theory may be anathema to the housekeeper, but, unrealized by her, practical socialism has taken possession of her kitchen.

Thus at one end, the family cook-book has been crowded out by commercialism in the forms of business efficiency and articles of food "ready to serve"; and at the other, by the projection of government activities into the home — it seems to have joined the great class of the "has beens."

But the cook-book has not perished altogether, — it has simply exchanged the service it once rendered the housewife for the service it now renders the student of history. This service, it is true, is somewhat recent. John Richard Green found no place for the humble cook-book in extending his history of the English people to cover literature. John Bach McMaster used ephemeral material of every kind, except the cook-book, as the basis of his *History of the People of the United States*. Yet no surer record not only of domestic concerns but of great national and international interests can be found anywhere that are found in this battered and worn household companion.

The most obvious record is that of language. What shows more conclusively the strength of the domestic ties that bound together the various members of the family than do the names given favorite recipes — Aunt Hannah's loaf cake, Cousin Lizzie's waffles, Grandmother's cookies, Grandma

Lyman's marble cake, Sister Sally's quince jelly, Mother's raspberry vinegar, Warren's cake, Jennie's gingerbread, Jack's oyster stew, Mercy's nasturtium pickles, johnny cake, brown betty, and carolines, while general domestic happiness must have emanated from sunshine cake, pop-overs, and roly-polys.

But domestic ties did not prevent the members of the family from visiting other localities, either in body or in mind, and on their return enriching the family cook-book with recipes for Lady Baltimore cake, Philadelphia ice cream, Irving Park cake, Bangor pudding, Berkshire muffins, Boston brown bread, Saratoga chicken, and Maryland chips. Some "put up" at famous hostleries and returned with glowing accounts of Parker House rolls, Waldorf salad, Delmonico cream, and maitre d'hôtel sauce, but how many veritably authentic recipes from famous hotels or chefs have found their way into the family cook-book is not clear. Some even traveled abroad and returned with recipes for Vienna coffee, Yorkshire pudding, Nuremburg cakes, Banbury tarts, Bavarian cream, Irish stew, Scotch broth, English muffins, and Hamburg steak. Every country visited by travellers makes its contribution to the cook-book — from India to Alaska; from Bolivia, Chile, and Mexico, to Iceland and Russia; from China, Japan, and the Hawaiian Islands, to the West Indies and the Canaries. The cook-book has become a universal melting pot. And the recipes have been but the forerunners of foreign articles of food that still further enlarged the culinary arts. Macaroni, spaghetti, sauerkraut, frankfurters, chili con carne, tamales, Devonshire cream, Neufchâtel cheese, chop suey, Brussels sprouts, all found at least a temporary home in the cook-book.

And if a long leash permitted travels into distant parts, domestic ties again brought the traveller home, and they are recorded in the recipes for family and seasonal festivities — birthday cake, bride's cake, wedding cake, christening cake, reception cocoa, barbecue ham, all find their place in the cook-book.

But domestic ties are but a part of the life recorded in the language of the cook-book. The Church receives its tribute in hot cross buns, lenten salad, lenten croquettes, eastern cream, nun's puffs, nun's sighs, angel food, cardinal mousse, hermits, twelfth-night cake, Scripture cake, Christmas cake, Quaker cake, Jerusalem pudding, and devil's food.

Its rival, the State, with its political questions, also takes toll from the cook-book, and election cake, civic cake, training-day gingerbread, Confederate army soup, Pilgrim cake, Independence day cake, cabinet pudding, diplomatic pudding, all give evidence of the invasion of the home, long prior to the passage of the nineteenth amendment, of questions beyond its confines. And however much we may cherish the love of democracy in the abstract, do we unconsciously pay homage to aristocracy in the concrete? For how shall we otherwise account for the presence in the humble cook-book of sultana rolls, imperial cream, royal custard, imperatrice ice cream, queen cake, royal icing, royal diplomatic pudding, Princess ice, and Queen Anne rolls?

So, too, great public characters, perpetuated by name in the cook-book, attest our adoption of high personages into the family circle where they play an important part in relieving the dull monotony of routine life. Washington pie, Jefferson stew, Robespierre omelet, Napoleons, Lorenzo canapé, Nesselrode pudding, Victor Hugo sauce, Chateaubriand steak, Prince Henry croquettes, Jenny Lind tea cake, and Queen Victoria soup may all be found on humble tables.

Higher education may not have adopted cooking into its curriculum, but the cook-book pays homage to it in adopting on its part the names of institutions of learning and giving directions for preparing Harvard pudding, Vassar fudge, Wellesley tea, and University pudding.

The work of the housewife may seem to have been one of unalleviated routine, but while her mind roamed abroad and returned with the names of lords and ladies of high degree which she attached to the products of her hand, was she not to that extent emancipated from the limitations of time and space? And if perchance her mind found congenial associations with the realm of nature, her imagination led her to compare her own handiwork with that of the outer world. Poetry enters the humdrum kitchen and transforms it through birds on canapés, bird's-nest pudding, floating islands, apples in bloom, shadow potatoes, cheese aigrettes, apple snow, snowballs, gossamer gingerbread, fairy gingerbread, aurora sauce, moonlight cake, lily cake, lady fingers, and amber pudding. And again, may she not, like the mediaeval worker in stone who loved the grotesque figures he fashioned, have found an outlet for her humor in fashioning in her turn "pigs in blankets," "angels on horseback," "bubble and squeak," and "harlequin balls"? May she not also find a humorous satisfaction in giving her economies the masquerading names of Welsh rabbit, Scotch woodcock, and English monkey?

The language of the cook-book again records a vastly different world from the one we know to-day. The sheltered life is recorded when the author, — or the "authoress," as she was called on the title-page — shielded herself from publicity and announced the book as written by "a lady," "a gentlewoman," "an accomplished housewife," or "American Cookery by an American Orphan." The orphan who shrinkingly concealed her name from the prying curiosity of the housewife is many stages removed from the modern up-to-date author who counts on the sale of her cook-book because it appeals, not the charity of the public, but to her own reputation as a cook, or as the head of a cooking-school, or as a recognized expert in the field of domestic science.

But charity appears in many guises, and if "an American orphan" has disappeared from the title-page of the cook-book intended by its sale to contribute to her slender support, the charity cook-book to be sold at church fairs is ever with us. Here no "modest violet" conceals her identity lest she imperil the sale of her book. On the contrary, the social prestige of the bearers of the names attached to the recipes is counted on to enhance the sales. The recipes themselves may have little or no intrinsic value, but the names of Mrs. Van Astorbilt and Mrs. Murdorf de Clementine are relied upon to float the book.

The cook-book again may derive its name not from the reputation of a distinguished author-cook, but from that of a city or a locality. The *Philadelphia Cook-book*, the *Bluegrass Cook-book, Cooking in old Creole Days*, the *Belgian Cook-book, Italian Recipes*, the *Jewish Cook-book*, all attest sectional, national, and racial, as well as individual, reputation in the art of cooking. To the French alone has it been given to enter the cook-books of every nationality and through its purées, fondus, souffles, compôtes, and the entire range of the language of the cuisine, to transform cooking into an art.

How far removed in time and thought are the cook-books of gentlewomen and orphans from those of to-day that appeal for support on the merits of their contents rather than on the poverty of the compiler! The family cook-book, "*especially intended as a full record of delicious dishes sufficient for any well-to-do family, clear enough for the beginner and complete enough for ambitious providers,*" blossoms out as the scientific cook-book fresh from the schools of domestic economy, household economics, or domestic science. Advancing theories of education are recorded in postgraduate cookery books, as well as in the high degree of specialization seen in *One hundred and one ways of preparing oysters, Fifteen new ways of cooking oysters, One hundred and fifty ways of cooking Indian corn, More than two hundred ways of cooking apples, My best two hundred and fifty recipes, Three hundred and sixty-five breakfast dishes, Three hundred and sixty-five desserts, Fifty soups,* and books devoted exclusively to recipes for preparing vegetables, eggs, fish, sandwiches, salads, or soups. And are not successive generations of varying aspects of "the staff of life" recorded in the names "mother's bread," "dyspepsia bread," "graham bread," "aerated bread," "Swedish bread," "Hoover bread," and "war bread"?

"Exhaustive manuals," "complete cook-books," and cook-books "covering the whole range of cookery" give place to *The Small Family Cook-book, The Cook-book of Left-overs, Made-over Dishes, Food and cookery for the sick, Food for the invalid and the convalescent, Hot weather dishes,* and *The dinner calendar for* 1912. *The White House Cookbook: A comprehensive cyclopaedia of information for the home, containing cooking, toilet, and household recipes, menus, dinner-giving, table etiquette, care of the sick, health suggestions, facts worth knowing, etc.* is far removed in thought, as well as in time, from *Food, fuel for the human engine; what to buy, how to cook it; how to eat it; the simple story of feeding the family, based on the Diet Squad experiment in cooperation with the New York City Police Department.*

Business has entered the cook-book, and its pages have been made up in the interests of a special brand of baking powder, a new variety of shortening, a great milk-distributing corporation, a standard brand of flour, or a well-known variety of chocolate. Both business and cook-book are under deserved suspicion when every recipe recommends the use of some special manufactured product — a special brand of molasses, or vinegar, or preparation of spices, and all the names in heavy, capital type.

Not less unerringly than in language does the cook-book record economic conditions. The royal hand that in the preparation of a single dish once used eggs by the dozen, thick cream by the pint, and butter by the pound has been succeeded by that of the business woman who estimates the cost of food in terms of dollars and cents. *The Economy Cook-book* and *Better Meals for Less Money* have displaced the *Queen's Royal Cookery* and *The Complete Court-Cook*. They give "first aid to the housekeeper in distress," and provide recipes for one-egg cake, poorman's pudding, emergency biscuit, one-egg muffins, half-pay pudding, cottage pie, and miner's hash. It would be more true to say that the attention of cooks is no longer concentrated on ways of preparing food for lords and ladies of high degree. Instead, interest has pressed downward and no circle of human life is too humble to be reached by the cook-book prepared especially to meet its needs. *Cookery for workingmen's wives and oatmeal food* has been made the subject of a consular report, *Economical Cooking, planned for two or more persons, compiled from many sources and especially designed to reduce the cost of living; The Small Family Cook-book; Key to Simple Cookery; The Cottage Kitchen*, all record the growing interest in "the other half." Substitutes and articles "just as good" enter the pages of the cook-book and record the high price of butter and other articles once deemed indispensable in the preparation of food, but not used to reduce the cost of living.

The shadow of war fell on the cook-book and nowhere are the privations of warfare more in evidence than in the cook-book with its recipes for meatless menus, wheatless breads, sugarless cake, conservation plum pudding, Hoover corn bread, liberty fig rolls, vegetable canning — conservation was everywhere the key note of daily life. Well might the healthy young appetite have cried out, "Conservation, conservation everywhere and nothing good to eat."

But the language of the cook-book has recorded much besides the strength of domestic ties, travels at home and in foreign lands, the influence of Church and State in all walks of life, and the eternal conflict between the abstract theory of democracy and the concrete admiration of aristocracy. Not only does it record changing systems of education; the invasion of the kitchen by questions of production and distribution, of specialization and cooperation, of war and peace, but revolutions in thought are everywhere in evidence.

An eminent philosopher-historian has classified minds into those who look to the restoration of the past for the attainment of the perfect life and those who find it in the progress of the future. Other antagonistic principles govern human life. One type of mind seeks always authority as the basis of action, while its opposite finds in investigation and research the culmination of inborn curiosity. The eternal conflict between the old and the new, between authority and research, is nowhere more in evidence than it is in the cook-book of the housewife. Authority rears its head in "tested recipes," "recipes prepared from experience," "the famous old recipes used a hundred years and more in the kitchens of the North and South are contributed by their descendants," "approved recipes," "favorite recipes," and in recipes for food "like Mother used to make." The love of exploration, adventure, investigation, and of discovering whatever has not been known before comes out in "my own recipes," "something different recipes," "modern recipes," and "household discoveries."

It is perhaps significant that by far the larger number of recipes are those based on the principle of authority. Thus the humble cook-book in the main runs in harmony with the conservative human mind as shown in other fields. Caution rather than adventure, fear of the unknown rather than the joyful quest for new worlds; adhesion to a safe past rather than voyages to far countries probably characterize the great majority of human kind. Is it for this type of mind that a recent cook-book has been prepared and entitled *Eating Without Fears*? Yet progressive liberalism is ever alert and its adherents choose to believe — it is not susceptible to proof — that the love of research is steadily gaining over the principle of authority, and they rejoice in the evidence of the reasonableness of this belief that the cook-book affords. If the old cook-book gave recipes for medicines for the sick, the new cook-book provides a balanced ration for the well. If *The Helping Hand Cook-book, The Infallible Guide*, and *The Whole Art of Cookery Made Easy* were prepared for the use of the sheltered daughters of an earlier day, the cook-book of to-day discusses principles and processes, it is written for the trained mind of the intelligent, self-reliant, independent housekeeper, and it illustrates in itself the complementary principles of individual specialization and collective cooperation.

Other changes are also recorded in the cook-book: A young college man was recently asked if the schools of engineering and of domestic science that formed a part of the technical university with which he was connected were open alike to men and women students. They were not excluded from either one, he replied, but while there were no women in the school of engineering, they might sometimes enter it, but no man would ever enter a school of domestic science.

History is always a safer field than prophesy. It is well to remember that Thomas Austin edited two fifteenth-century cook-books now in the British Museum — both written by men. When the closet of Sir Kenelm Digby, Knight, was opened, there were "discovered" "Excellent Directions for Cookery: As also for Preserving, Conserving, Candying, &c." The cook-books of the seventeenth and the eighteenth centuries were largely the work of men, — always excepting the *Art of Cookery* by the incomparable Mrs. Hannah Glasse that ran through successive editions for nearly a hundred years. It is in the family cook-book of the nineteenth century that the high-tide of womanly domesticity is reached. But it is in the cook-book of the twentieth century that the balance is restored and the cook-book records the growth by geometrical progression of the spirit of co-operation between men and women. If women have entered political life, men have returned to their former interest in domestic life and both men and women are giving their interest and energy to the field in which their individual ability lies. The cook-book records more than it realizes! At an early period cook-books were prepared by men and "*made most profitable and necessary for all men, and the generall good of this Kingdome.*" In the middle period, the field contracted and Mrs. Ellis's *Housekeeping made easy; or, Complete Instructor in all Branches of Cookery and Domestic Economy, containing the most useful and approved Receipts,*" indicated that the home was the sphere of women. The cook-book went even further than this and the domestic, social, and industrial philosophy of centuries was summed up in the descriptive title of a cook-book that was issued in many editions. It was called *The Whole Duty of a Woman: Or a Guide to the Female Sex from the Age of Sixteen to Sixty*, etc. . . . . *Also Choice Receipts in Physick, and Chirugery. With the Whole Art of Cookery, Preserving, Candying, Beautifying, etc.* Written by a Lady. And the eighth edition has an appropriate frontispiece, the woodcut of a woman at prayers and in the kitchen.

A radical change has come in the third period. The quest for knowledge is shared alike by men and by women and the cook-book of today records their mutual, cooperating interest in overcoming ignorance and in advancing the outposts of knowledge. A work of insight and of erudition on *Roman Cooks* comes from the pen of Cornelia Gaskins Harcum, and a distinguished American, recently an Ambassador at a foreign Court, discussed, in the pages of a leading American monthly, six recent books on cooking. Evelene Spencer, Fish Cookery Expert for the United States Bureau of Fisheries, and John N. Cobb, Director of the College of Fisheries, University of Washington, have cooperated in the preparation of a book on the cooking of fish. The directors of schools of domestic science may be indifferently men or women. Everywhere artificial arbitrary walls of demarcation are breaking down and the normal natural processes of human life are thereby promoted. The faded manuscript cook-book that was treasured by the house-wife who compiled it had been preceded by early manuscript cook-books written in a language unfamiliar to our grandmothers and by costly volumes printed on vellum. It has been followed by the cook-book that has been the result of investigation and research. The cook-book, from its early beginnings in ministering to the real or fancied needs of aristocratic circles, through its various stages of rendering aid to timid, inexperienced housewives, to its present preoccupation with the problem of the prolongation of healthful human life, has at all times faithfully recorded much of the life and interests of its age.

The cook-book has unconsciously revealed the characteristics of many countries, many times, and many classes of society, and the changes that have come in all. That the prodigal use of materials seen in a society emerging from the frontier stage of development was matched by the prodigal expenditure of the lives of women demanded in their preparation for the table the cook-book records. The natural interest of one people in expressing their thought in artistic form is illustrated in a highly developed art of cooking and of serving food that has characterized the French, and this too the cook-book records. The longitudinal interest in the cooking of a single nation, as recorded in *Italian Recipes* or *Russian Cooking*, has developed into a latitudinal interest in the varying ways of preparing the same articles as seen in the cook-books embodying recipes of every nationality.

The inexactness that once directed the housewife in making cake to "take a few eggs, a piece of butter, two cups of sugar, some milk, flour enough to thicken, give a good beating, and bake according to judgment" has been supplanted by directions given with the minuteness as to weights and measures found in a physical laboratory. The indifference as to the effects of "instinctive" cooking on the human body has been followed by prolonged study of this human body whose needs were once so ignored by the cook-book; investigation, experiment, observation, and research are now in control of the household. The education of to-day may be proclaimed a failure by the bumptious, self-assertive person, decrying every college because it does not give courses in cooking, and demanding what "mother used to make," but the cook-book itself knows better! Every page of every cook-book coming from the laboratory of an expert bears witness to the progressive thoroughness of education, to the importance attached to making the preparation of food serve the best interests of mankind, and to the emphasis it places on fundamental principles and the relation between cause and effect.

Theories of social relationships, of physical well-being, of mental health, of the meaning of all human life are spread on the pages of the cook-book of today as it is sent forth by officials of the government. Yet thus has it always been. From the earliest cook-book known; from *Closet of the Eminently Learned Sir Kenelm Digby Kt.*, of the seventeenth century; from Mrs. Hannah Glasse's *The Art of Cookery, Made Plain and Easy; Which far exceeds any Thing of the Kind ever yet Published*, of the eighteenth century; from *The American Frugal Housewife* of Mrs. Lydia Maria Child that ran through at least thirty-three editions in the nineteenth century; to the latest Government Bulletin issued on cooking in the twentieth century, the cook-book has recorded the development, by an ever-ascending spiral, of the interests of human life.

The City and the World of Objects

In a remarkable series of essays and pamphlets written during the early years of the twentieth century, Lucy Salmon formulated a historical methodology based on the reading of objects. Using the backyard and main street as test cases, she sought to find a way to integrate the everyday world of things into a comprehensive historical vision. She expressed this new methodology in a striking modernist writing style — broken, fragmented, cubistic — that captured her vision in irregular staccato rhythms or in lengthy encyclopedic lists. A photographer herself, it was as if these techniques represented the aggregation of isolated fragments of photographic detail. But unlike the photographer, who could only represent the surface, the historian could penetrate the surface and look into the past. Objects were reified history, and she set no bounds on this study. "The Economics of Spending," published in 1909, for example, reveals how carefully she observed the practices of shopkeepers and shoppers; a manuscript on women's fans describes how design and social practices interact. She taught her students to start their research by examining their textbooks, their library, and their classroom as objects. For Salmon herself, however, history was everywhere in a profusion that becomes almost comical. The family cookbook, changes in gym costumes (in "The Historical Museum"), and the form of parliamentary architecture, a subject discussed in "The Record of Monuments" (1933), but which she writes about as early as 1906, are all the objects of her interest. Indeed, in many of the essays in this volume she turns to objects in order to make a point, to prove just how complex history could be.

History in a Back Yard

Hope for a summer in Europe vanished into the dim background of "next year" while discouragement occupied the foreground. Where forsooth could one get new ideas except in Europe, where find a library outside of London or Paris, where study historical records but in foreign archives, where see the results of archaeological discoveries outside of European museums, where harvest stores of historical knowledge except in foreign fields? Winter quarters for nine months at home were endurable for the sake of three months of activity in other lands, but hibernation prolonged to twenty-one months — that was unthinkable. The calendar has indeed always seemed hopelessly wrong — were not the three months in Europe a full year of mental life, and did not the nine months of constant draft on mental resources at home shrink to a paltry week of growth? Did not three months of acquisition in Europe leave one rich, while nine months of constant depletion of mental capital at home left one bankrupt? If "fifty years of Europe were better than a cycle of Cathay," did it not follow that one-fourth of a year in Europe was better than three-fourths of a year anywhere else? It was all a tangle that might possibly have been straightened out after a summer abroad, but in June it was a hopeless snarl.

But the chance question of a friend put Aladdin's lamp in our hands and opened up before our eyes as large an undiscovered world as could be found in seven kingdoms. She had asked how she could study history in a back yard, and, lo, the whole past opened up at our door! Why search for hidden treasure abroad when the history of the world was spread out in the back yard? Perish the thought that we had ever sought knowledge elsewhere — we would study historical records in a garden seat, and search for archaeological remains in the summer house. If Mahomet could not go to the mountain, the mountain could summer in the back yard. The world was still ours to explore!

Our back yard is a parallelogram about thirty feet wide and four times as long. On one of the long sides a board fence separates it from the adjoining property and in that direction a series of fences marks the divisions of private property. On the other side of our yard, our kindly landlord and a genial neighbor agreed to take down the division fence between the two places, other neighbors on that side have followed their example, and thus a green park extends in the rear of the block half way to the corner. At the lower end of the yard, a very high board fence separates our yard from the one that joins it back-to-back and conceals from our view the vegetable garden of the neighbor in our rear.

Privately printed in 1912; reprinted in *Historical Material* (New York: Oxford University Press, 1933), 143–57.

Now it seems a very simple, commonplace thing to have a fence, or not to have a fence, and the question is apparently one to be decided by the common consent of the two adjacent property holders. If a fence is built, it means presumably that the property owners place a high value on privacy and seclusion, that they do not care for the unsought visits of children, that they do not wish to expose their flowers, their fruit, and their vegetables to the ravages of those too lazy to plant their own gardens, but not too lazy to profit by the industry of others, that they seek protection from the dogs, pigs, goats, and cows that in some localities still have the freedom of the town and in a not remote past had it in all. If the fence is surmounted by a row of spikes, it indicates not simply an aversion to certain undesirable conditions, but a positive fear of disagreeable visitors and of dangerous intruders, coupled with serious doubts about the enforcement of the law on the part of those charged with that duty. If a high hedge is selected to mark the boundary lines, it suggests not only a love of retirement and contemplation, but a desire for protection from dust while currents of air are not entirely shut off. The hedge also becomes a screen that separates the prosaic vegetable garden from the lawn or the flower beds. If, however, the hedge is placed behind a high stone wall, then indeed are all passers-by impressed with the love of solitude that characterizes the occupants of the place. The invitation "to loaf and invite the soul" becomes esoteric, not exoteric, and whoever braves the forbidding wall and hedge and enters within feels himself a candidate for the medal awarded the doer of "the bravest deed ever done."

If, on the other hand, no fence is built, or one already built is taken down, it may indicate a disregard of privacy and a desire to live more or less in the public eye, it may be an index of aesthetic ideals, or it may imply a growing desire to subordinate personal advantage to public good or an appreciation of how much is gained by neighbors who have interests in common rather than mutually repellent characteristics. The absence of a fence shows that laws are both made and enforced, restraining cattle from running at large — what community of interest once demanded, community of interest now forbids.

It is thus apparently a matter of option between neighbors whether or not property rights are indicated by an outward, visible symbol, and it seems equally a matter of option whether that symbol of private ownership shall take the form of a fence, a hedge, or a wall, or any combination of these three forms of enclosure. Moreover, it seems again a matter of option what variety of material is to be used in constructing the division-marker. The wall may be of brick because brick is cheap, or because it harmonizes with the architecture of the house and with its other settings; it may be of stone because the land needed clearing, or because the owner was able to gratify his taste and import stone from a distance. The material of which the dividing wall is built may indicate either one of the two extremes of necessity or of luxury, of resourcefulness of ideas or of abundance of means.

The fence in its turn may be a record of pioneer days when the first settlers cleared the forests and the stump fence became a by-product; the zig-zag rail fence is a later development of pioneer life, while the plain board fence and the picket fence were the plebeian and the patrician divisions between village lots. The lattice fence meant honeysuckle vines, while the iron fence meant the portly, prosperous merchant who was always up-to-date. The introduction of the barbed wire fence indicated the ravages that had been made on the timber supply of the country, while legislation against the use of barbed wire and the substitution for it of woven wire and other forms of wire fencing is a record of growing humanitarianism and the care that the state is coming to take for the protection of both animals and men. The still further depletion of the timber supply is recorded in the displacement of the wooden fence post by the concrete post, and thus the gamut is complete from a fence entirely of timber in some stage of development to a fence constructed without any timber whatsoever.

The character of the hedge as marking the division line is determined by its secondary object. Is this secondary object protection against the free passage of animals, the osage orange is called into requisition; is the land low and marshy and does it demand support, the willow hedge is set out; if wind and dust are special enemies, the hedge of evergreens results; if privacy is sought, the privet, the box, and the arbor vitae are in demand; if varied beauty is the ideal, the barberry is planted. The hedge, to a greater extent than the wall and the fence, not only serves as a line of demarcation, but it also renders a secondary service of beauty scarcely less important than its primary one of indicating boundary lines.

But, after all, wall and fence and hedge are but outward symbols of a crude method of marking private ownership. "The things that are seen are temporal, but the things that are unseen are eternal." The real boundary lines have been long ago established by the theodolite of the surveyor and they have been recorded in the office of the county clerk in the county court-house. Walls, fences, and hedges of every form and variety known to man may be set up, and taken down, but the surveyor's instruments and the recorded deeds are a court from whose decisions no appeal can be taken.

The unpretentious plain board fence that separates us from one of our neighbors has introduced us to the whole question of methods of marking boundary lines, to the complicated subject of surveying that has in the beginning determined where these boundary lines are to run, and to an elaborate legal system that has been developed for the purpose of establishing and maintaining the claims of rightful ownership.

On the other side of our back yard, there is no indication of private ownership of property—neither wall, nor fence, nor hedge separates us from our neighbor's apple-trees and rhubarb, we share his garden seats and his lawn swing, and we in turn offer him the hospitality of our berry bushes, our grapevines, and our summer house. We know indeed that the boundary line has been measured to the fraction of an inch and that its location has been duly described in the deeds of ownership of the two adjacent properties, and that these deeds are presumably deposited in two respective safe deposit boxes in one of the city banks. But as long as no fence obtrudes itself with its insistence on private ownership, we shall enjoy the fiction of joint ownership with our neighbor of all the treasures of two back yards. The fence means isolation, separation, and lack of common interest; the absence of the fence means community life, mutual aid, toleration, and joint pleasures and opportunities.

Who made the first fence and who gave him the right to make that fence? "Ah, there's the rub!" If the fence on one side of our back yard has introduced us to the realms of higher mathematics by way of the surveyor's line and compass, and to the Torrens system of recording deeds by way of the court-house on the corner, and to the question of public guardianship of personal property by way of the safe deposit box in the bank, the absence of a fence on the other side has brought us face to face with a question that antedates all the written records of history. Did private ownership of land precede communal ownership, or was land held in common and did enclosure follow? Over this question battles on paper have been lost and won, reputations made and shattered, and the final word in regard to it said with each and every recurring discussion of the subject. With a fence on two sides and no fence on the other two sides, our back yard maintains a discreet impartiality and refuses to commit itself on the merits of the controversy.

Our back yard has nothing that even by courtesy could be called a garden — a few spring bulbs blossom in the lawn, a row of rosebushes reminds us when June comes, bunches of old-fashioned artemisias announce the arrival of autumn, a trumpet vine all but conceals a rustic summer house, honeysuckles cover the lower branches of a mulberry tree, berry bushes and morning glories conceal in summer the long dividing fence, a high trellis for grapevines is at the lower end of the yard, immediately in front of the high division fence covered with woodbine. A long narrow strip of lawn connects the back yard proper with a passage-way that leads to a bit of lawn in front of the house where a rose of Sharon and a hydrangea are found and a wisteria that climbs over the front porch. A few spring flowering shrubs are planted along this very narrow strip of grass that connects the back yard with the passage-way, and a few annuals blossom for us wherever it is convenient to drop the seed in the spring. An occasional weed persistently comes up every year, apparently rather not to be forgotten than to be obnoxiously obtrusive.

It all seems very simple and commonplace and there is nothing that at first indicates its cosmopolitan character. But a study of genealogy reveals many surprising and interesting family relationships. The crocus comes from the Levant, the hyacinth and the narcissus bear Greek names, the daffodil is a native of England, the tulip in its name is allied with Turkey and in its history with Holland, the fleur-de-lis is the insignia of France and also of Florence, our lilac is Persian, the wisteria is Japanese, the asters Chinese, the rose of Sharon suggests Palestine, the ubiquitous thistle is Scotch, while cosmos in its name connects us with the order and harmony of the whole created universe. Could the nations of the world live together as peacefully as do their representatives in our back yard, international peace would be already an accomplished fact.

But our flowers and shrubs and vines bring us into contact not only with the nations of the world in this very concrete form, but they introduce us to the world-old union and conflict of realism and idealism, the literal and the imaginative. Realism confronts us in the names of the morning glory, the trumpet vine, the honeysuckle, and the tulip, while imagination and ideal-ism give us the heliotrope, the hydrangea, the narcissus, and the hyacinth. Yet it is the realism of the Greek that crops out in the names of the he-liotrope and the hydrangea while it undergoes a sea-change in becoming for us words of the imagination and idealism. Is it possible that the realism of one becomes the idealism of another? What if all our realism has its imagina-tive side and what if our idealism has its roots in realism.

We have never quite understood why there should be a mulberry tree in our back yard, but there it is and it makes a pleasant connection for us with that doughty Dutch patroon, Kiliaen van Rensselaer. He never saw the vast estates on the Hudson to which his name was given, but he managed the territory and the colony in his Amsterdam office at a distance of more than three thousand miles in space and four months' distance in time. Among other minute instructions sent out to his agent is one to the effect that he should be on the look-out for silkworms since they are likely to be found where there are mulberry trees. Whether the agent found the silkworms or not, the papers of Kiliaen van Rensselaer do not state, but we infer that he may not have done so since we have been on the look-out for silkworms for some years, and while in our search we have encountered fireflies, mos-quitoes, June bugs, and bats, no silkworms have been discovered.

Our back yard does not in truth have a Lombardy poplar, but it so natu-rally belongs there that we often look at a certain spot and lo, the tree is there. The Lombardy poplar was the emblem of democracy in the struggle between Lombardy and Austria and the very derivation of its name from *populus* gives it a democratic lineage. If princes and potentates take the rose and the lily as emblems of their authority, why should not humble social democrats take the Lombardy poplar with its double democratic lineage as the badge of their individual beliefs? And if the tree is not in reality in our back yard, but is there in spirit, is it not in the end the same?

Nor does our back yard number among its assets a Norway maple. Yet we have claimed kinship also with this. If at times we are all cowards, are there not other times when the blood of the vikings flows in our veins? If at times inertia keeps us in our accustomed places, are there not many more times when the zest for exploring the undiscovered realms of knowledge takes us into far countries? Our Norway maple links us with the venturesome voyagers of old who were ever seeking new paths across the trackless seas and it thus opens up to us the whole world of knowledge for discovery and exploration. The cherry tree outside of our back window is not ours — the robins take the fruit, other birds build their nests in its branches, winter claims its foliage, and we have no special feeling of affection for it; it is a plain, prosaic cherry tree, doubtless with admirable qualities, but it is a stranger to us. But our blood tingles with the glimpse of our democratic Lombardy poplar and our venturesome Norway maple. These bloom for us in perennial youth.

The grapevines at the lower end of the yard are not in themselves real additions to the place — the grapes rarely ripen, and when they do ripen they are small and tasteless. It is not for the sake of what they are, but for the sake of what they suggest, that every year we mend the trellis and trim the vines — for the grapevines connect us with the great revolutionary movement in western Europe and put us in touch with the company of young men who came to this country to seek the political liberty they had missed in their native land. Among the number was a young German who settled in northern Iowa, edited a newspaper for a livelihood, and cultivated grapes for recreation. Coming from the valley of the Rhine where the vines were grown on poles rather than on trellises, he became an ardent advocate of the advantages of the single-pole method of grapevine culture, and the merits of his grapes attested individually the virtues of his theory. But his theory of grape cultivation and the zest with which he advocated it were after all but an outlet for a genuine love of political liberty and social individualism — traits that characterized his family, another branch of which had given to the cause of liberty the Tyrolese patriot, Andreas Hofer. If we tend our grapevines and do not resent their thankless return for the care lavished on them, it is because we see behind them the German Revolution of 1848–1849 and back of that the Tyrolese uprising of 1809, and because our sympathies and interests are with the side that met temporary defeat in the struggle for political equality.

The English ivy does not thrive in our climate, but it sometimes maintains a precarious existence where it does not grow luxuriantly, and our back yard counts as its greatest treasure a modest vine grown from a slip taken from the home of Maria Mitchell at Nantucket. When discouragement comes and nothing seems quite worth while, the ivy becomes a veritable tent of Pari-Banou and quickly we are at her island home, we discover with her the famous comet that bears her name, we share her interests and her work, we sit in her observatory and listen to "the music of the spheres," and behold, all things are made new.

Our back yard has little in the way of furniture, but that little is an interesting record of the changes that have come even in our own day in the direction of greater naturalness and a more normal, healthy, wholesome life. The old love of fashionable adornment that found expression in iron dogs, stone deer, and garden statuary, and the love of ostentatious display that found an outlet in the importation of Italian seats, French fountains, and Spanish vases have given place to a genuine interest in out-of-door life, healthful exercise, and rational recreation. The old playhouse where the children quietly amused themselves with toys and dolls has given place to the sand box, the tent, the cart, the wheel, and the diminutive automobile. Tennis and croquet are possible even in a restricted space, and the bicycle is again coming into its own. The hammock, the garden bench, the seat with protecting awning, and the summer house all show the growing love of fresh air, and the appreciation of the back yard as a place for rest and refreshment. The change has extended even to animal life — the artificial bird house has disappeared and the birds seek their own location, while the dog kennel has vanished with the banishment of the large dog to the country.

Industrial changes are recorded in our back yard. Once the weekly laundry was displayed on lines strung between posts, then came the clothes reel, and now both have disappeared since the laundry is done out of the house. But our back yard joins back-to-back the yards of the two-family houses on the next street, and now we see, is it every day in the week? the line and pulley that show that the domestic "wash" is done in the limited space afforded by flat and tenement and apartment. Is there some maladjustment somewhere that demands that laundry work must be done in a space inadequate for it, while it is sent out of a house that has abundance of room for doing it? Will sometime the record show that laundry work is everywhere taken out of the individual flat, tenement, apartment, house, mansion, palace, and done under perfect sanitary and economic conditions?

Electric wires running in our back window show the cooling of the kitchen by an electric fan and suggest the future possibilities of the substitution of electricity for gas in lighting and in summer cooking.

The growing interest in sanitation has also left its record in our back yard. A disused cistern means an improved municipal water supply and the galvanized iron can with tight fitting cover indicates that garbage is collected by the city, though the pile of ashes in the back yard of one neighbor and the mound of rubbish in that of another suggests fields for municipal activity as yet but partially entered. The rain-water barrel in the back yard of a friend, with its coat of kerosene, suggests new ideas of sanitation and the mosquito.

Our back yard has a modest outlook over the back yards of our neighbors and in one we see the unused conservatory of a fine old place — unused, not because the flowers are loved less than formerly, but rather perhaps because they are more universally loved. The greenhouses of the florist have superseded the conservatory of the private owner, outside of large country estates, and former luxuries have become democratic necessities. The back yard of another neighbor has a bed of herbs, apparently containing every variety known to the botanist — a luxury to-day, but an interesting record of past time when every housewife of necessity grew her own herbs for savory flavorings and for the family medicine closet. The spring flowers and early vegetables of another back yard suggest the annual flitting of our neighbor and the summer flowers and late vegetables that await them at their country home. The orderly tool house of still another neighbor, with its lawn mower and roller, its variety of garden tools, and its hose reel all indicate the growing attention paid to the care of lawns, gardens, and yards, though the opposite tendency is indicated in the case of a neighbor who thinks that his proximity to a park frees him from the necessity of troubling about a back yard at all.

Our back yard has never had a barn or a stable, but as we look up and down the yards on the block we see recorded the passing of the stable and the coming of the garage, and not only the simple garage for the automobile, but the more elaborate one with "two rooms and a bath" for the chauffeur records the ever-ascending standard of living for employees as well as for employer. Not far away a single old-fashioned barn remains with its record of a cow as well as of a horse once kept, and with its chicken coop attached. If the family horse and carriage have become an automobile, if the family cow has been removed to the dairy farm, and the family chickens now lay their eggs on a poultry farm, will not the family washtub in time develop into the country laundry?

So our back yard has the records of all the ages within its narrow enclosure. Prehistoric questions of the ownership of land lie in our fences, classical mythology blossoms in our bulbs, the discovery of a new world rises in our Norway maple, affection for mother country blooms in daffodil and thistle, the Dutch West India Company lives in our mulberry tree, new trade routes are opened up in our lilies, commercial treaties are signed in our shrubs, Italian independence shimmers in our Lombardy poplar, political liberty and the downfall of tyrants climb over our grape trellis, and international peace is proclaimed in all that grows within our domain.

Sanitation is recorded in our garbage can, municipal improvement in our disused cistern, higher standards of living in the garage, education in the sand box, wholesome recreation in the tennis court, love of fresh air in the garden seat, summer migration in the abandoned garden, housing problems in laundry line and pulley, and progress in invention in electric wires. Genealogy is concealed in our flowers and biography in our vines; democracy lives in our trees and patriotism thrives in our weeds; economic theory lifts up its head in the single tax on land and economic research delves into enclosures, while over all broods the spirit of historical investigation.

What are the treasures of Europe in comparison with the wealth of the whole world that is ours by the right of eminent domain when claimed from the back steps?

The advantages of studying history in a back yard are manifold. Neither hot sun, nor pouring rain, nor driving winds interfere with the pursuit of knowledge on a back porch. No impertinent guides must be placated with fees, no taxicabs deplete our pocketbooks, no Baedeker proclaims us tourists, no foreigners practise their English on us, no one jeers at our efforts to speak an unknown tongue, no one gives us the wrong change or obsolete coins, rooms and meals are "just as good as they are at home." If work presses, or the bank fails, or a sprained ankle comes, or unexpected demands on time arise — seek the records of history in the back yard.

Main Street

And he showed me a street called Beautiful.

The main street of Apokeepsing is much like the main street of other cities of its size in the great river valley. It begins at the river, climbs a short steep hill, catches its breath on a shelving ledge, climbs another short hill, runs two miles or more to the boundary line of the city, and is later lost in the forked road that leads to the open country. The stranger who enters it from the railway station and traverses it the long distance to the outskirts of the city holds it in ill-concealed scorn, or makes merry over its evident attempts to rival the metropolis two hours away. The adopted citizens who are daily forced to use it as a thoroughfare find it dull and commonplace and endure with such resignation as is possible its shabby gentility and its sordid aspirations. Those who claim the city as their birthplace find it "not so bad after all." It is the politician alone who in the midst of a heated ward election finds it "fair and lovely, the most beautiful street in the world." At all other times, to all alike, it is just Main Street.

Yet Main Street and the streets that run parallel to it or that cross it at irregular intervals and at varying angles hold the records that connect Apokeepsing with the very beginning of time. From the records that have survived it is possible to reconstruct in a measure the history of the past, to interpret the spirit of the present, and even in a measure to anticipate what its future will be. Main Street may not rival in beauty Unter den Linden or the Champs-Élysées, but it is possible that it surpasses them in inherent interest. If beauty is an undefined, even an undefinable term, may not beauty be interpreted as including interest, and thus in a very true sense may not the main street of Apokeepsing really be "the most beautiful street in the world"? And if again the records seen on Main Street connect it with "the very beginning of time," may not Main Street make its humble contribution to the discussion of that perplexing question, "What is ancient history?" And if once more the beautiful must be useful, will not the usefulness of Main Street in making this slight contribution give it still another claim to the distinction of being relatively, if not absolutely, "the most beautiful street in the world"?

When did time begin? Ah, that we do not know! But we do know that the slates and the shales of the rocky foundation of Main Street take it back almost, although not quite, to the oldest geological formation known, and that their quarried blocks form the foundation walls of Main Street build-

Privately printed in 1915; reprinted in *Historical Material* (New York: Oxford University Press, 1933), 161–82.

Fig. 10. Illustration used in the original pamphlet publication of "Main Street" in 1915.

ings, and that out of them have been constructed the many miles of stone walls that mark the division lines between the farms of Dutchess County and between the great estates that border on the Hudson River. The great river itself becomes a record of primitive means of communication when the waterways were the great highways for the exchange of products as well as for personal intercourse both warlike and friendly. Nature helped man before man helped himself. Main Street also records the changing seasons in the permanent signs "skates sharpened," "furs remodeled," "sleds for sale," "buy an electric fan," "fireless cookers," "cold lemonade," and "hot coffee." Thus Main Street, in recording geological and climatic conditions, takes us back to the primitive records of nature, even to the very beginning of time itself.

What of the prehistoric period when the records of history were to be found in myth, legend, and tradition? Can Main Street contribute to these great classes of records that form the raw material from which history is derived before the records of history took on written form? Main Street, with its tributaries, does indeed take us far back to a period when mythology, legends, and traditions antedated written records. The Phoenix Horse Shoe Works, the Hygeia Ice Company, the figure of Bacchus so frequently represented take us back to a period of time when the myth — "the incarnation of the spirit of natural fact" — was the universal means of passing on beliefs in regard to the past. These are the records of classical myths that have come down to us and with scores of others similar to them preserve for us the continuity of our own times with those of a remote past.

But the formation of myth, legend, and tradition never ceases, and age is not a necessary characteristic of their existence, for they rise under our very eyes and quickly acquire the prestige of age and respectability. Many of the outside watch signs that designate the stores of Main Street jewelers show the hands pointing to 8:17 and the explanation almost invariably given is that the hands mark the hour at which Lincoln died. The tradition has become well-nigh impregnable and it does not occur to those accepting this explanation of the fact so frequently observed to notice whether all watch signs do so mark the time — at least three on the streets of Apokeepsing do not; whether the hour of Lincoln's death was 8:17; whether watch signs were so made prior to 1865; and whether they so indicate the hour in the southern states and in foreign countries. The very ready acceptance of traditions so easily proved to be false becomes in itself a valuable record of the mushroom growth of many traditions, and of the persistence of their survival. The task of the historian in separating tradition from historical fact is not always so simple as it is in the watch signs of Main Street, yet wherever found and whether it has or has not the kernel of fact, the acceptance of tradition at its face value becomes a record of the deep-seatedness and apparent ineradicableness of tradition.

Ancient history has been brought down to Main Street through the spirit and substance of myth, legend, and tradition. It comes down to us also in the score and more of secret fraternal organizations — Masons, Odd Fellows, Moose, and Red Men — that are but the appearance on Main Street of a time-old custom among men of banding together in the hope of achieving certain ends through mystery, initiation, and secret tie. The Eleusinian mysteries of Greece never die, but under other names and with other rituals are perpetuated wherever men are found.

The building materials and the building forms of ancient history have been uninterruptedly transmitted to us. The brick of ancient Egypt lives still in our buildings and our pavements, the concrete of ancient Rome, after a period of disuse, is so universally used that "the age of concrete" is becoming a designation of our own period, and the stone of the everlasting hills is still one of our great resources for building even as it was in ancient times. An imperfect model of a Greek temple overlooks Main Street from College Hill, Corinthian columns, Ionic columns, and Doric columns lift their capitals on more than one building of Apokeepsing, while Roman arches are seen on every side. It is to the descendants of the ancient Romans, the Italians of our own day, that we turn for the knowledge and for the practical construction of the enduring roads that have made Rome famous.

The languages of bygone days live on Main Street in perpetual youth. The signs of chiropodists, dentists, manicurists, oculists, opticians, osteopaths, physicians, surgeons, and veterinary surgeons; of dealers in agricultural implements, automobiles, bicycles, and motorcycles; of advertisers, architects, auctioneers, confectioners, contractors, electricians, engravers, insurance agents, intelligence officers, machinists, manufacturers, orchestras, photographers, stenographers, surveyors, telegraph and telephone companies, and the name of the Municipal Building, all show that the classical languages are not dead but rather live among us in undying vigor. What a void would be left on Main Street were all signs removed that bear words of Greek and Latin origin!

Ancient customs, too, live in Apokeepsing. Sundials in more than one garden still mark the shining hours; the placing of inscriptions on all public buildings goes back to earliest days; the urns for flowers, and flowers placed on the graves in the Rural Cemetery have fellowship with the burial customs of ancient time; every marriage ceremony performed in Apokeepsing gathers up into itself customs extending back to primitive times. The ancient custom of distinguishing by dress, age, occupation, and social station is perpetuated on Main Street. The uniform of the postman, the policeman, the conductor and the motorman of the trolley line, of the conductor and the trainmen of the railroad, of the messenger boy, of the bank janitor, and of delivery boys of business firms all record responsibility to public, corporate, or private business; the white suit of physician, dentist, and milkman records a belief in the virtues of sanitation; the clerical dress of the clergyman sets him apart from others and gives record of an ever-present readiness to serve others.

The term "medieval" often connotes to many the so-called dark ages, but the records of the medieval period burn bright on Main Street. Narrow crooked streets, houses with the upper story projecting over the lower, high stone walls, basement rooms, gratings in front of basement windows, iron gates, iron grillwork outside of entrance doors, stone pillars, wooden turrets, stained glass windows, small panes of glass, window shutters—all go back to a period when danger lurked on every side.

Main Street in its numerous rebus signs records a mediaeval period when illiteracy prevailed and education was the prerogative of the Church. The barber pole, tea-kettle, fish, watch, key, boot, shoe, last, foot, pair of glasses, large eye, horseshoe, head of a horse, wooden horse, wooden hat, shears, three balls, red flag, saw, anvil, chair, wooden Indian, large awl, and other emblems all record a medieval period when it was necessary to identify every trade and occupation, not by the name of the proprietor of the place which could not have been read, but by the symbol of the trade. The emblems of political parties placed today on election tickets are but survivals of ancient medieval rebus signs. Thus Main Street records the meeting of social extremes in its rebus signs on stores and the coats of arms seen on its automobiles — both once a guide to the illiterate.

Main Street records the trade organizations of a mediaeval time. The Chamber of Commerce finds its prototype in the great commercial leagues of Italy, the trade unions seem the outgrowth of medieval guilds, the order of the Knights Templar finds descendants akin at least in name in the Knights of Columbus and the Knights of Pythias, and even the system of militia may make connection with military organizations of a medieval time.

A medieval industrial system survives in the terms "merchant tailor" and "journeyman tailor" that record the rank of workers in the medieval guilds. Representations of the Nativity are carved in wood in Apokeepsing, as for long ages they have been in Germany. Hand looms, carpet weaving, farmers' markets stretch over long periods of time.

Medieval customs hold sway on Main Street. The man who takes the outside of the walk when walking with another person perpetuates the spirit of protection that once was demanded in parlous times. The man who tips his hat assures the person he meets that, in medieval language, he is removing his helmet and therefore has no fear, and when he extends his right hand he declares in the same medieval tongue that his sword hand is free and that the person he meets need have no fear. All those who dine *table d'hôte* at any Main Street hotel are figuratively dining at the host's table — a custom that prevailed down to modern times and is still perpetuated in parts of Europe, although on Main Street, as elsewhere in America, it really means the way in which a meal is served rather than the place where it is served.

Medieval superstitions are recorded in the horseshoes that are seen over more than one doorway on Main Street, and in other superstitions that flourish undimmed by age.

The records that originated in a more recent period are numerous and interesting. These records concern first the names and the external appearance of Apokeepsing. Once known as the "city of schools," its educational interests have been supplanted by its commercial interests as indicated by the names "Bridge City" and "Queen City," and its confidence in itself is recorded in its advertisements of itself and of its resources through name and sign at the railway station. That it has entered on a period of expansion is recorded in the existence of the numerous suburban extensions found in every direction, while names like Fairview Heights, Fairlawn Heights, and Oak Dale Park suggest the attractions held out by real estate development companies to induce suburban residence.

The external records show an excess of individualism — streets have been laid out without plan, there is no common architectural or civic center and no town hall, and these negative records indicate the lack of a common civic purpose. The very name "Main Street" records the lack of imagination and ease in following the line of least resistance — nearly a thousand cities and towns in this country have a "main street." The names of other streets record a desire to honor its citizens of all nationalities — Adriance, Bayeaux, Delano, Du Bois, Livingston, Zimmer. Political influence and interest are seen in the streets named Clinton, Franklin, Hamilton, Jay, Jefferson, Lafayette, Roosevelt, and Washington — the latter name, like Main Street, shared with nearly a thousand cities and towns. Geographical situation is recorded in other street names like Water, Front, Prospect, High, and Cataract. Accidental and temporary features are recorded in the names Academy, Mansion, Market, Mechanic, and Mill.

Connection with the family of one of Apokeepsing's wealthy benefactors is recorded in the names of Vassar College, Vassar Brothers Institute, Vassar Brothers Hospital, Vassar Old Men's Home, and Vassar Street. That advantage has been taken of the prominence of this connection is seen in the large number of names that have been adopted from the Vassar name without family connection with it and presumably used through a desire to cater to the various Vassar institutions, as Vassar Pharmacy, Vassar Ladies' Tailor, Vassar Novelty Shop, and many other establishments that have adopted the name of Vassar.

The railway station at Apokeepsing records the passing of the railway restaurant. The ceiling of the waiting-room plainly shows the shifting of the partition that has diminished the size of the restaurant and increased that of the waiting-room, and this records the increasing use of the dining car, as this use in its turn records a desire to economize time by "killing two birds with one stone."

The street signs indicating the names of streets record changes in method and time of travel.[1] The cross-post signs on the outskirts of the city record the beginning of country roads and slow methods of travel, while the street sign in the city has changed its location from fence to house, to business block, with occasional visits to the sidewalk, and now, on Main Street, it is found on the electric light posts — a record of travel by night and the necessity of signs and of lights that give information and warning to speedy travelers.

That Apokeepsing has become an industrial rather than a purely residential city is recorded not only by its factories that fringe the river bank and border its outskirts, but by the general appearance of its main and tributary streets. Two-family houses and flats have sprung up by the hundred, while small, cheap stores, cheap restaurants, furnished rooms, cheap amusements, and more than a score of public laundries record a population industrial in character and more or less floating in its domestic life. Congestion of population in more than one section of the city is recorded in the evident change of one-family into two-family houses, in the numbering of houses 20-a or 21½ showing that houses have been erected on the yards originally attached to other homes, in the large number of covered tenement-house outside stairways that have been attached to older residences, and in the architectural excrescences that have been thrown out for business purposes from many small but substantial houses.

The citizens of Apokeepsing have left on Main Street many records of their origin and of their interests. The great original colonizing nations — the Dutch, the French, the English, the Germans — have all left their records here in architectural forms, in customs, in names, and in language. The new nationalities that have been later introduced through immigration — not fewer than forty-two different nationalities can be counted in Apokeepsing today — are also leaving their records in dress, in language, in physiognomy and in customs. The red fez of the Turk, the white turban of the Hindoo, the shoulder shawl of the Italian and a score of other forms of national dress have all been acclimated for a more or less temporary period on Main Street. The needs of different races and religions are met by restaurants of Chinese, Italian, Roman, Greek, Hungarian, German, Austrian, and kosher characteristics. Practically every special national dish can be eaten on Main Street from the cookies and the roelichies of the first settlers to the fritto misto and chop suey of later comers.

Main Street also records the other extreme of national influence that has come through importation. Travel abroad, fashion, commercial competition have introduced a thousand and one articles and customs that have been grafted on those indigenous to America. French modes, Robespierre waists, Dutch collars, Irish lace, Hardanger embroidery, regal and queen quality shoes are foreign to the thought of the native American, but have come through a widening of the industrial and social circle. Main Street also records race prejudice — until recent legislation at least two of its business houses posted the notice "colored trade not wanted," while churches and clubs for the negro and negro orchestras show a color line of cleavage among the citizens, perhaps in itself a survival from the time when slavery existed in Dutchess County.

Main Street with its double trolley tracks, its never-ceasing line of automobiles, delivery trucks, and vehicles of every description and motive power, its constant stream of pedestrians, its trim sprinkling carts and street sweepers, its regular lighting-posts, its uniformed policemen, and its commodious fire-engine houses seems sufficient unto itself and perhaps so thinketh itself. Yet on every hand there are the records of its connection with forms of government external to itself. The dependence of Main Street on the federal government is recorded in the post-office building, in street mail boxes, in uniformed carriers, and in the mail wagons of the parcel post delivery and of the railway connection. With every postage stamp bought, every letter mailed, every letter received, the man on the street maintains a friendly relation with the seat of government in Washington. Posters calling for recruits for the regular army and navy and flags designating recruiting offices indicate a volunteer rather than a compulsory military service. The license displayed and the revenue stamps affixed to certain articles purchased record the connection between federal expenditures and the taxpayers of Main Street. The federal Geological Survey has certified the official altitude of Main Street in the inscription affixed to the Municipal Building. The Department of Agriculture scatters broadcast seeds for the back yards of Main Street and it publishes daily reports and forecasts of weather conditions, the alien citizens of Main Street received their certificate of arrival through the Department of Labor, passports are issued by the Department of State, federal census statistics are collected through the Department of Commerce, patents are granted through the Department of the Interior, pensions for military service are paid, government reports distributed, examinations held for appointments to federal offices, while every American coin and every American bank note that passes through the hands of every citizen of Apokeepsing has its origin in the federal government. These are but suggestions of the immediate and intimate connection, both voluntary and involuntary, maintained between Main Street and the great executive departments of the federal government. With the legislative department of the federal government the voting citizens of Apokeepsing have also established friendly relations through sending one of their number to represent them there. To many citizens on Main Street the material capital of the nation seems far distant, yet is not its spirit ever present, and ever ready to perform a thousand services for them that they are unable to perform for themselves?

Many records connect Main Street with the government of the State of New York and indicate the watchful care the State maintains over its citizens — to protect them from themselves, to protect them from all who prey on weakness and ignorance, to help them do for themselves co-operatively what they are unable to do for themselves individually. Diplomas "conspicuously displayed" in the offices of physicians, dentists, and pharmacists are but a single illustration of the care taken by the State to protect the health of every individual citizen from ignorance and quackery. Factory whistles at five o'clock and the crowds of operatives pouring out from mill and factory record the purpose of the State to protect every working man and woman from those willing to take advantage of the necessities of labor. The great State Hospital nearby is a record of the desire of the State to care for one large class in society unable to care for itself and needing the expert care that can not be given in the individual home. The public highways that branch off from Main Street are records of the wish of the State to co-operate with its citizens in promoting all facilities for intercommunication between all the Main streets of the State. Albany is not so remote as is Washington, and the records of its interest in Main Street are evident to all its voting and its observing citizens.

Dutchess County is still closer at hand and in material form it finds embodiment in Court-House, in nearby Fair Grounds, in County House, and in the group of officials whose headquarters are at the corner of Main and Market Streets.

At every turn on Main Street are the records of the oversight given the citizens of Apokeepsing by the city fathers chosen by the voting citizens. Protection to life, health, and property are recorded in the lists of offices posted on the walls of the Municipal Building, care for education on the walls of the old high school building, interest in wholesome recreation in public parks, and in playgrounds and school gardens for children, — these are but illustrations of the innumerable records of Main Street that show the control of the city by its own representatives.

Thus wheel within wheel — federal government and state government, county government and city government — is the machinery arranged that cares for the complicated life on Main Street.

There are other records of present-day conditions to be seen on Main Street besides those that indicate its external appearance, the nationality of its citizens, and the various forms of governmental control. Main Street is an epitome of all the records of industry and of commercial methods that are known. Records of home industries are on every hand — "hand-made shoes," "home-made bread," jostle hard with "shoes mended by electricity" and the great bakeries operated by electric power. The drift towards great industrial combinations is seen in the signs of the National Biscuit Company and of the Union Pacific Tea Company, while international tendencies are seen in the advertising signs of the American Express Company and the great telegraph companies; while still another development is recorded in specialized industries like those of "Paper Box Factory," and "Queen City Underwear." Concentration of like occupations has taken the tailors to Garden Street and the doctors to Mill Street.

The evolution of business is clearly recorded on Main Street where at every turn the old jostles the new. The early stage of irresponsible business is seen in the stores that display food on the sidewalks, or exposed on counters, the stores that are heated by antiquated coal-stoves and lighted by kerosene lamps, where change is made from a till under the counter, where the windows are cluttered with samples of nearly everything offered for sale, and the owner of the stock is often salesman and errand boy combined. Newer methods have moved eastward on Main Street and heating plants, cash registers, overhead cash trolleys, protection of articles offered for sale from the dust and dirt of the street, package groceries, and arrangement of windows that "say something," all show higher standards of business.

Yet side by side with these records are interesting survivals of still earlier methods of business. Royal patronage has, over seas, been the allurement held out to encourage custom, and the privilege of announcing "shoe-makers by appointment to H. M. the King" has presumably meant solid increase in sales made to the general public. Main Street records the same belief in the frequent use of the name Vassar, Eastman, and Glen Eden. The pseudo-coats-of-arms seen over cafés record an early transference to inn and tavern of the free hospitality once accorded by mediaeval castle. These and other illustrations are a record of business dependence on some outside patronage of an office, a social class, or an influential element in the community.

One of the newest classes of records introduced on Main Street is that of keen business competition. Human ingenuity seems fairly inexhaustible in the devices used to attract the custom of the passersby. The bargain-hunters are earliest on the street and for them are offered the advantages of seasonable sales described in all the terms of the calendar months, and also as "mid-winter," "spring," "Easter," "mid-summer," "harvest," "harvest home," "autumn," and "fall" sales. Special day sales appear for every day in the week from Monday to Saturday and the special day expands in Hallowe'en sales, Thanksgiving sales, Christmas sales, and holiday sales. Time sales are devised and "ten days' sales," "six days' sales," "morning sales," "one hour sales," "five minute sales," and "as-long-as-they-last sales" greet the early shopper. "Anniversary" sales are modest reminders of the personal element still left in business, but they are, unless accompanied by special attractions, presumably less effective in securing "results" than are other more sensational descriptive terms. According to size and characteristics, Main Street describes its sales as "big," "great," "gigantic," "mammoth," "mammoth publicity," "record-breaking," "sale of sales," "clean sweep," and "stirring." Main Street becomes "a business weather-vane" in recording general business conditions of the country at large as well as of the community. Sales are announced as "bankrupt," "sacrifice," "money-getting," "reorganization," "expiration of lease," "dissolution," "inventory," "removal," "auction," "closing out," "cost," "below cost," "fire," "flood," "insurance," "damaged goods," "reduction," "what's left," "shovel 'em out," "liquidation," "salvage," "eviction," "evacuation," "receivers," "forced," "cut price," "last call." Other appeals are recorded in sales announced as "remnant and pound," "drummers' samples," "mill-end," "good luck," and "horseshoe." Colors are pressed into service and sales announces as "red tag," "yellow tag," "green tag," and "white." And amid all this bewildering variety of sales, Main Street occasionally offers a plain, humble "sale."

Keen business competition is also recorded in the huge, unsightly billboards that line upper Main Street, in the business devices of guessing contests, trading stamps, and other methods of attracting trade. The trail of the advertising spirit is seen in the appreciation of what appeals to buyers — stores are named on the one hand "Imperial," "Emporium," "Globe," or "Majestic," or on the other hand "People's," "Economy," or "Square." Another appeal is made by places denoted "Smart," "Up-to-Date," "Up-to-the-Minute," "Beehive," or "Busy Bee." Proneness to attach unusual merit to articles originating away from home gives rise on Main Street to "Paris Confectionery," "Boston Candy Kitchen," "Philadelphia Millinery," "Rochester Academy of Music," "New York Waist Store," "Hudson Lunch," "Yale Lunch," "The Plaza," "The Manhattan," and "The Mohican." The invasion and conquest of language by business is recorded in commercialized names like "restu mattress," and "uneeda biscuit." With the passing of the domestic parlor there has appeared on Main Street the commercialized parlor — "icecream," "shoe-shining," "shampooing," "tonsorial," "massage," "beauty," "hair-dressing," and "manicuring" — all of them probably preserving the original meaning of the word *parlor.*

Monopoly lifts up its head on Main Street in the wagons of the Standard Oil Company, the Gulf Refining Oil Company, of the various national express companies and of the great packing houses of Armour, Morris, and Swift. A variant of the single monopoly is found on Main Street in the representatives of the great chain stores seen in the Five and Ten Cent stores, the various tea stores, the United Cigar stores, and others with fewer links in the chain.

If competition and the natural development from it of advertising as a business in itself are so plainly seen on Main Street that he who rides in the trolley may read the records, other records scarcely less visible are found. The great majority of those who frequent the stores of Main Street are themselves wage-earners or they are purchasing supplies for those who are wage-earners. The appeal is made to this class of purchasers to "buy on the installment plan" — a fixed weekly wage apparently makes this an easy way of making weekly payments on staple articles. But the Main Street merchant is wary, and while the installment plan or even the credit system may answer in the purchase of household furnishing and even of clothing, the merchant takes no chances on groceries but installs a cash register and tickets his store "cash grocery." Coupons, trading stamps, and dividend stores are devices for securing trade that appeal especially to the wage-earner and may be used with payment by installment, cash, or credit.

That a large proportion of the population of Apokeepsing are wageearners is recorded in the numerous bakeries, delicatessen stores, restaurants of every description, public laundries, stores for the sale of ready-made clothing for men, women, and children, stores where standardized articles are sold as in the 5, 10, and 25 cent stores and the variations seen in the 3, 9, and 19 cent stores, in automatic scales, in street slot machines for obtaining candy, nuts, and chewing gum, and in slot gas meters.

Thus Main Street holds the records of all the changes in the industrial and in the business world that have come since every Main Street was. Individualism, competition, and co-operation are all recorded, as are the domestic and the factory system of manufactures, the transference of the work of women from the home to the factory, the rise of a great wage-earning class with fixed wages, definite hours of work, and consequent circumscribed opportunities, and the long, long train of results that have followed.

How may we reconstruct the past of Main Street from all these records, ancient, mediaeval, and modern? We can not indeed reconstruct the history of Main Street in its entirety if by history is meant a chronological account of what the corporate city has *done*, but we can reconstruct its changing and successive interests, the different problems with which it has had to deal, and it is possible thus to know the mind and spirit of Main Street more perfectly than we can know it through formal history. We may reconstruct its means of communication with the outside world and see how these have been evolved, with all their ramifications and accompaniments through river, boat, steamer, ferry house; farmers' sheds, harness shops, horse-blocks, hitching posts of wood, iron, stone, simple and grotesque; stages, cabs, taxicabs, and jitneys; carriages, buggies, victorias, landaus, broughams, sulkies, and wagons; push-carts, bicycles, bicycle racks, bicycle repair shops, motor cycles; automobiles of every size, pattern, and purpose, for business or pleasure, with their long train of garages, repair shops, gasoline stations, and supply stores; baby-carriages and children's carts and express wagons; horse-cars, trolleys, and railroads; trail, log road, plank road, cobble stone pavement, dirt road, macadamized road, and pavement of every variety — all means of transportation and all routes for transportation may be made to live again on Main Street.

The history of Apokeepsing's enlarging interest in education may be written not only from its new high school building, but from the transformation to other uses of the large number of buildings once used as private schools. The State has enlarged and improved its facilities for education, the private school is disappearing, and a newer system of education and a newer organization of education is being developed. The collective state is doing for the individual what the individual can not do for himself.

The results of the improvement in educational methods may be written from the records of the demands for even greater facilities and the response to these demands. Night schools, schools for foreigners, special classes maintained by different organizations, lecture courses, increasing size and use of the public library, the size of the post office, the increasing number of newsstands and of newsboys — all this and more shows that education thrives by the very demands it itself creates, offers, and satisfies.

The history of Main Street's progress on the road to health may be written from the records of hospitals, the board of health, the health officer, the health warden, doctors' signs, health notices in public places, quarantine signs, milk stations, sanitary fountains and drinking cups, an inspected milk supply, and through other records, while it also shows the untraversed road ahead with its food exposed for sale unprotected from dust, cemeteries within the city limits, buildings uncondemned, nuisances uncorrected, tenement-houses insufficiently controlled, as well as minor offenses against public health tolerated or excused.

The records of Main Street enable us to reconstruct the changing ideas of charity and in a measure to forecast the direction future changes will take. Many of these show that the early so-called charitable institutions were private benefactions and were palliative in their nature — they represented efforts to care for the wreckage of life but showed little constructive work for social betterment. Later records show a growing sense of responsibility on the part of the community as a whole towards all of its citizens and an appreciation of the advantage of preventing social, civic, and industrial ills rather than curing them after they have arisen.

The records of Main Street enable us to reconstruct its religious beliefs and the organization of its ecclesiastical bodies; to see the development of its amusements, sports, and recreations; to interpret its ideas of patriotism; to become intimately acquainted with its hopes, its aspirations, its ideals, as also with its fears and its discouragements; to realize that Apokeepsing has not escaped the world-old struggle between the forces of good and of evil and that the forces of evil have not seldom been triumphant — Main Street still bears the scars of conflict.

All times, all races have contributed their records to Main Street and have made it what it is to-day. Whether seen from sidewalk or from trolley, the records unfold into a vast panorama far more wonderful than those of reel and of scenario. There is nothing of it that doth fade,

But doth suffer a sea-change
Into something rich and strange.

The Record of Monuments

All passes, Art alone
   Enduring, stays to us,
The Bust outlasts the throne, —
   The coin, Tiberius.
            —*Austin Dobson*

. . . Italy embowered in a belfry, a fresco, the scope of a piazza, the lilt of a stornello, the fragrance of a legend.
            —*Maurice Hewlett*

We have perhaps read the past aright but we have not yet learned how to see it.
            — The Nation

The records that have thus far been considered may seem in a sense elusive and intangible. But a vast mass of historical records of concrete substantial character has been left in the form of material monuments. These are in the main the work of artists, artisans, and craftsmen who have been unconscious of being the preservers of historic records. Since the primary object of the artist has been artistic rather than historic, he has not always hesitated to subordinate accuracy of historical fact to the requirements of artistic presentation and the record left by him has often been incidental to his main purpose as an artist. But the record thus left gains an added value from having been made unconsciously.

These material monuments lie all about us and he whose eye has been trained to read the record they contain finds the dead past instinct with new life, even as the ivory image of Galatea became a living human being under Pygmalion's sympathetic touch. Art in all its manifold forms records the daily public and private life of the past — it tells of the temples men have built in honor of their religion, of the gods they have worshipped and of their belief in a future life; it tells of the buildings in which men have lived, of their occupations, their industries, their commerce, and their trade routes; art everywhere records in enduring stone and brick, bronze and ivory, gold and silver, in temple and basilica, in statue and fresco, in stained glass windows and in illuminated manuscripts, in lace and in tapestry the ideals of the past, and the evolution from these to those of the present. The eye of the historian is thus being trained to receive ideas through the medium of art as well as through the medium of literature and so to read not only the language of letters, but the language of vase-painting and statuary,

Historical Material (New York: Oxford University Press, 1933), 113–39. Copyright 1933 by Oxford University Press, Inc. Used by permission of Oxford University Press, Inc.

of heraldry and armor, of coins and of medals, of rugs and of blankets, of every form of monumental evidence. The study of botany once consisted in dissecting a flower and by this means finding its name in a botanical classification — it now means a study of plant life in its habitat and its relations to other forms of life. The writing of history once meant a narration of the heroic deeds of military leaders and for history of this character the records of tradition or the printed record sufficed. History to-day attempts to reconstruct the life of the past in its entirety and the historian seeks the records of the past wherever they have been left by the hand of man. He thus endeavors to understand not only the external life of the past but life in its varied meanings.

This monumental historical record serves various ends in the study of history. It gives a basis for an imperfect, incomplete skeleton of history during those periods and in those countries where literary evidence is lacking. It is not indeed possible to reconstruct the history of the past from monumental evidence alone — "material monuments take a place, important or unimportant, in the historian's reconstruction of the past according as they can be interpreted well or ill by comparison of the monuments of letters"[1] — but, as in the case of the Orient and the Mycenaean age in Greece, they afforded a picture of the civilization of an era and of a people for whose connected history the literary remains are either lacking or are as yet undecipherable.

Monumental evidence must also be relied on to illustrate and to supplement the written evidence. Description can never be a substitute for reproduction, nor can the printed page compensate for the lack of illustration. A view of the Arch of Titus, or a photograph of it gives a far better, truer, and quicker conception of it than will many pages of description unaided by a sight of the object itself. Many problems in ancient history must remain forever unsettled if the historian relies exclusively on his studies of Greek and Roman literature. Greek history has not been changed by the discoveries of Schliemann and Dörpfeld, Hommel and Evans, but our knowledge of it has been made more complete through the wealth of monumental evidence placed at the disposal of historians through their archaeological explorations. Pausanias must be the *vade mecum* of every scholar in Greece, but the record made accessible by the archaeologist in Greece must also be read. The statistician may have left an obviously inaccurate record of the population of an ancient town, but it may be computed from the size of its ampitheater and the circumference of its walls.[2] The chronicles of the mediaeval monks narrate much concerning their daily life, but the ground plan of a mediaeval monastery is a necessary supplement to the written record. At every turn it is seen how interlaced are the literary and the monumental records and how indispensable to the historian each record is.

Fundamental records on a large scale that may be classed as monumental are found in the arrangement of farms in all agricultural sections of the country and in the ground plans of all villages and cities. The great primary questions of land enclosure and common holdings; the later questions growing out of these that are found in the German agricultural communities, the Russian mir, and the English manorial system; the more recent phases of the subject involved in questions of absenteeism and tenantry, agricultural processes and conditions like rotation of crops and exhaustion of the soil, the extensive agricultural system characteristic of new countries and the intensive system of long-established communities, all of these are records that must be utilized by the historian in the reconstruction of the past.

No more important records are found than are those on the ground plans of cities. The primitive walls that recorded the fear of external foes have been razed and their sites have become boulevards and promenades; the fear of to-day is that of internal foes — unsanitary conditions, occupational diseases, hazardous employments, exploitation of human life in the interests of greed or selfishness, and the risks incurred by ignorance or bravado. The ground plans of the modern city record everywhere the spread of interest in all classes of society — the development of parks and of breathing places in crowded sections, the growth of playgrounds and athletic fields. Everywhere the external features of the city record the socializing of life, the widening circle of responsibility, and the constructive efforts made for the improvement of society, even in the midst of devastating wars.

How much is recorded by material monuments may be suggested by a consideration of architecture — in every form and in all times it gives a record of the evolution of men's ideals in public and in private life. Religious architecture records the varying changes through which men's conception of the purposes of a religious edifice have passed. The Greek temple was designed to honor the image of the deity to whom it was devoted, the Roman basilica with its tribune became the place of assembly for the Christians, the elongation of the tribune into the choir marks the development of church ceremonial; the reaction against excessive ceremonial and the belief in the saving merits of faith rather than of works is recorded in the primitive simplicity of the Puritan church, and the Friends' meeting house; the emphasis on sermon rather than on service gives the amphitheater arrangement of seats, the passive reception of religious truth is indicated by the substitution of opera chairs for benches; the evolution of the modern social church with auditorium, chapel, session room, Sunday school rooms, Christian Endeavor rooms, committee rooms, balcony, foyer, parlors, dining-room, kitchen, pantries, closets, rest rooms, lavatories, social rooms open daily, reception rooms for wedding parties, kindergarten, nursery, class rooms, gymnasium and drill room, arrangements for stereopticon and moving pictures, theater, study, library, and museum records a belief in the organic nature of the church society of to-day; while the latest form of

ecclesiastical edifice that adds to all the features of the social church those of
assembly hall with stage for concerts, banqueting room, apartments for
sexton, fire-proof vault, church museum, administration floor, and office
building is but the reflection in ecclesiastical form of the modern idea of
business efficiency.[3] The ground plan of a church or a monastery may give a
truer record of its ideals than do the statements of its church manual or its
articles of faith, and thus it may have greater value in a reconstruction of the
past than does a representation of its exterior form.[4]

Our knowledge of the power of the mediaeval Church would be incomplete had not the mediaeval churches and cathedrals survived, nor should
we understand so clearly the variations of the Church in different countries
without the illustrations of these variations in differences between the
French, the English, the German, and the Italian cathedrals. But not only
does the development of church architecture record the development of
religious beliefs, it also illustrates the relation of the Church to contemporaneous society. When civic discord prevailed and danger lurked on every
hand, the church, as well as the castle, was armed for defense and the
battlemented walls of Ely and of St. Denis still record that a church was a
fortress as well as a cathedral, a place of refuge for the oppressed. The
towers of the churches of Glamorganshire and of Bedale church[5] attest the
disorder of the border lands, while lodgings in steeples[6] are survivals of
the watchmen who kept watch and ward in a material way as the clergy
watched over their flocks in a spiritual way. The deep porches for teaching
record the control of the Church over education.[7] Individual churches
sometimes show in themselves the evolution of centuries of change,[8] the
growth of monasteries reflects the development of a complex life from early
simple conditions,[9] the influence of mediaeval guilds on ecclesiastical buildings has many interesting records,[10] while in minor ways ecclesiastical architecture bears many curious records.[11] These records may be misinterpreted
through lack of knowledge, or lack of observation, or lack of a vivifying
imagination — it is not so much the function of the historian to vivify as it is
to verify the records of history — but such misinterpretations do not invali-
date the records themselves.[12]

The subsidiary parts of ecclesiastical architecture contain equally important records of changes in belief and in ceremonial. The evolution of the
rite of baptism as practiced by the early and mediaeval Church is clearly
indicated in the decline of separate baptistries, in the change of form and
size of the baptismal piscina, in the dwindling of the piscina to a small font
on a single pedestal, and in the ultimate use of the metal or earthen basin.
These changes clearly show the decline of interest in adult baptism from the
first centuries when men in large numbers gave up a former religion and
friends and neighbors witnessed the ceremony, to the eighth century when
infant baptism became common and "out of very love of children the es-

timation of the sacrament of Baptism was inevitably lowered." Baptism became of secondary interest to the sacraments since the rite was administered
but once, while the Eucharist was frequently administered.[13]

The relation of the baptistry to ecclesiastical architecture has been vari-
able, but the relation of the window has been permanent, since "Glass
inevitably follows the architecture of the period."[14] Shape, size, design, and
general features of the window are but the artistic parallel of the building
itself; it is in the stained and the painted glass, especially of the mediaeval
period, that the interests of the time and the beliefs of the Church are
recorded. In the absence of the printed page, all religious instruction not
oral was conveyed through pictorial means and the stained glass window, the
most effective means at hand, was used as long as the need for it existed.
Recorded in it therefore are found all the religious beliefs of the Church,
the mutual relations of Church and State,[15] the militant tendencies of the
times, the gradual decline in the dependence on the window as a means of
inculcating religious belief and teaching biblical history, the development
of varied and secular interests,[16] and the present use of the stained glass
window for decorative and pictorial effect.

Choir stalls, with their misericords and other accompanying parts, have
been utilized, as have been other parts of ecclesiastical buildings, to teach
religious history and beliefs, yet dim light and the exigencies of position and
location have made them less useful for this purpose than other parts of the
sacred edifice have been; hence they have often served as an outlet for the
expression of the artists' personal feelings. Satire and ridicule, skepticism,
criticism, and possibly revenge have all found expression in these grotesque
and whimsical figures that show "a wonderful sort of hideous beauty and
beautiful deformity." The biblical scenes are few,[17] but animals of every
variety known to the bestiaries are carved on the seats occupied by those
attached to the service of the Church and possibly the personal peculiarities
of the contemporary occupants of the stalls may have consciously been used
by the artist to add to the grotesqueness of the original.[18]

The pavement is an important part of cathedral and of church and this
too has been utilized to convey to worshippers what has been believed to be
religious truth. Mosaic as a form of artistic expression has been used for
pavements and in its most elaborate form, as in the pavement of Siena, it has
shown the interesting confusion of mythological, biblical, apocryphal, and
secular subjects that has grown out of imperfect knowledge, literal interpretation of traditional subjects, and a certain child-like guilelessness that
finds expression in unusual forms. The pavement of Siena shows the story of
Moses and the tables of the law, of Absalom, of Elijah, of Samson, and of
other Old Testament characters; of New Testament parables and of events
described in the Apocrypha; of mythological sibyls; of fortune's wheel with
portraits of Euripides, Seneca, Epictetus, and Aristotle — of the seven ages of
man;[19] of abstract virtues, as prudence, justice, courage, and temperance; it

gives the civic emblems of Siena and of her twelve confederated allies; and it represents other subjects of apparently secular but now unknown import, as the relief of Bethulia. The incongruities of the expulsion of Herod from a mediaeval Italian hill fortress is of far less interest than is the supposition advanced that the scene alludes to the expulsion of Pandolfo Petrucci from Siena,[20] and the representation of the massacre of the innocents on the portico of an Italian palace where it is viewed by Herod seated on a Renaissance throne is of less moment than is the suggestion that the scene was designated "as an object lesson to recall to the public mind, through the medium of a Scriptural Tragedy, the horrors to be endured at the hands of the unspeakable Turk."[21] Whatever may have been in the minds of the artists and of those who commissioned them, the pavement remains a valuable record of the political independence of Siena and of its interest in civic affairs. The church pavement in many minor ways records incidentally the position of the Church on important questions,[22] it shows the migration of workmen from country to country,[23] and in the use of stone instead of mosaic it gives a foundation and a background for the wealth of monumental brasses that become in their turn records for the service of the historian.[24]

The walls of the church have given great opportunity for conveying religious truth and from the earliest Roman basilica the opportunity has been improved to the utmost. The wall mosaics of Ravenna give almost of themselves opportunity for a complete reconstruction of both Arian and Athanasian theology and incidentally they show the influence of Byzantine art. The simplicity of the symbolism used in this early period of Christian art gives a point of departure for the development of symbolism as a necessary means of conveying religious truth until it reaches its climax in the highly complex, luxurious, religious symbolism of the present.[25]

It can not be repeated too often or with too great emphasis that prior to the invention of printing in the middle of the fifteenth century books were the luxury of the Church and of the wealthy, and that the only language used by the Church to communicate with its members was the language of art in all its multifold forms. Of all these forms it was painting that was the most effective and that was most frequently used as the language of the Church.[26] By the use of a simple symbolism as easily understood as are the letters of the alphabet to-day, walls and ceilings of cathedrals, churches, chantries, chapter-houses, monasteries were used by the Church to portray biblical history and episodes in the lives of the early Christian martyrs and of mediaeval saints — painting was the open book known and read of all men. To the historian the subjects chosen become important records of the beliefs taught by the Church. Whatever the special medium employed, whether wall fresco, stained glass window, wall or pavement mosaic, the Church, as long as through its wealth it controlled the work of artists, taught theology and biblical history. Thus the historian, even more than through formal creeds, reconstructs the teachings of the mediaeval Church from its conscious portrayal of them. But he finds other records of equal moment. Religious belief has not been stationary, but it has changed from century to century, from generation to generation,[27] and it has been accompanied by corresponding changes in ecclesiastical ceremonial. The choice of subjects clearly shows that in the early Christian painting the emphasis was placed on subjects from the Old Testament and on the representations of Christ as the Good Shepherd.[28] It was during the mediaeval period that the Church as an organization developed, especially through painting, an elaborate martyrology and hagiology[29] and thus fixed in the minds of its worshippers the teachings of the Scriptures and the traditions of the Church.

Painting not only records the beliefs taught by the Church at different periods of its development, but it also indicates the special phases of religious belief that most appealed to different nationalities. In Greece, while there are numerous representations of all the greater and lesser divinities, there are no representations of a regular priesthood. In the Christian Church, Christ is represented in the East as a king, with the nimbus, the symbol of power, seated on a throne of gold and precious stones, and surrounded by angels, principalities and powers, while kings grovel at his feet; in the East he is the Son of Man, while in the West he is the Son of God.[30] Different aspects of the Church are recorded in different countries—in Spain it is the harrowing rather than the devout aspects of the Church that are recorded, evidently a record of religious persecution.

Civic architecture shows how different political theories have left correspondingly different records. England has party government and builds assembly halls where the members of its parliament are seated in opposing ranks, and public questions are settled through debate—every member of the House of Commons faces his opponents and attempts by argument to win them to his side.[31] France is governed by faction and the architecture of its legislative halls permits an extreme right, a right, a right center, a left center, a left, and an extreme left, with varying combinations among the parties, while the tribune encourages harangue rather than debate. America is governed by committees and the committee system is built into the national capitol as well as into the capitols of different states. Its legislative halls with huge galleries invite the legislators to address the occupants of these rather than their fellow legislators. The corruption prevalent in political life has left its permanent record in the "jobs" built into public edifices. In New York State the passing of the Raines law in 1896 resulted, all over the state, in the conversion of small and unimportant buildings into architectural monstrosities that record the attempts of legislators to square the circle—to restrict the sale of liquor through extending its use.

In a similar way municipal architecture everywhere unconsciously records the ideals of its citizens—political, artistic, economic, social. The great mediaeval town halls found everywhere in northern Europe are conspicuous records of the remarkable work carried on by free and independent com-

munities; that to-day many of these play a much less important part in civic
life than was once the case is silent testimony to the development of the
larger national life. The stately modern city halls that arise in European
cities to-day, like that of Copenhagen, give impressive evidence of the coming of new conceptions of the functions of the city and the enlargement of
its horizon to include constructive social work.[32] The civic center, so much
desired in American cities and attained by a few at great expense because
the desire for it has come long after its early beginnings, finds in the city hall
the center of civic interest, while other communities emblazon on their city
halls in gaudy electric lights, "X Bids You Welcome," and thus record their
interest in visiting conventions as convenient money-bringers to the munici-
pality and their own paramount concern in material prosperity.

The varying ideals of domestic life are shown in the domestic architecture
of different countries at different epochs. The semi-publicity of the Roman
house, the mediaeval castle built for defense, the house in southern Germany without windows on the public highway, the typical English basement
house, complete in itself and cut off from all communication with its neighbors, the huge city apartment house of the French containing a dozen
families, the French suburban villa removed from the highway but with
summer house to enable its occupants to see without being seen, the lofty,
cheerless mediaeval palace in which many modern Italians find their abode,
the latticed windows of the Turks, the detached house with every modern
convenience without dividing fences and with lawns of every size found
everywhere in America, the balconied homes in the extreme south, the
quarters for the slave found wherever slavery existed, all show how the spirit
of the times leaves an enduring record in brick and stone.[33]

The changes through which buildings have passed leave similar records.
Mediaeval castles built for defense and the châteaux of half-forgotten kings
have been transformed into historical museums for the tourist,[34] the châ-
teau has become the summer home of the merchant millionaire,[35] it is used
for local administrative offices,[36] it has become a home for aged soldiers,[37]
the castle is now the seat of an educational institution where young men
dine in the old banquet hall of princes and have their private rooms in
Norman galleries that date from the twelfth century.[38]

Similar changes in modern buildings record as unerringly the transformation in the ideals and opinions of our own times. The series of brown-
stone fronts give way to the huge apartment house, the small apartment to
the palatial hotel; the old time house with its "best room" and with its
"spare room" adjoining the parlor, and the room for the "help" next to the
kitchen, has been transformed into the house with its first floor all open, its
guest room practically eliminated, and its "help," now become a "maid,"
transferred to the upper story.

The growing increase in land values is recorded in the shrinking of the
individual detached house into the apartment, with small rooms, and an

entire reconstruction of domestic and social life. Small space for books
means books printed on india paper and the increasing use of the public
library.[39] The lack of provision for storage means, and the small flat, apples
packed in boxes, canned meats and canned vegetables purchased at the
corner grocery, while in the large apartment it encourages the purchase of
fresh fruits and vegetables brought from a distance long in advance of their
local season; a small kitchen means for children that candy is no longer
made in the home but in factories and packed in boxes by paid workers, that
home-grown nuts are no longer cracked in the kitchen, but, instead, nuts
grown in France and in Italy are cracked by machinery and the meats picked
out and packed in city tenement houses.

No part of the house records more unerringly than does the plan and
arrangement of the kitchen the swift but silent changes that are transform-
ing domestic life. The old kitchen with its fireplace, crane and brick oven,
with its low ceilings and heavy beams,[40] with its cooking utensils of heavy
iron, earthenware and wood, has been transformed into the modern compact efficient kitchen significant for what it does not contain quite as much
as for what it does.[41]

A single architectural feature like the porch in its various forms of sun-
parlor, screened porch, sleeping porch, and porch furnished as an out-of-
doors room attest the interest in fresh air, sunshine, and health, as the large
porch, with its rocking chairs, of the once fashionable summer hotel recorded not simply leisure but inertia and idleness.

The domestic architecture of the day seems everywhere an exemplification of the advertising phrase, "You press the button and we do the work."
The ground plan of the modern house shows that all processes of domestic
manufacture have been taken out of it — work that ministered to the necessities of the household collectively, as well as to the individual members of it.
This change has involved corresponding charges elsewhere; as the individual house has dwindled architecturally, the factory, the department store,
and the hotel have expanded. The factory, in its beginning scarcely more
than a barrack, records in its latest development an awaking business and
social conscience, the enormous strides taken by science in its study of
questions of health and safety, and an appreciation of the value of attention
paid to the aesthetic side of factory building. The department store has
developed from the nucleus of the old retail store with additions made from
time to time as needs arose to the department store of the hour planned to
forestall every conceivable desire or need on the part of customers, employees, and business management.[42] The expansion of hotels has developed by leaps and bounds until the statement that $20,000,000 is to be
expended on a hotel in a city already counting by the hundreds its expensive
well-kept hotels scarcely arrests attention.[43]

The changes in domestic architecture thus record the removal from the
individual house to the collective factory of the manufacture of practically

every article of domestic consumption, the necessity of purchasing at retail these commodities made by the wholesale, and the transference of much of the productive labor thus released to the idleness and luxury of hotel life. How complete the change has been still other records of a different character clearly show. The castles and large manor houses of the late Middle Ages and early modern period show in their construction the fear of danger to life in the *salle des gardes* and the placing of few windows on the first floor, the presence of the tower and the dungeon for the discovery of enemies and their punishment when taken, while if those approaching prove friends rather than enemies the great halls record hospitality, the huge rooms the absence of clearly marked social classes, of no provision for the comfort and convenience of women and children, of lack of specialization in labor, and an almost complete lack of sanitary ideals. The influence of the Church on domestic life is recorded in the chapel attached to manor house, the decorations with their use of ecclesiastical emblems and symbols, and representation of biblical history. The modern house with its locked doors and burglar alarms records fear for property rather than for life and the change of property values from lands and houses to bonds, jewelry and easily transportable valuables, as this in turn records the existence in society of a distinctly criminal class that has taken the place of the euphemistically termed "soldiers of fortune" of an earlier day. Even the changes in architectural details, as in the construction of staircases and the formation of inside and outside shutters and blinds, as well as in their use or absence, all record the ever-changing ideals and purposes of collective humanity.

Nor are such changes in ideals recorded only by the architecture of our own times — Demosthenes pointed out to his contemporaries the change in the ideals of Athens from the greatest period in her history when her noblest buildings were erected in honor of the gods and for public purposes to his own time when some of his fellow citizens had "provided themselves with private houses more imposing than [the] public buildings; and the lower the fortunes of the city have fallen, the higher theirs have arisen."[44]

Gardens have always been important accessories of private and of public architecture and their records have often paralleled those of architecture while showing their own individual records. They have fluctuated in general type from geometric, elaborate and formal, to natural and simple; they have been sumptuous in Spain, they have been terraced in Italy, secluded and exclusive in England; they have been surrounded with high walls, or they have been unprotected by either wall or fence; they have been laid out in labyrinthian mazes to conceal a royal tomb or to become the sanctuary of a god,[45] they have been approached through a lodge, often fortified and provided with an alarm bell, and they have been denominated "old fashioned," without a too strict definition of what is connoted by the term. The garden wherever found records the prevailing architectural theories and taste of its time, and the records of its accessories are in harmony with it;

dove cotes, beehives, bird houses, and bird fountains mean love of animal life; hanging gardens and roof gardens mean restricted space; ponds in mediaeval monastic gardens mean fish and ducks for monks and nuns; gardens of medicinal herbs mean primitive ideas of health; tables and benches mean feasting; religious statues are found in monastic gardens; topiary work with its fleet of ships in Queen Elizabeth's garden may record the victory over the Spanish Armada, or ladies with flaring skirts record prevailing fashions, the twelve apostles the influence of the Church, and hunter and hare the love of sport; gardens with statues of Greek gods and goddesses record enthusiasm for classic art and literature, as the mid-Victorian period is recorded in garden statues of small slave boys, deer, dogs, lions, and Rogers' groups; early sun-dials mean absence of watches as later sun-dials mean fashion; the weather vane means the dependence on the weather of occupations like agriculture, commerce, or fishing, as it also records the absence of a scientific weather bureau; shell-bordered flower beds are found in the gardens of seafarers, and their records are transferred to the white painted stones that form the names of towns at railway stations.[46] Records of still a different type are found in tree, in shrub, in flower, in vine, in the plant life that the garden exists to foster—records for the most part of international intercourse and the opening of new trade routes.[47]

Is the question of the record of modern domestic architecture with its estates and gardens summed up by a reviewer of an important work treating of the subject when he says: "But if the houses say nothing about the owner (except that he is very wealthy) they are eloquent of the training and the technical skill of the men who have designed, decorated, and furnished them . . . whether we regard [the] books as a record of contemporary domestic architecture of a certain sort, or as a contribution to sociology, it will be of scarcely less interest a hundred years hence than it is to-day."[48]

How Far Can the Past Be Reconstructed from the Press?

Avant que ce siècle soit fermé, le journalisme sera toute la presse, toute la pensée humaine. Depuis cette multiplication prodigieuse que l'art a donnée à la parole, multiplication que se multipliera mille fois encore, l'humanité écrira son livre jour par jour, heure par heure, page par page; la pensée se répandra dans le monde avec la rapidité de la lumière; aussitôt conçue, aussitôt écrite, aussitôt entendue aux extrémités de la terre, elle courra d'un pôle à l'autre, subite, instanée, brûlante encore de la chaleur de l'âme qui l'aura fait éclore; ce sera le règne du verbe humain dans toute sa plénitude; elle n'aura pas le temps de mûrir, de s'accumuler sous la forme de livre; le livre arriverait trop tard: le seul livre possible dès aujourd'hui, c'est un journal.

— *Lamartine*, 1831

I look upon the common intelligence in our public papers with the long train of advertisements annexed to it, as the best account of the present domestic state of England, that can possibly be compiled: nor do I know any thing, which would give posterity so clear an idea of the taste and morals of the present age, as a bundle of our daily papers.

— The Connoisseur, 1850

If I desired to leave to remote posterity some memorial of existing British civilization, I would prefer, not our docks, not our railways, not our public buildings, not even the palace in which we now hold our sittings; I would prefer a file of *The Times* newspaper.

— *Edward Bulwer-Lytton*, 1855

I do not think there will be any novels or romances, at all events in volume form, in fifty or a hundred years from now. They will be supplanted altogether by the daily newspaper. . . . As historic records the world will file its newspapers. Newspaper writers have learned to color every-day events so well that to read them will give posterity a truer picture than the historic or descriptive novel could do.

— *Jules Verne*, 1902

The man who writes about himself and his own time is the only man who writes about all people and about all time.

— *G. B. Shaw*, 1918

The attempt has been made to show to what extent the press can be deemed authoritative, but essential as is authoritativeness in all material used by the historian, other considerations must enter in if the periodical press is to be used as historical material. Nothing is more persistently urged on the press in season and out of season than the injunction to "tell the facts," but the belief that the press can not be used to reconstruct the past because of its manifold inaccuracies, is not well founded. It is true that the press may

The Newspaper and the Historian (New York: Oxford University Press, 1923), 468–91.

claim accuracy for itself, but in the very nature of things it is and must be inaccurate. But it must be remembered that it is possible to make a fetish of accuracy. Literal accuracy, as has been seen in the case of verbatim official reports, interviews, and illustrations, may often be misleading and in essence untruthful; a specious accuracy is perfectly compatible with a genuine fundamental misconception of an existing situation and with ignorance of the real truth. On the other hand, it is perfectly possible for an inaccurate report to be fundamentally authoritative. The press does for the most part give the facts faithfully and well, as has been indicated in the numerous direct and indirect guarantees, voluntary and compulsory, given in, by, and for the press. But for the purposes of the historian something more is needed. Edward Dicey points out that if "a foreigner were to read the *Times*, and half a dozen other English newspapers, daily for years, his knowledge of English life and politics would be extremely incomplete and erroneous, unless he had actually lived enough in England to have acquired what may be called the key to the English press," and while the "Hieroglyphics contain the history of Egypt . . . to understand the history, you must be able to read the characters."[1] It is not sufficient "to tell the facts" — all the facts may be accurately and truthfully told in regard to any event and yet the account of it may give little understanding of its real meaning — the mind of the seer, the poet, the philosopher is needed to interpret these facts, for without interpretation they are but dry bones. This power of interpretation may come to a periodical through the force of a single dominating character, or it may come through the absolute suppression of all personalities to such an extent that the resulting paper is altogether impersonal, but through whatever channel it comes, it must be the breath of life that vivifies the press. This does not mean that the editor, the reporter, and the correspondent must express their personal opinions on all subjects brought forward in the press — far from it. It does mean that the newspaper as a whole must itself so understand and so convey to its readers a sense of relationships, so respect values and relative proportions, and so discern the meaning of the times that its value will be rendered permanent. In spite of its name, the chief function of the newspaper is not to give the news, it is not even exclusively to reflect public opinion, — important as this is — but it is to record all contemporaneous human interests, activities, and conditions and thus to serve the future. What the historian wishes from the newspaper is not news — that always ultimately comes to him from other sources — but a picture of contemporary life.

But not only must the newspaper interpret the events that it consciously reports, — it must in its turn be interpreted by those who use it in a reconstruction of the past. It must be evident that not all of the parts of a newspaper are of equal value to the historian, or will be of equal value — the proportion shifts from year to year, even in the same paper; the country weekly has one value in a reconstruction of the past, a quite different value is attached to the metropolitan daily. Much that passes as news and fills the foreground of the present will later on lapse into obscurity and be of no service whatever to the historian. The reader on his part must have the seeing eye and the understanding mind.

The parts of the press that are most obviously of immediate service in reconstructing the past are the editorial, the illustration, and the advertisement.

The editorial serves in a measure to reconstruct current opinion, yet its value is somewhat lessened by the tendency of some editors "to keep an ear to the ground," a tendency that must in part vitiate the value of editorials on political questions and other mooted subjects, like preparedness. Lamartine spoke of the scum that rises to the surface when the nation boils and the editorial sometimes reflects the superficial rather than fundamental public opinion. But no part of the press has been so frequently reprinted as has the editorial column. Various collections selected from leading London papers "present in a new light a series of occurrences that have in their day been subjects of public recognition and journalistic record,"[2] and they thus give an almost complete collection of material for the study of certain phases of nineteenth century English history. The editorials in American newspapers while perhaps less significant must still be reckoned with by the historian. James Ford Rhodes has written, "I can emphatically say that if you want to penetrate into the thoughts, feelings, and grounds of decision of the 1,866,000 men who voted for Lincoln in 1860, you should study the New York weekly *Tribune* . . . it was the greatest single journalistic influence in 1854 with a circulation of 112,000." And again he writes, "The story of the secession movement of November and December, 1860, can not be told with correctness and life without frequent references to the *Charleston Mercury* and the *Charleston Courier*. The *Mercury* especially was an index of opinion and so vivid is its daily chronicle of events that the historian is able to put himself in the place of those ardent South Carolinians and understand their point of view."[3]

The illustration is the most conspicuous feature of the press that suggests present or past conditions and it is of special value as an interpretative record. The cartoon in particular through its insight into the past interprets the present for the future; the cartoonist and the historian are thus kindred spirits. Since the newspaper in its illustrations tends to the form of the caricature, the cartoon, and the photograph, it has as a rule greater value for the historian than have the illustrations of the magazines that, outside of the advertising pages, tend to the purely ornamental.

One of the greatest values of the illustration to the historian is its comparative freedom from authority. In political cartoons especially, much is tolerated and even welcomed that would probably not be permitted in the text. *Punch* has more than once shown weak spots in the methods of canvassing at a general election and it has thus been an ally on the side of purity of elections. The cartoon in Germany has seemed to be under less restriction than have other parts of the press. In *Bradley's Cartoons* there is much interpretation of the widespread aversion to war and of the conviction that war was futile as a solvent of the world's troubles. The same freedom of expression in other parts of the press would at least have been deemed "indiscreet." It has been said that "the cartoon thrives best in the fertile soil of democracy" and this may perhaps be accepted even in the face of the great uncertainty as to what democracy really is and whether it has anywhere ever been achieved. The illustration certainly often guides rather than merely reflects public opinion and it does it through the power of interpretation that gives it a prophetic character.

If, as has been seen, it seems possible to reconstruct from the pages of *Punch* the attitude of at least a part of England towards America during the Civil War,[4] the rule works both ways and *Harper's Weekly* well indicates the reciprocal feeling of America towards England. The press discloses little effort made in either country to remove prejudice and to arrive at a better mutual understanding. If *Punch* during the recent war showed an impatience with America for not earlier entering the war, but threw the blame of it on the president, *Life* showed America and England smoking the pipe of peace.

The press has sometimes been accused of being "anti-social" in its tendencies and influence because readers on trains and trolleys are absorbed in their newspapers and do not converse with their neighbors. But it is rather to be said that the newspaper enlarges the social circle and that readers thousands of miles apart are by the newspaper brought into oneness of mind or ranged in opposing columns far more effectively than they would be through the chance conversation or the monologuing of those in their immediate physical proximity.

It is the illustration in particular that enlarges the social circle and that shows everywhere the tendency towards luxury — views of spacious homes, summer residences, city hotels; distant countries reached by luxurious railway trains and steamer service; the automobile in infinite variety, elaborate clothing, household equipment — a thousand and one illustrations in the daily press and in weekly and monthly periodicals all show prosperity and the ability on the part of many to gratify every desire, whim, or caprice. These are all the unconscious representations of the life of the wealthy, illustrated through the appeals of business houses for the patronage of the rich. If "we make the thing we buy," the illustration shows infallibly the enormous production of everything that contributes to a life of ease on the part of some members of society. It shows with equal clearness the development of the similar appeal made by all transportation companies — speed, comfort, luxury, amusements, strange sights, unusual scenery, opportunities for business, "safety first," politeness and consideration for both employees and passengers. The limousine in its turn is always illustrated in appropriate surroundings.

But just as unerringly the illustration shows the opposite extreme. This, however, it does consciously—no one seeks through illustration the patronage of tenement-house dwellers. The illustration is used, not to sell to those who can not buy, but to show overcrowding of tenements, lack of space, air, and light, the unwarranted use of fire escapes, unsanitary conditions in passage-ways, areas, and back yards, and violations of decency, order, and law. The illustration becomes a conscious co-operator with the forces in every community that make for righteousness through its service in showing negatively undesirable, positively objectionable conditions of life. The illustration presses upwards into the homes of the rich to seek their patronage, but it also presses downwards into the homes of the poor to show to the rich conditions they have it in their power in part to relieve and prevent. Both extremes are abnormal, the illustration faithfully depicts each class, but each from opposite motives.

The great middle class is more normal in its conditions and its interests and these the illustration also faithfully represents. It is interested in time-saving inventions, in ready-made clothing, in prepared foods, in victrolas and piano-players, in bicycles and runabouts—all of these interests are standardized and represented through the illustration.

But the illustration shows far more than passive conditions of living—it shows the enormous development of new interests, the changing relationships between different elements in society, the quickening of the social conscience, and the widening sense of responsibility for all conditions that can be improved. New interests are seen in the illustrations of baseball crowds, college "bowls," golf links, open-air theaters, folk dances, playgrounds, and all conditions that show the development of out-of-door life and wholesome recreation. With equal clearness the illustration shows the dividing line between those who take their amusements vicariously, as in the views of opera houses with capacity audiences, and those who find their recreations in active participation with others in community singing and in other forms of collective activity.

But with this somewhat superficial jolting of society out of its traditional grooves through the development of new interests, the parallel illustration shows how other conditions move with glacier slowness towards perfectibility. The illustrator who satirizes modern society shows how universal and apparently fundamental are certain human characteristics; the braggart, the snob, the tuft hunter, the flunkey, the poseur, the social climber, the miser, the spendthrift, the slacker in peace as well as in war, know neither time nor country. Is it strange that this form of social satire has its complement in the illustrations that everywhere show the prevailing social and industrial unrest?[5]

The prevailing feeling, often however contradicted, that the relative position of children in society has changed, finds confirmation in the illustration. Once inconspicuous in the illustration, represented as dressed like their elders, evidently restrained in their actions, the newspaper now gives children their own illustrated pages, illustrates their own special fashions in dress, in toys, in amusements, in books; it represents the part they take in fashionable society, and shows them everywhere in the limelight.[6]

That this is the woman's age the illustration unerringly shows. The early illustration did not represent women outside of the fashion magazine or ballroom and society scenes. To-day it shows her engaged in every form of professional, business, and industrial activity; in all enterprises for the promotion of public welfare; taking a prominent part in out-door sports and recreations; putting her housekeeping on a scientific basis; gaining her training for every occupation through colleges, universities, technical, and professional schools.

The illustration shows the changes in fashions not only in clothing and in architecture, but in the accessories of life. The large dog once illustrated as guarding the lonely farm house, or drawing a cart for village children, has been supplanted on the farm by the telephone and in the village by the bicycle; in the restricted space of the city apartment he has become a toy and plaything—the illustration shows the fashionable breed of dog of each generation, a fashion changing not simply with whim and caprice but necessitated by changes in manner of living.[7] And it is the illustration again that reconstructs the services rendered by the dog in time of war where he is trained to act as scout and rescuer.

The tendency towards specialization is clearly seen in the illustration—specialization not only in all industrial and educational lines, but even in the smaller matters of every day life. The jeweller in the advertising columns illustrates a dozen varieties of forks, of knives, of spoons; the department store illustrates a score of different articles of china and silver; the housekeepers' column illustrates their use and shows the development of an elaborate table service with special dishes for each particular article of food.[8]

The illustration also shows the changes that have come in the temper of the public mind, the effect of the interest in psychology, and the widening of the circle of interest from the individual to the community, while the individual becomes concrete. Illustrations of games and of athletic contests are now from photographs that show the whole event, both players and spectators; individual athletes are shown rather than drawings of any man running, or playing ball, or with wings on his feet; the symbolic and the conventional has changed to the specific and the individual illustration, while the individual is shown in relation to a larger whole.[9] A single periodical like *Life* shows within the range of a few years the decline in the use of fabulous and prehistoric animals and the use made of representations of the devil.[10]

The illustration in its own character shows the cleavage between those to whom an appeal is made by the crude humor of the comic supplement and the sporting page and those attracted by artistic effects both of process and of scene. Thus the illustration shows the change in fashions of humor as unerringly as it records the changes of fashion in material things.

The illustration reflects the prevailing interest in all questions of sanitation and of public health. It shows the plans and the interior arrangement of hospitals, the uniform of surgeons, physicians, and trained nurses, and it spreads far and wide specific knowledge of sanitary conditions.

The illustration serves the investigator in disclosing the conditions of tenement house life where piecework is done, in showing the peculiar features of casual occupations like those of berrypicking and the canning industries, in making known the effects of overwork, of child labor, and of occupational diseases.

The illustration may also serve the cause of justice through enabling the officers of the law to detect and to identify those who have violated the law. The snapshot may have great value in the courts. Often it is so clear that no person could prove an alibi if represented by the camera as forming one of a group of strikers, or taking part in mob violence, or disturbing the peace. It may show incontestably that many of the participants in strike riots have been mere boys, presumably encouraged by their elders to take part in them.[11] The illustration is thus of service not only in reconstructing the past but also in reconstructing the present.

Nothing shows so conclusively as does a comparison of illustrations through a series of years the changes that have come in the way in which holidays are celebrated. The "safe and sane" Fourth of July with its appeal to a new nationalism and internationalism is far removed from the flamboyant, bombastic celebrations illustrated fifty years ago. The early illustrations of Christmas depict family scenes, later come the illustrations showing the results of late Christmas shopping, while to-day Christmas sales have become the conspicuous feature of December advertising. "What is Easter?" or what is the popular conception of the meaning of Easter, is perhaps better answered by the illustration and by the advertisement than it is by the Church, and sectional differences may be seen in the much greater influence of Easter on the illustrations and advertisements in the New York than in the Boston press.[12] Nothing more clearly indicates how widespread is the love of luxury to which particularly the advertisement appeals than do the advertisements of expensive clothing for men and women, gifts, jewelry, flowers, confectionery, restaurants, music, amusements, and excursions to all expensive resorts arranged for the Easter season. War, here as elsewhere, is utilized as a motive for commemorating the day — "Easter services are to reflect loyalty," "we are mobilizing the serried ranks of Easter's army." To the child the differences between Christmas and Easter are specially illustrated in the gifts for them advertised at that time, — if one brings dolls and drums, the other brings chickens and rabbits.

The extent to which the illustrations of the press may be used to reconstruct the past may again be tested through using the press printed in a
foreign language. Much may be gleaned in regard to business, social, military, and political conditions in contemporary Greece through an examination of a file of Athenian newspapers by one not familiar with modern
Greek. The language of the illustration, unless it is that of a not self-
explanatory symbolism, is a universal one.[13]

The most significant change in illustration has been its introduction into
advertising. An examination of the illustrated papers extending over a series
of years shows the ingenuity used in combining the illustration with the
advertisement and its increasing use in every field of business enterprise;
both advertisement and illustration take advantage of current interests and
profit by them. The current interest in athletics has been constantly utilized
to illustrate and to sell innumerable articles. Twenty-five years ago the bicycle was illustrated, but only later was the figure of a woman introduced and
then shown on the wheel; men and women were later shown riding wheels
and the illustration used to advertise a brand of soap; men starting on a race
or putting shot illustrate a patent medicine; a sailor in uniform advertises a
smoking tobacco; a horse jumping a hurdle illustrates a camera advertisement and is one of the first illustrated advertisements to use the photograph
itself; the automobile appears, but without occupants; later, the automobile
appears with women seated in it, and still later, with a golf course in the
background, with picnic parties in the foreground, with parties of elegantly
dressed women appearing from palatial residences, all, not simply to advertise automobiles and their accessories, but to advertise quite different articles.[14] But not only is the interest in athletics utilized to advertise and to
push the sale of articles that may be but remotely connected with them, but
the prevailing interest in athletics and sports of every kind, in all their wide
ramifications, can be completely reconstructed from the illustrated and the
unillustrated advertisement.

The agile advertisement everywhere is in the van in anticipating new
demands, in creating new interests, in realizing new conditions, and in
being prepared to meet them. The prevailing weather and the climate of a
particular section may be reconstructed from the advertisements of articles
for sale adapted to every degree of temperature, atmospheric conditions of
wind, moisture, dust, and even a knowledge of the state of the highways and
of a particular road may be gained from noting the advertisements of articles offered for sale adapted to these conditions.

The object of the advertisements of a great department store is obviously
to sell its merchandise, yet if the advertisements of a single such establishment are examined day by day throughout a year in a single metropolitan
daily it will be found that they have done far more than set before possible
customers the advantages of purchasing goods at this particular store. Quite
incidentally and unconsciously they have narrated much of the history of

the business, they have shown the extent of the business, the foreign and domestic markets from which and to which goods are shipped, the business methods employed, the spirit that actuates it, and its relations to both employees and patrons. It is possible to gain from such advertisements a wide knowledge of foreign and of American geography, as also of many of the facts of ancient, mediaeval and modern history and of current events; to become acquainted with the names of the great masters of all time in the fields of music, art, and literature and with the names of their chief works; to understand somewhat the nature of the industries, occupations, and professions that occupy men; to gain an introduction into the social life and customs of the very rich, and to know the conditions of the average household; to realize the progress made for the householder and housekeeper in matters of sanitation and hygiene; to come into contact with the great problems of education; to acquire much information in regard to the natural resources of the country and many facts of natural history — much is given in regard to weather and climatic conditions, different varieties of woods and their uses, fruit, flowers, vines, shrubs, trees, birds, animals, leather, and furs — and finally to have an insight into the qualifications needed in the writers of advertisements in order to produce successful advertising.

How do these advertisements fail to reproduce the life of the time? The advertisement of the great department store in its appeal to persons of wealth and leisure looks out on a world where all is fair and smiling — it has no hint of disaster, of hard times, low wages, lack of employment, poverty, sickness, misfortune, political struggles, tariff controversies; for it, crime, evil, and sin are non-existent; fire and flood, tornado and earthquake, the horrors of war pass unnoted.

Yet the advertisement records unerringly all of these conditions. Fire destroys a great building and within twenty-four hours advertisements referring to it appear. They concern insurance and safe deposit companies; fireproof buildings, vaults, cabinet safes, and floorings; metallic doors and interiors; automatic sprinklers; bonds covering burned securities; office rentals with immediate possession; offers of free rooms for limited periods; removal notices; night and day service for the furnishing of offices of those burned out; new addresses of former tenants asked; club privileges extended to the members of a club burned out, and library privileges offered those whose professional libraries have been destroyed.

Do the advertisements of great establishments ignore strikes and all labor troubles? The advertisements of others lay bare their difficulties and disclose their methods of dealing with strikes. The advertisements "we break strikes" show the frequency of strikes, the necessity felt of breaking strikes promptly, the inability to cope with a strike situation unaided, the hostile attitude towards trade unions, violence attending strikes, the attempt to establish the open shop, and the difficulty suggested of lodging and boarding imported workmen.[15]

Are men and women out of employment? The "want ad" columns answer the question — "willing to work at anything," "unfortunate, without work, good worker," "well-educated man needs work," "carpenter, wants any kind of work," "man, 40, former steamer steward, wants any kind of a job" — so the list lengthens into column after column, day after day, throughout the year.

Why are men and women out of work? The "help wanted" column in part answers the question — "thoroughly competent bookkeeper wanted," "experienced salesman, willing to go on the road," "ambitious man, not tired of life, can get permanent position," "hustlers only need apply," "office-boy, willing and ambitious," "best of references demanded," "applications considered only from sober men," "no boozers need apply," "applicant must dress well and have good personal appearance," "small capital needed" — and so this list, too, goes on, suggesting in every line the difficulties employers have in securing the help of well-trained, competent, ambitious workers.

Is war menacing the world? All articles advertised for sale are urged on buyers with the statement that they are to be used in some way connected with the war — sewing machines will make garments for soldiers, and piano-players will play martial music; "personals" are used to communicate with absent friends or to locate wounded relatives;[16] Kurt Schwarz in London advertises that he has changed his name to Curtis Black, while Schmidts become Smiths, and Müllers, Millers; "want ads" in English papers are printed in the French, Dutch, and Russian languages; newspapers offer to translate foreign advertisements into English, and the reverse; "situations wanted" become "situations needed," and they indicate that the loss of occupation is most felt at first in what the English call the middle class — "stranded Englishman, expelled from Germany needs work"; innumerable sales are advertised of clothing, jewelry, furniture, automobiles, pianos, houses, and of pets of every description; firms advertise that they look for lost luggage, and others that they will discover the secret of making articles hitherto made in Germany; books are advertised describing the countries at war, as are also maps, photographs, and plans of cities; advertisements call for cooks for the army and electricians for the navy.

The advocates of war urge that it develops courage, manliness, and all the cardinal virtues, but the advertisements of the press record quite different developments and they reflect the very worst traits in human nature — every opportunity is improved to take advantage of the necessities of others, and every necessity is magnified in order to impose on the generosity of others; gifts of motor-cycles are solicited in order that the recipients may join the motor-cycle corps, and the gift of an aeroplane is desired; loans of harriers or beagles to be used by officers until ordered abroad are asked for; an agency announces to clergymen that it will supply them with sermons every week, "new, fresh, simple, and drawing lessons from the war"; "A Continental chaplain unable to return to his work on account of war would be grateful for temporary hospitality for Wife and Himself"; "Gentleman, Austrian by birth, but naturalized British subject since 1908, debarred through present war from use of his club (a leading West End Club) would like to join a club offering similar conveniences"; many bare-faced advertisements asking for personal gifts of all kinds are signed *Pro Patria*. Even more sordid conditions are recorded in the advertisements for the return of stolen goods and offers from legal owners to buy at full value stolen surveying instruments or other implements of a profession or trade. Numerous fortune tellers ply a lucrative trade in time of war, hedge lawyers offer their services on all "war questions," and "fences" seem immune in advertising columns.

But it is the advertising that also unconsciously reveals the very real sufferings and privations entailed by war. The Swiss boarding-schools for boys that advertise in Berlin papers and hold out as a special inducement for patronage "abundant food"; the photographers who furnish life-size photographs of those who have fallen; the compulsory auction sales of household goods; the small business for sale cheap because the husband is at the front; the insurance against explosion, bombardment, and riot, and life insurance without restriction or extra premiums—a thousand and one similar advertisements from European papers indicate the genuine misery and sorrow that follow in the wake of war. They are in striking contrast to the light-heartedness of the advertisements in countries less immediately concerned with the war where deftness of phrase may veil the real meaning of war while using its language for commercial purposes.[17]

The press has everywhere been a potent witness to the transformation wrought through war in industrial society. The messages from the governors of twelve states calling on women to enter industrial and business service indicate a significant change from the somewhat recent time when the slogan was "woman's place is home."[18] Advertisements of fashionable hotels for waitresses to take the place of waiters whose services had been requisitioned by the government "for essential industry" have given an insight into important changes in the industrial world.[19]

Not less significant are the changes in social conditions recorded in the announcements of births, engagements, annulment of engagements, marriages, and deaths. During the war it was noticeable that into the notices of engagements and marriages there was incorporated much information in regard to the military affiliations of the contracting parties. The army rank of one was given in detail and the Red Cross or training camp activities of the other were mentioned; the distinguished lineage of both parties was noticed; details given in regard to probable delay in the wedding— "Lieutenant X has been called to the colors"; the plans for the honeymoon and for future residence, as well as the occupation of the bridegroom, were stated, as was also the college of the young man, his college fraternities, his social clubs, and his business connections. Since the close of the war, much of this information in regard to ancestry, previous life, and future plans has been retained.[20]

Advertising columns give one of the best records of the progress of the temperance movement, even before the adoption of the Eighteenth Amendment. Men sought work and stated that they were sober, or total abstainers, and one of the leading demands in the "help wanted" column was for men who were sober. Through the advertisement information is given in regard to legislating liquor out of Canada[21] and on the other hand the advertisement has been used to combat the further spread of the prohibition movement — liquor firms increased the number and size of their advertisements in such papers as did not exclude liquor advertisements; in covertly advertising beer as the best temperance drink, they recognized the progress made by the Anti-Saloon League; and they used the advertisement as propaganda to promote in every way their private business interests.

The newspaper is not necessary to reconstruct the books printed, the works of art produced, the new music written — these presumably survive and the historian can examine them himself. But the newspaper records the impression made on the public by the appearance of new works of literature, art, and music. It reflects even more perfectly than do statements of the number of editions issued and copies sold to what extent the impression left has been purely ephemeral, how far it has been relatively permanent, how far a work has at first apparently been a failure but later has come into its own.

The press, considering all of its departments collectively, may be used to reconstruct in a measure the daily life of different classes in society,[22] though the lack of proportion in the conscious description and the unconscious reflection of these classes must somewhat impair its usefulness in this direction — the life of one class must seem to be filled with weddings, dances, dinners, charity balls, and of another with drunken brawls, murders, crime of every description, while the life between these two extremes passes unnoted.

These differences are evident in the country press and in the metropolitan press. They are illustrated by a comparison of the society columns in these two classes of papers. The country weekly gives both relatively and sometimes absolutely a larger proportion of its space to purely social events than does the daily of the large city. Every trifling event is chronicled and its importance magnified, yet while its exaggerations are prone to be excessive, they are easily detected and discounted. All weddings are described as pretty, all brides are beautiful, all bridegrooms are successful, both are always popular in the community, the wedding repast is sumptuous or elegant, and the presents received are numerous and valuable. The facts may often be precisely the reverse, but in a small community the rhetorical descriptions deceive no one and presumably will not mislead the future historian.

These elaborate descriptions of social events are found in the metropolitan dailies only in exceptional cases — the vast majority of weddings and of social events go unchronicled by the press. In such as are chronicled, a different set of conventional phrases is used. Barring change in names, the society columns vary little from one social season to another. The historian is rarely concerned with the names that fill these columns, the inaccuracies that inevitably creep in do not vitiate his use of them in his reconstruction of the past since this reconstruction must concern itself less with the individual than with the type. The dinner party or the theater party may supplant the ball, skating may take the place of *thé dansant*, new experiments in social entertainment may be introduced to whet the jaded appetites of the professional social classes, — it is with this that the historian is concerned in his reconstruction of social life rather than with the individuals through whom they are carried out. The genial editor who describes in florid language the social events of a country village is in effect not so much describing these events as he is recording his own natural characteristics, the family ties that bind together all parts of the village, the common desire to give every one "a good send-off," the intimate relationships that prevent the naked truth from being told in public places, the concealments that do not conceal — all of these conditions are faithfully portrayed by descriptions that in themselves are wholly unreliable, yet are absolutely trustworthy records of the state of mind, the intellectual interests, the friendly relationships of the rural community. It must also be remembered that conditions in a poor, backward community can also be in part reconstructed from what the paper does not contain as well as from what it publishes. The country press as an interpreter of rural and village life is best described by William Allen White who says:

Therefore, men and brethren, when you are riding through this vale of tears upon the California Limited, and by chance pick up the little country newspaper with its meager telegraph service of three or four thousand words — or, at best, fifteen or twenty thousand; when you see its array of countryside items; its interminable local stories; its tiresome editorials on the waterworks, the schools, the street railroad, the crops, and the city printing, don't throw down the contemptible little rag with the verdict that there is nothing in it. But know this, and know it well: if you could take the clay from your eyes and read the little paper as it is written, you would find all of God's beautiful sorrowing, struggling, aspiring world in it, and what you saw would make you touch the little paper with reverent hands.[23]

The reconstruction through the newspaper of the life of the small community seems simple, — the reconstruction of the life of a great city is a more complex matter. The rural community knows itself, it is interested in reading about itself, and it makes the necessary modifications of all local accounts given. But a huge city does not know itself — "the people in one part read with eagerness about the other part of which it knows not. The society debutante will read of the temptations of the Bowery and of Chinatown, while the shop girl pores over the descriptions of Mrs. K's jewels and the latest entertainment or the newest scandal in the upper set."[24] Yet as one star differeth from another in glory, so the metropolitan press of different countries and of different sections of the same country have their own variations. A historian of the press finds that "the local news in Berlin and other large cities is written with the minuteness and the familiarity of style of a village chronicle, and gives the impression that every one is occupied in observing the doings of his neighbor."[25] An England reconstructed from the advertisements of the *Spectator*[26] of Addison is a very different England from the England that it would be possible to reconstruct from the advertisements of to-day.

Many extracts from early Australian newspapers make it possible to reconstruct social and industrial life in Australia during the first part of the nineteenth century, although not political conditions since "there were but two classes, those who ruled and those who obeyed." Although the first fleet for Australia carried out a printing press in 1787, no one in the colony was able to set type and when the first paper was issued in 1803 it was found that Australia had not only inherited all of the press disabilities of the mother country but it had added to them the trouble of securing paper and ink as well as compositors since ships were sent out but once or twice a year. "Being under the strictest censorship," the Sydney *Gazette* "did not attempt to discuss public matters. Officials of all grades, when mentioned at all, were spoken of in terms of the most fulsome flattery."[27] The press is the limelight that illumines, as do no other sources, the hardships of frontier life as well as the courage with which they are met.

The newspapers that come to-day from Australia, the Fiji Islands, Hawaii, and the Philippines are invaluable in reconstructing present-day life there — even to the extent of showing how long the advertisements linger of patent medicines announced as cures for cholera.

In *The Voice of the Negro*, R. T. Kerlin, through a compilation from the negro press of America for the four consecutive months immediately succeeding the Washington riot in 1919, has shown how the negro feels in regard to national affairs, what his own grievances are, as well as what are his hopes and his aspirations.

The contemporary accounts of the battle of the Yser that have been collected from the press of England, France, Russia, Holland, Switzerland, and Austria, in the opinion of the editor, "deserve to be presented for the edification of future generations."[28]

The reconstruction of the exploits of Paul Jones in English seas during 1778–1780 has been made from the contemporary accounts collected from English newspapers.[29]

These various reconstructions of the past and the present that have been made indicate the great opportunities afforded by the press for an insight unconsciously given into conditions seldom consciously described.

The press itself is the best refutation of the conventional judgments passed on America, and presumably of those passed on other countries. The advertisement everywhere rebukes the assertion that Americans are superficial — it records to-day precisely the opposite tendency. A genuine desire to reach foundations is recognized by the advertiser who shows the construction of the automobile engine and illustrates the inmost foldings of the tire. Tools, implements, instruments with which work is done are portrayed as evidence that work is thoroughly done. Laws are cited in advertisements showing that banks are permitted to act as executors, administrators, guardians, and testamentary trustees. The statements made that in filling such positions preference should be given the impersonal bank are supported by citations in advertisements from court decisions showing that estates have often been squandered through the mismanagement of the private executor. Recognition of a desire "to know the law" is given in the information frequently conveyed through the advertisement of the latest legislation on important matters. Extracts from debates in Congress are given in advertisements to satisfy a desire to know tendencies in legislation proposed. The advertisement repeatedly gives unconscious testimony to the universal desire to get at the bottom of things, to have guarantees of the reliability of statements made, to ask for evidence and proof that things are as they seem to be.

The press gives indisputable evidence of the growth of the principle of co-operation. During the war different industries co-operated in raising war loans, and in promoting the sale of war stamps. "Working with Uncle Sam" became a persuasive slogan and wide circulation was given the phrase of Secretary Franklin K. Lane's — "We are but beginning to learn the art of co-operation in the United States."[30] Kipling's lines —

> It is not the guns or armament
>> Or the money they can pay,
> It's the close co-operation
>> That makes them win the day —

recorded the universal belief in the effectiveness of co-operation.

The sentences carried by the press — "This is heatless Monday," "This is meatless Tuesday," "This is wheatless Wednesday" — were illustrative of the efforts toward national co-operation as well as privations entailed by the war, and they are more impressive in reconstructing the conditions of the time than would have been a statement of the request to forego the use of coal, meat, and wheat.

The press everywhere announced the formation of scores of alliances, councils, federations, leagues, societies, and unions — all formed to co-operate with the government in the prosecution of the war, as similar alliances to-day exist to promote peace.

Collective advertisements[31] and international advertisements are again significant illustrations of the growing spirit of co-operation.

The value of certain parts of the press to the future historian may be tested by an examination of the accounts given by different reporters of any contemporaneous signal event in a community. How far is it possible to reconstruct from the press a series of events, running through several days, attended by thousands of persons from different sections of the country and by delegates from foreign countries? Such reports, to those who have taken an interested and sympathetic part in the events, must often bring depression and discouragement. If the reporters are instructed to send in "snappy stuff," the instructions are assuredly literally obeyed. With every possible opportunity to gain information in advance and at the time, often no preparation whatever has apparently been made, and the reports show not only ignorance of the events to be commemorated but a general rudimentary ignorance. Errors innumerable are made due to a failure to understand the significance of the event, to a lack of knowledge of local conditions easily obtainable, and to a perverted notion that every report must be "a good story." Attempts at reconstruction from such reports encounter at one end innumerable but needless inaccuracies of statement, exaggeration, flippancy, frivolity, sensationalism, and many positive errors of omission and commission. At the other end, they encounter a failure to see the general plan of the events, the unifying principle that binds together all parts of it, the subordination of the individual to the whole and the spirit of co-operation that has made it a success, and a lack of appreciation of the dignity and seriousness of the occasion. The resulting report, in spite of a straining after the spectacular, is a prosaic, unbalanced account that might well serve as an illustration of Buckle's "golden age of successful mediocrity." It fails to provide material for an adequate reconstruction of an important series of events, but in so doing it unconsciously records the tendency of even reputable journals to encourage reporters to add their own personal views to their reports of news; it records a belief on the part of the press, that the reading public wishes only to be amused and that therefore it must be amused at any cost; it is an unconscious kodak of the standards of that part of the press that "follows the crowd," that "gives the public what the public wants" and that thereby fails to interpret the times in which it lives.

The analysis of the periodical press that has been made, it is hoped, may indicate that the actual value of the newspaper is far beyond all that could have been anticipated when the presses close, the papers have passed into the hands of their readers, and have then been cast aside as having served their purpose. The suggestions that have been made of its ultimate value to the historian through the infinite range of reconstructions of past time made possible by the press have presupposed a press under normal conditions. A press regulated or censored by authority, a press under governmental control, a press used by governments to promulgate its special doctrines is not a free press, and a society reconstructed from a press thus limited by external conditions is but a caricature of what should be a normal society.

For this study of normal life the newspaper — abnormal as it itself may seem with flaring headlines and blurred pages of illustrated advertisements, with all of its limitations, its inaccuracies, its unworthy representatives, its lack of proportion, its many temptations — not always resisted — to throw prismatic colors instead of the white light of truth on its accounts of the day, the periodical press still remains the most important single source the historian has at his command for the reconstruction of the life of the past three centuries.

Schools and Citizenship

Lucy Salmon was totally engaged with education and with the educational institutions where she worked. She remained in contact with friends from her days as a high school teacher in McGregor, Iowa. Her devotion to the University of Michigan, where she took her B.A. (1876) and her M.A. (1883), was lifelong. She formed close intellectual and personal relationships there as a student, sought news of her classmates, and participated regularly in reunions and alumni gatherings. In 1926, at her fiftieth reunion, the university awarded her an honorary degree. She showed similar devotion to Vassar College, where she began to teach in 1887. Her early years there were spent living in Main Building in the heart of the campus following along with the routines of her students' lives: meals, chapel, and study hours. Later, as her responsibilities were defined more closely to history and as the department expanded, she remained the central figure in its development, a status that she achieved not only through intellectual authority but through her extraordinary popularity with the student body.

Students' lives were transformed by contact with Lucy Salmon. Her methods were shocking to middle-class women students raised on the practices of memorization and rote learning and accustomed to speaking in public only in answer to questions. Miss Salmon, as she was called, assigned them themes and sent them to the library to conduct research. There they learned to take notes, to muster evidence, and to supply multiple sources and when they returned to the classroom they had to construct an argument in public. She also urged students to read newspapers, and she invited alumnae to send newspapers to her from around the country for use in the classroom. Later still her "ubiquitous laundry lists," as they were called, grew into a collection that was used to teach students to see how the most banal of documents could be analyzed for their significance. Yet what seems to have given Salmon's methods special purchase for her students was that she effectively turned the classroom experience back toward self-examination and self-reflection and forward to life after college. After mastering the techniques of analysis and learning the historical background, the students were invited to examine and criticize their own environment: the campus plan, the college catalog, the newspaper, the house or community in which they lived. No surprise that her students, many of whom had led the sheltered life of late-Victorian America, should have been stimulated by this liberated view of their own possibilities.

That connection between the classroom and the wider world was integral to Salmon's view of education. Education is neither about the accumulation of knowledge nor about the practice of historical methodologies either on their own or together, but about bringing both to bear in our communities: "The basis of all good work [is] the ability to make knowledge effective," as she wrote in 1905. From her master's thesis on the appointing powers of the president, her earliest significant work, one sees an interest in the political implications of historical knowledge, a position that is repeatedly reinscribed much to the irritation of the conservative president of Vassar College, James Monroe Taylor. She lectured to reform societies and women's groups, large and small, and she wrote letters to the editor. Even her decision to move from the comparative isolation of the Vassar College campus in 1901, where she had lived for more than ten years, into a house on Mill Street in downtown Poughkeepsie, becoming thereby a citizen of Poughkeepsie (albeit without the right to vote) was a statement of her own commitment to action within the world.

Examinations in Theory and Practice

Examinations—primarily library examinations—were discussed at the December meeting of the Long Island Library Club in a manner that brought out points of interest to library workers. The subject was presented by Miss Lucy Salmon, professor of history at Vassar College, in an informal talk, which was followed by general discussion. Miss Salmon's address was, in part, as follows:

There are two kinds of examinations—first, the class of entrance examinations, and second, the examinations that come at the completion of a course of study. The purpose of one is for selection, the purpose of the other is educational. Examinations for entrance are to determine the qualifications of persons to do a certain class of work, such as Civil Service examinations, college examinations, examinations for library assistants, etc. College examinations are for the purpose of selecting students who are qualified to do college work, library examinations are for the purpose of discovering persons who are qualified to do library work. This class of examinations is necessary where an examining board does not know the candidate's ability, and those who give the examinations are entirely unfamiliar with the applicant's qualifications. The question is simply to find out whether the candidate has sufficient knowledge to do certain things. For the purpose of selection, then, the question is, What can the person do? Then the other question that comes in connection with the examination at the close of work would perhaps be the companion question, What has this student learned to do? Both are perhaps different forms of the same question, How can you make your knowledge effective? That is the basis of all good work, the ability to make knowledge effective.

Applying the question then first to the library, it seems to me the fundamental object of entrance examinations as put by a library board would be first of all to weed out incompetents—the young woman who wants something to do; the decayed gentleman who is seeking for congenial occupation; the teacher who failed, but who wishes to keep her social position; the widow who enjoys reading. Having weeded out the incompetents, the second object of the examination is to determine the *best* material there is among those who have been labeled competent. The problem is to find out who are the most competent. Obviously the question is less, "How much does the candidate know?" than "What can the candidate do?" There are apparently three classes of qualifications for librarians and library assistants:

First, what may be called the luxuries of librarianship, creative ability, invention, great executive ability, ability to receive a new idea without pain, editorial ability, knowledge of a great many languages, this ability which has been called the sixth sense — the ability to read mss. without great and laborious study. These qualifications can never be determined by an examination, and when found entitle the possessor to occupy a foremost rank in librarianship.

Second, personal qualifications, taste in dress, neatness, pleasing manners, ability to keep one's temper, physical and mental endurance, patience, moral qualifications. These are not determined by examination; some of them are discovered instantly by inspection, others by trial.

The third great class, mental qualifications, can be determined by examination — alertness, concentration, accuracy, order, adaptability, versatility, literary taste, judgment, power to reason. These can be determined by examination, and the examination that can bring out these qualifications will enable the examiner to answer the question, What can the candidate do?

How do the examination questions meet the situation? Sometimes they meet the conditions, obviously they do not always meet the test.

In looking over various examination papers for entrance to library work there seems to be a certain grouping of subjects. One paper is usually History and General information, another Literature, one on French and one on German, and one even on Arithmetic.

From the standpoint of a teacher of history, it is difficult to see how the chasm can be filled which separates general information inorganic in character, from history organic in character.

Many of the questions asked under the head of General information seem rather useless questions. In examining the questions, it was my plan to take illustrations of good questions from library questions and illustrations of poor questions from my own department of history. The criticisms that are to be passed upon examination questions concern both the form and the substance.

What questions are to be avoided? One class, those which do not help the examiners in any sense to answer the question, What can the candidate do? Special questions that should be ruled out are: 1, Questions which are not questions at all — "Napoleon," "Julius Cæsar," "War of the Revolution." The applicant who is being examined is expected to know what the examiner wishes him to do with these various words or phrases. 2, Questions that can be answered by simply "yes" or "no," as "Has the legendary history of Rome any value?" 3, Questions which imply the answer, those ending "If so, why?" "If not, why not?" 4, Another class, those which cannot be definitely answered or about which there may be a difference of opinion, as "When did the Reign of Terror end?" 5, Questions involving unrelated points. 6, Indefinite questions, "Give some," "Discuss a few," etc. 7, Another sort of questions, which we sometimes find at the end of text books, written in what Carlyle called the past potential subjunctive, "If France had not helped the colonies, would they have defeated England?" 8, A great many questions which you may call historical puzzles, such as "Who was the youngest soldier who fought in the Revolution?" "How many presidents have served but a single term?" "How many vice-presidents have succeeded to the presidency?" 9, Generalizations which involve a premature judgment — based on an insufficient command of facts, such as "Mention the effects of Alexander's conquests on civilization." These are far beyond the ability of any person to answer inside of five minutes. 10, Generalizations beyond the probable reasoning powers of a high school pupil, such as "Give your estimate of the Athenian Democracy." 11, Questions encouraging on the part of the candidates undue confidence in their own judgment, such as "What are the possible annexations to the possessions of the U. S.?" "Do you regard further annexation as desirable?" 12, Ethical questions of which examiners are sometimes fond, such as "Did Cæsar deserve the death he met?" These are neither history nor general information. 14, Another class of questions may be called drag-net questions, "Write a page on what you know about the history of your own state." 15, Another class is that of scrappy questions, "Name five cities occupied by the English during the Revolution," "Five French generals," "Five Russian authors." It is obvious that students could pass examinations of this character and yet be absolutely worthless as civil servants, college students or library assistants.

What shall we say of the examinations to be taken at the end of a course of study? There are two theories in regard to these. One is that they shall be a test of what the student does or does not know, and by them a student shall stand or fall. In a way they might be considered a form of punishment for the sins of omission committed by the idle, the lazy, the indifferent. On the other hand the examinations may be considered to have an educative influence just as valuable as class-room work. They should clinch the work of the class-room, and in an educational way should be as valuable as the daily work. They should cover the whole ground and bring about the unification of the knowledge gained, and should be a test of a person's ability to utilize the knowledge which he possesses. The situation is like that of a person who has taken lectures on first aid to the injured. If he does not know how to apply his knowledge when he is brought face to face with a case of poison or drowning, the lectures are of very little use. What is desired at the close of a course of instruction is not a restatement of the instruction received, but the application to specific cases of the knowledge that he has gained during the period of study.

This might be illustrated by a series of parallel lines which never meet. These represent the work from day to day. When it comes to a review, we may make these parallel lines meet and then we may combine the reviews into an examination and bring to a focus all the work of a semester. Any examination which does not put all the work of a semester before one in a general way seems to miss its mission. An examination at the end of a term is not an examination of a student, but is an examination of the subject which the student has been studying to show the student what he has gained from the subject; to test his ability to deduce conclusions; to see what a candidate does not know as well as to see what he does know. We may say then that it is always the proper function of an examination to give new ideas and it may be the means of imparting knowledge. Sometimes such examinations will make havoc of a marking system, but — ! It is sometimes perhaps a very good plan, in order to accomplish all of these various objects, to ask a student to make out a set of questions himself. This will be a very good test of a student, and will show what grasp he has of a subject.

Examinations are three-fold in aspect, intellectual, physical and moral. They are sometimes opposed on the ground that they are actually harmful, that they make the persons taking them nervous and subject them to a great strain. The person who gets nervous is not educated, he has not learned to hold his faculties in control, he has not properly trained himself, and does not choose the right conditions. I remember some years ago dining with a friend of mine in Paris, and at the dinner were some young men who had taken a five years' course of study and were to take examinations the next day. About half-past eight these young men excused themselves, and as they were hurried away by the host, he explained that they were to have these examinations the next day, and it was very important that they should be asleep by nine o'clock. Rest was considered imperative that they should be in the best conditions. Having come into good physical condition the mental part takes care of itself. The excuse that students are nervous would be a valid one against their being permitted to take the examinations. The test of an educated man is his ability to meet crises. In meeting an expected crisis a student is being prepared to meet unexpected crises. If the examination has an educational value nothing can be more illogical than to excuse from examinations students who have obtained a certain percentage. This may not enter into consideration in the library field, but is quite prominent in college circles.

The third question is essentially a moral one. The honor system should prevail, and students should be free from watching and the sense of supervision. Years and years ago it used to be the fashion for persons to go around to see that students were not cribbing nor using helps. The assumption always was that the student was doing something he should not do. This is in direct violation of law that a person shall be assumed innocent until he is proved guilty, and examiners should give the students the benefit of that assumption.

The examination is beneficial to the teacher, as it enables him to revise and correct his own work. In giving examinations at the end of a course of study, one of the most helpful questions I find is, "How could this course have been more useful to you?" From the answers to this question I have learned much, and it has been very influential in determining changes and improvements. Every person who prepares an examination is himself under examination. The mental ability of the examiner is indicated by the questions quite as much as that of those examined is indicated by the answers.

If all of these qualifications before enumerated are to be brought out through an examination, and the student is to prove what he can do, certain essentials must be borne in mind. First there should be absolute quiet, quiet inside the room and as far as possible quiet outside also; physical conditions must be met by having reasonable arrangements for short periods; reasonable time for lunch and recreation; freedom from inspection, absolute quiet and calm.

What, then, shall we say are some of the characteristics of a good examination? As to the paper as a whole, there should be a certain uniformity, one idea should run through its various parts; variety in the questions; brevity, definiteness, logical sequence, comprehensiveness. Those questions are good which show clearness on the part of those taking the examination, and would bring out the qualifications which the librarian is seeking, such as adaptability, literary taste, accuracy, ability to meet emergencies, knowledge of books, etc. We should say that questions like the following were very well adapted to the purpose:

"Describe the system of classification with which you are most familiar so that it would be clear to a person who was not familiar with it."

To bring out the ability to meet emergencies, "What would you do if a reader should address you in a foreign language?"

Literary taste, "What books do you reread from time to time for pleasure?"

Breadth of outlook, "What are the opportunities for usefulness in a town library?"

Judgment, "What books would you give under such and such circumstances — persons fond of fiction who wish something about the French Revolution, a student who wishes something about wireless telegraphy."

Adaptability, "What periodicals would you select for a high school library to be used by both students and teachers?" "How would you change the list for a reading room in a settlement in an Italian quarter of New York?" "What books would you select to describe points of interest for a foreigner travelling in America?" "What five or more books would you select for a traveller going to England to acquaint him with town and country life?"

Reasoning power, "How would you answer a borrower who argued that if a tax-payer asks for Mary J. Holmes' works, the library ought to supply the demand?"

To test the candidate's executive ability, "Arrange a time schedule."

All these questions, taken from various library papers, seem to indicate this, that the questions given to library students are given at an age when there is a beginning of a creative ability, and the questions are adapted to those who are able to create and able to improve upon the facts given them.

It is sometimes said that a very good definition of an educated man is one who knows what he knows, is not ashamed of what he does not know, and knows how to find what he wants to know. The last part is perhaps adapted particularly to librarians, and an examination that would find out what a candidate can do, whether he knows what he knows, is not ashamed of what he does not know, and knows how to find what he wishes to know, would be the best method of selecting the ideal assistant which all head librarians are seeking for.

The discussion was opened by Miss Foote, of the New York Public Library, who asked in which of the two classes of examinations examinations for promotion belonged? Promotion examinations had been objected to, she said, as useless on the ground that the librarian-in-charge could tell best about the quality of her assistants from their work, but the examination is valuable, first, because it makes a uniform test against which there can be no fair complaint, and the personal equation cannot enter in; secondly, because the examinations for promotion are an incentive to study on the part of the assistant. Miss Foote advocated questions that involved short answers, as making for condensation and clearness, on the part of the assistant, and making the papers easier to correct.

Miss Hawley, of the Brooklyn Public Library, said: "In preparing examination questions, do not read over other examination papers to get questions from them, but try to think what you want to get from *people*, not only in the examination, but in subsequent work. A very good test of an examination is to take it yourself after making it out." Miss Hawley took issue with Miss Salmon on the "scrappy question" in library examinations. "Scrappy information," she said, "is not scholarly nor good for self-culture, but it has a very important value in library work. It is hardly possible to give unity to a library entrance examination, as it is necessary that the candidate must have a wide range of information."

Miss Rathbone agreed with Miss Hawley on this point, adding that there was a psychological reason for the scrappy question, as the library worker must have the sort of mental ability that can turn quickly from one subject or train of thought to something entirely different, and the "scrappy question" was an excellent test of that sort of mentality.

Miss Plummer said that in a library examination we want to find out what a candidate *is*—what is his stage of maturity, that being not a matter of age merely, his vocabulary, his power of expression. Many traits of personal character can be discovered from an examination; orderliness of mind, neatness, clearness, sense of proportion, common sense, intellectual honesty (the candidate who tries to conceal his lack of information by abundance of words, or who wilfully misunderstands the questions, stands convicted on that point). Specialized information is not called for in a library worker, hence there are many branches of knowledge, as the sciences, that can be slurred over; some understanding of their terminology being required, and some idea of the recent progress in science. The best general examination, added Miss Plummer, is one that cannot be crammed for.

Miss Hume recommended the dictation of difficult English as a good test of accuracy. She held that the report of the librarian-in-charge was of the greatest value in determining promotions.

Miss Lord made the point that examinations for admission to a library would not fall under either of the heads Miss Salmon had given. "They are not," she said, "entrance examinations in the sense in which Miss Salmon had used the term, and they are not tests by those who are going to direct further study. Neither are they examinations at the end of a course, given by the directors of the course to find out how far the students have grasped the work of the course. They are indeed a sort of mixture, being given at what is practically the end of a course — at the end of the candidate's preparation for the work, by a person who has had nothing whatever to do with the candidate before. This complicates the question of type." Miss Lord also asked whether it was not possible to prevent the admission to examinations of candidates who would in no case be accepted on account of personality. She said that it seemed to her hardly fair to admit a person to the examinations and practically tell them they had a chance, when it was already definitely settled that that person could not in any case be given the position. It saved trouble for the examiners to admit every one, and then to bring down the mark of the undesirable candidate by including "personality" in the marking, but was it fair?

The question was asked Miss Salmon whether she advocated a time limit for examinations. She said that she did not, that the sense of hurry that a time limit induced was detrimental to the best results of an examination. Miss Hawley objected that speed was a very important quality in an assistant, and that an examination ought to show it. Miss Salmon suggested that a certain part of the examination might be made to show this quality without injury to the paper as a whole.

Miss Salmon said in conclusion that she was much interested in seeing in how many points library conditions differed from conditions in colleges making library examinations in many ways a very difficult problem.

On the College Professor

The most humble of all persons is the college professor. Assigned by his official superiors a small field to till, watched by his colleagues lest he cross the line that separates his assignment from theirs, dubbed by his fellow citizens a visionary and a theorist, the college professor quickly learns "to know his place." At times when he has looked up from the plow and he has ventured to hope that long experience has taught him how to plow deeper and to draw a straighter farrow, the college student and the newspaper reporter have been at hand also to see that he keeps his place, but he plows on cheered by the inner consciousness that he has at least not willfully wandered from the straight line that marks out his small plot of land. But when at other times his humility has been merged into a profound discouragement that has threatened to paralyze his hand and cause him to drop the plow, he has sought hope and encouragement from his friend the librarian, "the sun that shines for all."

But even this last refuge is failing him, for does he not read in the *Library Journal* that "college professors do not realize the value of their libraries; do not make adequate use of them; do not impress their students with the importance of skill in using books and libraries, and do not insist that that skill be acquired in the four years of the college course."[1]

The question may at least be raised whether these kindly strictures on what the college professor does not do to teach his students the use of books as tools as well as a love of books as literature are really deserved; whether a too hasty generalization has not been made from the one professor who does not do the things he might do; whether this generalization has not been equipped with unlimited expansive powers and thus made to cover all college professors, most of whom at least are trying to do the things they should do; whether the city librarian really knows how much the humble college professor ought to do and might approve if he knew it were being done.

The worm turns! The humble college professor begs for a hearing and for a chance to explain what he is trying to do along library lines to increase the facility of college students in the use of books, to foster a love for books that shall be as deep and as personal as is the love for a living friend, to create a college and a civic responsibility in the use of books, to substitute first-hand acquaintance with the great books and the great records of past time for indirect information about them that has been culled by others, and to bring it about that every student before leaving college shall have been impressed with the importance, indeed the absolute necessity, of skill in using books and libraries.

Library Journal 36 (February 1911): 51–54.

The college professor craves patience while the explanation is made in some detail of what is being done by one professor in one college, and asks the possible reader to believe that it is but an infinitesimal part of what is being done in colleges the country over to achieve the end so ably set forth in a recent number of the *Library Journal*.

Every student in Vassar College is required to take here, unless she has had a similar course in another college, a course in European history that comes three times a week and runs through the year. About three hundred students take the course every year. It is optional whether the course is taken in the first or second year; about sixty per cent take it as freshmen and forty per cent as sophomores. The three hundred students are divided into twelve sections averaging twenty-five each.

At the beginning of the college year, the second time each section meets, every section is met by the head of the history department and an illustrated lecture given on the library and its use. This lecture shows that the library building must be studied as a record of conditions that have passed away, that it must be studied as a building on whose walls history is written, and that it must be studied with reference to the use it serves.

The Vassar College library building is of the ecclesiastical type and its students are shown that this type is a record of the time when all learning and all education were controlled by the church and libraries were for the most part attached to ecclesiastical foundations and controlled by them; that books were at first kept in the cloister; that when separate buildings were erected, libraries were public only in the sense that all connected with the foundation had access to them.

The steps in the development of the library are explained from the first stage when books were very costly and kept chained, and when it was the chief object of the library to preserve its treasures, to the second stage when with the advent of printed books the chains were removed but the idea of preserving books was still retained and they were placed on shelves inaccessible to the general public. The third stage came when the multiplicity of books compelled attention to the question of storage and from this resulted the stack. But the multiplicity of books has resulted in a corresponding multiplicity of readers and from this results in turn the question of how to make the large collections of books most serviceable to numerous readers. The answer to the question is — the open shelf. The students are thus made to see that the college library building is in itself a record of the changes that have come from the old ecclesiastical library with its chained books to the new ecclesiastical type of building with its open shelf; that the barriers that have at different times intervened between the reader and the book — the chain, the inaccessible shelf, the stack, the attendant page — have all been the accompaniments of an aristocracy of learning that is disappearing before the democracy and the responsibility of the open shelf.

But our college library is not only a record — it has also much history written on its walls. The great west window emblazons in stained glass a part of the history of the Lady Helen Lucretia Cornaro Piscopia who received the degree of doctor of philosophy at the University of Padua in 1678. Carved on its walls are the college and university seals of the great educational institutions of America and England. Hanging on the walls of the great entrance memorial hall is a series of tapestries narrating the history of a meeting of the council of the gods on Mount Olympus. Its windows contain in leaded panes the printers' marks of all the early leading printers of England and the continent.

It is hoped that every student will thus see in the library building itself a record and a history of the past.

But the building is but the means to an end — the means of providing a home for the books the students are to use. The students are therefore given full information in regard to the ground plan of the building — its basement, main floor, galleries, and seminary rooms; the general contents of the three main divisions of the building, the location of magazines, newspapers, manuscripts, and the rooms used by the library staff. This supplements in another way the information put in the hand of every new student the first time she enters the library — a brief pamphlet describing the location of the general classes of books, together with a card showing the ground plan and arrangement of the library.

The question of the library catalog is then considered and the general evolution of the present card catalog system from the writers slips on the end of the mediæval book stalls. This includes a discussion of the various forms of a catalog both as to its subject matter and as to its external form, while the evolution of the card itself from the card written by hand, the card printed by hand, the card printed from type, to the distribution of printed cards from central bureaus, like the Library of Congress and the American Library Association, is all indicated.

The lecture is accompanied by lantern slides that are fully explained. They include a view of the exterior of the college library; the interior of the library of the University of Leyden from a print of 1610 — its resemblance to one of the wings of the Vassar College library is very close; the interior of the Laurentian library showing the chained books; a view of one of the incunabula in the Vassar library; the city library of Poughkeepsie, illustrating the civic type of library architecture; the stack of a public library; the stained glass window of the Vassar College library; one of the tapestries on the wall of the entrance hall; the Vassar College seal; the seals of Oxford, Cambridge, Harvard, and Yale; various printer's marks used by William Caxton; a part of the college library showing the location of the table where the newest acquisitions of books are shown; a corner of the hall showing the card catalog; a drawer of cards showing the various guide cards used for the general subject of *history*; a series of sixteen catalog cards illustrating the special features used in cataloging a work defining history; a paper on history included in a series of papers, the difference between a *see* card and a *see also* card, an author and a subject card, a translator's and an editor's card, the method of cataloging *Periods of European History* and the *Cambridge Modern History*, the *Century Atlas*, and Spruner's *Atlas*, the *English Historical Review*, and Barnard's *Companion to English History*—all of the features on these cards are explained even to the smallest detail of punctuation; a slide showing the book-plate of the Vassar Alumnæ Historical Association; the title-page of Mr. De Vinne's work on *Title pages*; and a page from Robinson's *History of Western Europe* showing the use of different kinds of type to bring out specific meanings. The lecture as a whole is intended to make the students familiar with the conditions of the library and to establish friendly relations between them and the books contained in it.

In addition to this lecture on the library building and the use of its contents, every student beginning history has a pamphlet called *Suggestions for the Year's Work*. This pamphlet devotes one of its first sections to the library—its history, its description, and the meaning of its exterior and interior form. It also includes the ground plan of the library, it discusses the card catalog, and it reproduces from the library catalog the card for the textbook to be used as the basis of the year's work. The meaning of every word, and every figure and every punctuation mark used on this card is carefully explained by every instructor in charge of a section of the class. Moreover the pamphlet suggests the questions that arise in connection with the use of any book; its author, his nationality, residence, education, occupation, politics, religion, and personal characteristics; its general form—the meaning and use of title-page, copyright imprint, preface, table of contents, chapter headings, headlines, sidelines, margins, signature, footnotes, illustrations, maps, charts, diagrams, genealogical tables, appendices, and index; its structure; the date of authorship; its authoritativeness. The pamphlet suggests that the students study the bibliography at the end of each chapter in the textbook used and underscore with ink all titles of books they personally own and with pencil all books accessible in the College library. The students are also given in the pamphlet very explicit directions as to how to use books in the preparation of their history work, and specimen analyses of pages or chapters are given, as are also illustrations of footnotes and references to authorities, and directions for making bibliographies. It also suggests a series of principles for testing the authoritativeness of histories used and this is accompanied by an elaborate specimen chart. The pamphlet also gives a very full section under the caption *Helps*. This includes first *bibliographies*, and second *works of reference*, comprising the general classes of general reference works, dictionaries, encyclopædias, periodicals, year books, atlases, and autobiographical and biographical material, and ecclesiastical, political, economic, and art reference works. In connection with each class from one to five illustrations are given. The pamphlet also gives three pages of grouped titles of books, with prices stated, from which the students are urged to buy according to their means.

This pamphlet of nearly thirty pages printed in whole or in part is intended from the first page to the last to show the student how to get the most possible out of one class of books — histories; how to use these books with the greatest ease and facility; how to begin the formation of an historical library; how to judge of the value of histories; how to prepare bibliographies; and in a word, how to learn the use of the tools with which they are to work. In all of this work on our part we have been cheered and encouraged by the words of President Hadley, cited by President Lowell in his inaugural address, Oct. 6, 1909:

"The ideal college education seems to me to be the one where a student learns things he is not going to use in after life by methods that he is going to use. The former element gives the breadth, the latter element gives the training."

But the first lecture, the lantern slide illustrations, and the pamphlet are all merely the beginning of our efforts to teach the use of the tools. The history students are directed to library shelves containing books about books and they are encouraged to read them; they are given the first week or ten days of the first year numerous brief questions to answer through books, and these are intended to secure quickness and readiness in handling books; they have frequent individual conferences with their instructors who talk over with them the best ways of finding what they are looking for in books; they are given stated times for meeting their instructor in the library and looking over the bookshelves with them; they have had prepared for their use by their instructors in history a large number of classified bibliographies that are arranged in the tin boxes of the Library Bureau and placed in the history alcoves — these boxes supplement but do not duplicate the library catalog cards; they are required to hand in carefully prepared bibliographies with every written topic presented in history, and these bibliographies are talked over with the students individually and with the classes collectively; they are encouraged to read book reviews and to prepare occasional book reviews themselves; they are introduced to the questions involved in editing books and manuscripts, and to the use of photography in editing manuscripts; they are given reprints of articles on books and reading, as for example one on "Pace in reading," for study and analysis; they are given talks on rare histories or rare editions of histories; they are asked to prepare lists of histories suitable to be purchased by their own town or city libraries for children of specified ages, for adult foreigners of different nationalities, for adult study clubs, and for various other possible combination of needs; they are encouraged to buy books, to preserve with care all printed material found in their own homes and to deposit in their own town libraries whatever is of especial local value; they are encouraged to make their outside reading bear on their college work and they are asked to report from time to time what outside reading they have done that bears on their history work; they are referred to elaborate lists for summer reading prepared by the history department, and the first week of the college year they are asked to report in writing the reading done during the summer; they are given frequent topics to prepare in history that are systematically planned to introduce them to every *class* of historical literature and every kind of historical document found in the college library, — this of course can be done only for those students who continue their history beyond their first year; they hear occasional lectures given them by officers of other departments, as for example a recent lecture by an instructor in English on "The making of a book"; they are given occasional talks on the great historical collections in the libraries of this country and of Europe; every expedient that we can devise is employed to teach the use of books and to foster a love for them.

The humble professor would also bid his kindly critics bear in mind that the library activities of any one department must be multiplied by those of every other department in the college if they are to appreciate fully the sum total of what is done for, by, and through the college student to acquaint him with the use of the tools he is to use not only during his college course but in all his after life, to cultivate a sense of responsibility for the library work of his own home community, to minister to his appreciation of all that is best in books, and to find in books the realization and expression of his own highest ideals.

But again, and finally, the college professor must bid his critics remember that no one so keenly realizes his own shortcomings as does the college professor himself; that he does not reach his own ideal in pointing out to others standards of perfection; that if he climbs the mountain side, he sees far above and beyond him unscaled heights never to be reached by him, strive though he may with might and main; that when he measures the distance yet to be traversed with the distance over which he has passed, he realizes that both he and his critics are as one and that thus "all's well."

Democracy in the Household

A few years ago a gentlemen in early middle life with the fresh color of youth and the white hair of age entered a dining-room somewhat late for his midday meal. Rubbing his hands gleefully, he exclaimed, "I'm perfectly happy. I've just begun a piece of work I know I shall never finish."

The zest that attends perpetual search and constant effort awaits all who enter upon a discussion of the nature, the effects, and the desirability of democracy in any of its phases. No question of the day is of greater antiquity or of greater complexity than is this. From the time of Plato to our own, men have attempted to define democracy, and they have attributed to it all the virtues of an ideal condition of society, or they have held it responsible for all the ills from which mankind has suffered. Men have built up on paper ideal forms of mutual relationship that they have called democracies and they have given their lives and their fortunes to found ideal communities where they have hoped to realize democracy in material form. Yet in spite of countless attempts at definition and hundreds of attempts to establish democracies, we are apparently today as far removed as ever from a consensus of opinion in regard to the nature of abstract democracy and from a unanimity of desire to achieve democracy in the concrete. The work that has been begun will apparently never be finished.

In attempting therefore to consider the nature of democracy in the household we are dealing with a problem whose most fundamental factor is elusive and baffling. We do not know clearly what we mean by the term "democracy," or what we mean by its special application to the state, to society, to industry, to education, to the household.

It is, however, not difficult to see certain reasons that have heretofore prevented us from formulating a satisfactory definition of democracy. One reason has been our assumption that democracy has been everywhere and at all times always the same, and we have consequently failed to realize that it has had a growth and a development that have changed its aspect. We have thought of democracy as being something fixed and permanent, yet our conceptions of it, if we but stop to consider, have changed from time to time. Theodore Parker's famous definition, "Democracy means, not 'I am as good as you are,' but 'you're as good as I am,' " is certainly far removed from that of Mazzini, to whom democracy meant "the progress of all, through all, under the leadership of the wisest and best," and both are equally far removed from the more recent definition of J. T. Dye, to whom democracy "stands for equality of opportunity, freedom of individual growth, and social helpfulness."[1] As each individual looks at a distant object from a different

angle, so each individual has had his own conception of the nature of democracy, and these conceptions have changed from time to time since they
have naturally been affected by the ideals of the generation in which they
have arisen. "The equal life," "the intellectual life," "the simple life," "the
strenuous life," all indicate the changing ideas, the unattained, and perhaps
unattainable, collective ideals of successive generations.

Democracy in its partial realization in the state shows a corresponding
change. The democracy of Athens was not the democracy of New England,
yet they probably had more in common than either had with the democracy
of the French Revolution. Both in theory and in practice, democracy of the
day before yesterday was very different from the democracy of yesterday and
of today, and a form of it that satisfies one generation does not satisfy another. We have failed to realize that what men individually and collectively
have thought about democracy has changed from age to age and that in the
future it will apparently be an equal impossibility to give a hard-and-fast
mathematical definition of democracy.

Another reason for our failure to define democracy has been the confusion of democracy with other abstract principles that have an external, but
only an external, resemblance to it. We have confused democracy with
equality, democracy with liberty, and equality with liberty. "The deepest
cause," says Lord Acton, "which made the French Revolution so disastrous
to liberty was its theory of equality. Liberty was the watchword of the middle
class, equality of the lower."[2] Equality and liberty are really mutually antagonistic in spite of the coupling of the two terms on all the public buildings of
the French Republic, and neither the one nor the other is a necessary
accompaniment of democracy. It has been repeatedly pointed out that all
men are equal only as the liberty of some is restricted, and that if all men
have liberty, inequality results. Only as we distinguish between democracy
and other principles that have been confused with it shall we be able to
understand the real nature of democracy itself.

Yet if an exact, scientific definition of democracy has not been and probably cannot be formulated, it is not impossible to determine some of its
characteristics. One of these is assuredly the equality of opportunity that it
offers to all. Yet equality of opportunity must not be confused with sameness
of opportunity. The opportunity to secure a technical education or a musical education, to buy a farm, to own a mill, to manage a railroad may mean
success to one, failure to another. Equal opportunity means only the opportunity for all alike to make the most possible of the talents given in the
beginning, whether the number was one or five. Another characteristic of
democracy is flexibility and adaptability, as opposed to rigidity of condition—a capacity for change, for growth, and for development. We may
indeed think of democracy as possessing all the characteristics of a growing
organism, and this means an active rather than a passive state. This must
mean in its turn that democracy has its responsibilities, and that it attains its

fullest development only as it is permeated by the spirit of co-operation and mutual aid. Democracy therefore can never be a monopoly — all must share in its privileges, opportunities, and responsibilities, as we recognize the right of all to happiness and contentment. But just as our happiness and content-ment is affected by that of those about us, so our democracy is affected by the democracy of others. The perfume of a neighboring flower garden added to that of our own garden enhances the enjoyment of both, while a noisome odor from a gas plant detracts from the pleasure of both. Moreover this happiness and contentment must be positive and active — chloroform dulls pain but does not remove its cause. The righteous discontent with the present may lead to the attainment of genuine democracy in the future.

If we think of democracy as affording equality of opportunity for all, of having a capacity for growth, of bringing with it responsibilities, and of securing advantages for all alike, it must be remembered that these are after all but external manifestations and accompaniments of democracy. Sir Launfal in his search for the Holy Grail found it, not in distant lands, but within himself, in his own attitude of mind toward his fellow-men, and in his willingness to share himself and his possessions with his fellow-men, instead of bestowing in charity on others the gift that "without the giver is bare." Even more explicit is the statement of Holy Writ: "The Kingdom of God is within you."

We may therefore say that democracy is an attitude of mind toward our fellow-men, and that, like virtue, it is its own reward. This is today our conception of democracy; what democracy may mean to us tomorrow we do not know.

If we are to think of democracy as an attitude of mind, accompanied by certain outward expressions of this mental condition, we need not be sur-prised to find that democracy has not developed equally on every side. Thus a child, as we know, may develop physically very rapidly, but mentally very slowly, and always remain spiritually in a state of arrested development; the man with misshapen, deformed body may have a precocious intellect; the saint may have reached the heights through no help from a frail body and an untrained mind. If we have sometimes been impatient with the slow progress made by democracy, the explanation must be found in our confu-sion of political, industrial, and social democracy and the consequent ex-pectation that democracy in all these forms would develop *pari passu*.

Democracy has probably made its greatest progress in the field of politics, but that even here it has been as yet but imperfectly attained is evident when the existing restrictions on it *de jure* and *de facto* are considered. Restrictions of race, of nationality, of sex, of property, of education still prevent its complete realization. Yet we have been sufficiently near the attainment of political democracy to feel the effects of reaction and to question whether democracy has after all been a success.

That industrial democracy has not yet been secured is apparent from a study of the long history of the struggles of craft guilds, merchant guilds, trade unions, monopolies, and other forms of industrial combinations.

That social discriminations against certain occupations, as occupations, though not always against the same occupations, have always existed has been self-evident. These discriminations, it must be remembered, have been against the occupations as such, not against the individuals connected with them as individuals, not against the success or failure with which the duties of the occupation have been performed, not against the personal character of the individual. The late Mr. Charles Dudley Warner some years ago wrote an article to explain why teachers have no social position — the fact that they have none was to him not even open to question. "You do not want your son to call on a cook," is the triumphant argument used when the social position of houseworkers is discussed, though we have progressed so far toward social democracy since Mr. Warner's article was written that we do not object if our son calls on a teacher of cooking. The social objection is now apparently not to cooking as an occupation in itself, but to the personal relationship that goes with it. A cadet at Annapolis was recently reprimanded because he had invited to a hop the daughter of a distinguished professor in one of our greatest universities, on the ground that she was a governess in the family of a member of the Annapolis staff. Here the social objection, in the mind of the officer giving the reprimand, was clearly to the occupation itself. We all have acquaintances who tell with gusto of their embarrassment in mistaking the butler for the oldest son of the household when a guest for the first time in a family of recent acquaintance. Here again the social discrimination is against the occupation, although no external mark of dress or of demeanor serves to distinguish son from butler. We all know the head of a boarding-school who amuses his friends with the story of how he greeted most cordially the valet who accompanied to the school the young son of a household, under the mistaken impression that the valet was a member of the family. We have all read in the catalogues of private schools the announcement that the pupils must not bring automobiles or saddle horses to the school, since this would be a violation of the spirit of democracy that has always prevailed there, yet we may chance to know that in these very schools a sharp social line is drawn between those connected with the educational side of the school and those connected with its housekeeping side. Here complete democracy may prevail within the educational circle, but many within speaking distance are without the pale. At many schools for girls, chaperonage is regarded by the head of the school as one of the duties of the teachers of the school, but the members of the housekeeping staff are not permitted to act as chaperones. The teacher finds the duties of chaperonage irksome, while the matron of the school would welcome the opportunity to act as chaperone, even with all its attendant irksomeness, since it would apparently indicate an advance in social position. At one time or another every occupation has come under the social ban, though it is today for the most part confined to those who perform personal service for a remuneration.

Current fiction, with its social strugglers as heroes and heroines, shows conclusively, if other proof were lacking, that social democracy, like political and industrial democracy, has also as yet been but imperfectly attained.

The development of industrial and of social democracy has indeed been so backward that democracy is almost synonymous with political democracy; the great writers who have discussed the subject have almost without exception confined their discussions of it to its political manifestations. Yet it may be encouraging to note that the partial achievement of political democracy has not come by leaps and bounds. In its origin it was probably largely obstructive in its purpose — it was used as a means of preventing tyranny rather than of carrying out a policy; it was obstructive rather than constructive. The question may at least be raised whether the democracy of whose ill effects we have complained has not been this obstructive democracy. But today political democracy has reached a constructive stage; it is formulating a definite policy in order to accomplish certain definite results.

We may well believe that if the feudal system and the system of slavery were not abolished until long after a constructive political democracy had been at least partially achieved, the outlook is not discouraging for the future realization of a constructive social democracy. Industrial democracy seems indeed to have already entered into the stage of construction — it was but the other day that the head of a great industrial combination proposed that the federal government should abandon its policy of restriction and obstruction toward the steel industry and begin a policy of legislative regulation that would prove of mutual benefit.

There is apparently little connection between these large and possibly somewhat abstract conceptions of political and industrial democracy that have occupied the attention of the great publicists and social democrats of our time, as well as those of an earlier day, and the household, with what we call its dull routine of ever-recurring petty tasks, its impassable chasm between its members who are hourly thrown into intimate external relationship, yet may be world-wide apart in all those internal relationships that make for a common purpose and unity of action.

In attempting to consider the nature of democracy in the household, we are confronted not only by the difficulty of defining democracy, but also by the difficulty of knowing just what *household* connotes. On its external side it may mean the farmhouse with its "hired man" and "hired girl," or the village house with its "help"; it may mean the country estate with its small army of employees, or the city establishment of eighteen or twenty "servants"; it may mean the average town house with its census family of two adults and three children and its cook and "maid." On its internal side, it may mean the head of the house, or the parents, or the children, or the employer of the household labor, or the employee; it may mean all the persons living under the same roof, or it may mean those living under the same roof who are bound together by ties of blood and lifelong association. The household has probably at different times meant any one of these varying conceptions. But in this discussion of democracy in the household, we may consider the household as meaning one located in a small city and composed of parents, three children, and two employees.

Assuming therefore that today democracy means an inward feeling toward others, involving in the household a desire that all of its members should have equal, though not necessarily the same, opportunities, a recognition of the capacity and a desire of all members of the household for growth, and also of the right of all for normal development, the question follows, What conditions prevail, or should prevail, in the average household, if that household is to realize perfect democracy?

The household has as yet probably not been thought to provide a congenial soil and atmosphere for the growth of democracy; we have considered it at short range and thought of it only on its private and personal side; it has seemed to us to be quite apart from the great public activities by which it is surrounded but with which it seems to have no connection. Yet the isolation of the household is apparent rather than real and the great movements with their ebbs and flows that have carried us nearer and nearer to the attainment of political and industrial democracy have not left the household unaffected by them. If in this discussion of the subject emphasis is placed on the special relations between the employer and the employee in the household, it is in part because democracy in other parts of the household seems to have made more progress, while democracy in the relationship between employer and employee has not only made no progress, but even seems to have retrograded. It is also in part because the recent discussion of *Woman and Labor* by Olive Schreiner seems to render superfluous at this time any special consideration of the general question of woman's right to labor, and Emily James Putnam's historical essays on *The Lady* have shown the chasm that has always existed between the woman and the lady.

It is easy to see why democracy has as yet been more imperfectly realized in the household than elsewhere.

It is possible, first of all, that our theology has been in part responsible for the all-too-common belief that work is a curse rather than a blessing — "In the sweat of thy face shalt thou eat bread" has been interpreted as casting disfavor on work itself. While men as a class, and women in occupations outside the household, have emerged from the shadow, it still lingers on and darkens the lives of many engaged in household occupations for remuneration.

A second reason is very closely allied to it, and that is the fact that the question of democracy in the household is at base an economic one. We find in the household as a rule, as in no other occupation, a complete separation between the money-earning and the money-spending functions. In the mill, in the office, in the store, the young woman is working for someone who is himself a worker, but in the household she works for someone who does not work for money compensation — often for someone who never works at all. The household may indeed not infrequently shelter several members who do not work either for or without remuneration. Apparently the one who spends the money for the household does not earn the money that is spent and this creates an almost impassable barrier between the wage-earner and the money-spender.

A third obstacle that has prevented the realization of democracy in the household has grown out of the mistaken feeling that all questions concerning the household are summed up in the personal relationship existing between different members of it. The husband and father of a household may feel that if the wife and daughters are personally happy and contented and that if their bills for food, clothing, and amusements are promptly paid for them, democracy has been realized for them.

The *Report of the Bureau of Industrial and Labor Statistics* issued by the state of Maine for 1910 devotes eighty-two pages to a discussion of "the household servant problem in Maine." It includes one hundred and fifty letters from housekeepers giving their personal views in regard to "the servant-girl problem." In the opinion of one-third of the writers, the difficulties are summed up in the statement, "Girls don't understand their work, expect too much, and are impudent." The views of the other two-thirds are expressed in the statement, "I have never had any trouble because I always treat my servants well; they always stay with me until they marry." "The better you treat them, the more they impose on you," is the verdict of one-third. "Observe the Golden Rule in all dealings with them and you will have no trouble," is the opposing verdict of the other two-thirds. Nor is this opinion peculiar to the state of Maine. A few years ago on every table in one of the famous restaurants in Copenhagen was a printed card begging the guests not to wrangle with the waiters or to treat them haughtily, but to consider how they would wish to be treated were they themselves the waiters. Yet it must be apparent that the attainment of true democracy, with its "equality of opportunity, freedom of individual growth, and social helpfulness," will never be realized in the household as long as only the harmonious relationship between the members is considered.

A fourth reason for the absence of true democracy in the household grows out of our own mistaken notions of democracy. It is possible that the employer does not really desire it in his own home because it seems to him to mean a condition where the members of the household must do precisely the same thing — sit at the same table at meals, receive all guests in the parlor, share the same living-room, have the freedom of the piano and the automobile. It is probable that he fears, and perhaps with more or less reason, that the employee confuses democracy in the household with the right to be rude, blunt, and impertinent in manner, extravagant in dress, and selfish in spirit. For assuredly if the employer often mistakes false democracy for true democracy, it is not to be expected that the employee will have any truer conception of its nature. It may indeed happen that the head of a household may be a democrat in spirit while the employee may have the characteristics often attributed to aristocracy—race prejudice, class consciousness, personal selfishness, and hauteur of spirit and manner. It is often the employee who boasts of the millionaires for whom he has worked or whom he knows through his employer. It is the Negro employee who is proud of working only for "quality folks." There are social strata within the general class of household employments—in large households the distinction is carefully drawn between the chambermaid and the waitress, between the upstairs maid and the downstairs maid, and in general between the cook and the general household worker. It is possible that the employee may not desire democracy in the household, since to her it might not mean so much equality between herself and her employer as between herself and her fellow-employees. We all know maids who wish to take Wednesday or Friday afternoons off because most maids go out on Thursdays, and who resent being asked to be friendly with other maids just coming into the neighborhood.

We shall not attain democracy in the household by having all members of it do precisely the same thing, by having all share the same occupations and the same recreations. The greatness and the magnificence of the forest depends quite as much on the diversity of its various parts as it does on its external uniformity; the forest would cease to be the forest could all its parts be measured by a tape measure. External similarities do not constitute democracy. The tree grows from within, through its own secret, vital power; it does not grow by binding on it the bark from another tree, nor does the fruit artificially hung from its branches ever become a part of the tree. Democracy in the household is not to be feared on the score of uniformity.

A fifth explanation for the absence of democracy in the household grows out of this imperfect conception of its nature and it is found in the presence of the artificial barriers that we have either consciously or unconsciously set up in the hope that we may stay its dreaded advance. Probably the most important of these artificial barriers is the so-called "tip" that lowers the self-respect of both him who gives and him who takes. The tip is social, not economic, in its origin, and in this lies its strength as a barricade against the progress of democracy. We give a tip to one whom we consider a social inferior, we accept a tip from a social superior, but we neither give nor accept a tip from a social equal. No one so quickly resents anything that even remotely resembles a tip as does the waiter when it is offered by his social equal, yet he grovels in the dust for it before a social superior, and in his turn, when about to take a trip to Europe, gives interviews to the press on "the etiquette of tips." The giver of the tip salves his conscience in giving it by asserting its economic necessity—the low wages received by waiters must be supplemented by a gratuity. But the tipper usually speaks without knowledge, and inquiry at headquarters might show him his mistake. A recent examination of the payroll of a large summer hotel showed that every employee received from the proprietor wages in excess of what he would presumably receive in private houses for performing similar service. Yet the proprietor has been constantly losing ground in the fight against tipping on the part of his guests who while ostensibly tipping for economic reasons have in reality done so for social reasons. "Tipping is but little else than the giver's endeavoring to make the receiver believe that the former has more money than he knows what to do with, and more than the receiver possesses." If the giving of tips grows out of a desire to express social superiority, it is assuredly a lack of self-respect that is responsible for the acceptance of tips. The whole evil of tipping can be met, not by abolishing tips, but by increasing the self-respect of those who now accept them. Unpaid service ought not to be the special privilege of the rich, or of the well-to-do, or of the person of leisure; it is a fine flower that must bloom for all if we are to have genuine democracy. If "our 'New Patriotism' has no room for the receiver of tips," the new democracy has no room for either the giver or the taker of tips.

Another barrier to democracy lies in the use of the Christian name in address, a use that had its origin in the democratic nature of the household of an earlier day but has been retained long after even the semblance of democracy has disappeared; and there seems to be no special reason why a respectable, efficient waitress of mature age should be called Mary and be expected to call the ten-year-old daughter of the household Miss Mary, except that it emphasizes the social distance between employer and employee.

The use of the word *servant* as applied exclusively to the members of the class of domestic employees must also continue to stay the progress of democracy in the household.

If the tip, the Christian name in address, and the use of the word *servant* are all visible barriers to the advance of democracy in the household, the most fundamental and therefore the most serious barrier is the prevailing attitude of both men and women toward the whole subject of work for remuneration as it concerns women. To the freedmen of 1863 emancipation from slavery meant emancipation from work. It is but today that the Negro at the South is emerging from this attitude toward work and realizing what its possibilities are. We shall have a situation parallel to that of 1863 if women as a class come to believe that through marriage, or through the accumulation of wealth, or through inherited wealth they are either released from the necessity of productive work or deprived of the opportunity for work. The release of women from domestic activity through the industrial changes of the last century means a degradation, not an elevation, of domestic life, if its one result is to increase the amount of time it is possible to give to the round of petty social activities. Lincoln said that the Union could not exist half free and half slave. Nor can society today exist half active and half idle. If one-half of womankind live without labor, the other half of womankind must be overburdened and underpaid. Democracy in the household must mean the opportunity of all members of it to work for remuneration and the privilege of all members of it to work without remuneration. There can be no democracy in the household so long as the women members of it spend their lives in unproductive activity—in a ceaseless round of teas and calls, bridge parties and theater parties, automobile trips and steamer excursions. As long as our national ideals seem to be at least in part reflected in the universal greeting, "Have you had a good time?" we need not wonder that the cook, the butler, and the parlor maid fall under its spell and translate "having a good time" into "having nothing to do."

We have fought and won a great national political battle in the interest of a single monetary standard and have thereby gained the respect of the honest nations of the world. We are constantly urging the abolition of a double standard of morals, and this in the interests of a higher morality. We have yet to win the struggle for a single industrial standard for men and women, for the equal right of men and women to work for remuneration, and for the equal privilege of both to render unpaid service. When this struggle has been won, democracy in the household may not indeed have been gained, but at least progress toward it will have been made.

It has been seen that the tip, the use of the Christian name, the designation of household employees by the term "servant," and the double industrial standard for men and women seem effective obstacles to the realization of democracy in the household. Other artificial conditions are found that are apparently barriers but are not such in reality or of necessity. The uniform of the livery, for example, is not necessarily democratic or undemocratic—it may level up as well as level down. Democracy is not achieved when host, guest, and butler all wear conventional evening dress; the advent of democracy in the household is not stayed because the waitress wears a black dress and white apron while hostess and guests appear in reception dress. Class distinctions are quite as much emphasized by academic costume, military uniform, and diplomatic dress as they are by household livery; if we look upon one as a somewhat harmless desire for pageantry, we need not be distressed by the effective uniformity of the other. The meal taken alone is the lot of the solitary everywhere and is not of itself a foe to democracy. The lack of a place to receive company is not necessarily undemocratic; it is a condition met by every occupant of a hall bedroom, and by practically every young woman whose home is in the conventional flat of "five rooms and a bath."

It has been suggested that real barriers to the advance of democracy in the household may be found in our inherited theology, in the economic conditions within the household, in our assumption that the personal relations between the members of a household are the only ones that exist, in the mistaken ideas of the nature of democracy on the part of both employer and employee, and in the artificial barriers set up to prevent the advance of the undesired, because misunderstood, democracy. At least four others must be considered.

One of these is the fact that however much we may approve of a remote theoretical democracy, we dread the inconvenience of it in its close application in the household. The large political democracy with its equal rights for all appeals to us. We favor industrial democracy because we disapprove of special privileges. But democracy in the household "seems different." That "liberty, equality, and brotherhood" that seem so ideal when graven on the walls of the official buildings of France, that equality in community life that results in clean streets, good pavements, protection from fire and from crime, and hence seems so desirable and is so much appreciated — this long-range democracy has much to commend it. But it is over the question of whether we shall have the fish baked or fried, the eggs boiled or scrambled, that the happiness of the household is wrecked. It is when democracy seems to demand some personal sacrifice, when its virtues are not apparently appreciated by others, that its unlovely side seems disclosed to us; it is when the cook with a headache wishes to serve the cake made yesterday rather than make a fresh cherry pie; when the butler plans to be married the evening we had settled on for an elaborate dinner party; when the laundress complains of extra table linen in the Monday wash, although she had an extra day off the week before; when the parlor maid is "huffy" because Christmas brought her a new dress of an undesired shade; when the waitress is "grumpy" because the theater tickets given her are for Thursday evening and she preferred to go Friday evening — then, indeed, do we question the applicability of abstract democracy to our concrete household. But are the relations of the employer and the employee within the household necessarily any more irksome than they are outside of the household? Is it possible that we expect an ideal relationship between employer and employee in the household when this relationship does not as yet exist between employers and employees in other forms of industry? Is it possible that we look for an ideal relationship between employer and employee when that ideal relationship does not always prevail among the members of a household who have been born into it? Are domestic employees the only persons who do not always appreciate the efforts put forth in their behalf? Do we sometimes hear that husbands do not appreciate their wives, that wives do not appreciate their husbands, that children do not appreciate their parents? Is there not, indeed, a somewhat universal complaint of the general failure of everybody to appreciate what is done for everybody? Democracy in the household may appear unlovely if we look only at its outer garb, but the real character of a hero is not always disclosed by the cut of his garments.

Another obstacle lies in the fact that many who see somewhat clearly the true nature of democracy do not honestly wish social democracy in any form, even that species of it which we call "democracy in the household."

Our ordinary language unconsciously reflects our inherited, or our acquired, or our affected, or our apparently necessary tendencies toward social aristocracy. We are unwilling to send our children to the public schools "because they are so mixed." We avoid the trolleys because "everybody uses them." We move "in the best society" at home and away from home we meet only "the best people." Every generation contributes its phrase to the language of social aristocracy — "the cream of society," "the upper crust," "the upper ten," or "the four hundred" are all alike expressions of our social aspirations. In *The Tender Recollections of Irene Macgillicudy*, Miss Macgillicudy tells us that her mother, of plebeian ancestry and newly acquired wealth, was very democratic toward all those who were socially above her, and very aristocratic toward those below her. This movable line of demarcation between aristocracy and democracy with a tendency ever upward is not confined to fiction or to satire; its convenience is everywhere attested in everyday life.

Plato's perfect man was an aristocrat and his perfect state was an aristocracy. Even the consuming desire of the French Revolutionists for political and social democracy halted at democracy in the household — the constitutions of 1791, 1795, and 1799 gave as the only disqualification for the right of suffrage "to be in a menial capacity," viz., that of a servant receiving wages, though this restriction has sometimes been explained as coming from a desire to punish men who were willing to serve the nobility, rather than a discrimination against household service in itself.

If, then, there has always been a considerable element in society, an element where the intelligent man and the idealist is represented as well as the social climber, that has honestly doubted the efficacy of democracy as a social solvent, it must follow that such measure of democracy as has as yet been secured has come only after prolonged and serious struggle.

Still another barrier in the path of the attainment of democracy in the household is found in the disorganized nature of the household itself. The business man who pays an expert $100 a day to help him put his business on a scientific basis has not yet turned his attention to the household. Not only in the individual but in the collective household we find lack of organization, of co-operation, of apparent capacity for growth. Such improvements as have come have been superimposed on it from without through business activity, commercial enterprise, and inventive genius; they have rarely been developed from within. It has, indeed, probably been unfortunate that such organization as the household has received has been superimposed from above rather than normally developed from within. Wherever organization comes exclusively from above, there must always be many connected with the occupation who feel smothered, cramped, and fettered. It was probably quite as much a protest against the hierarchy of the church as an organization as it was against the theology of the church that led to the various degrees of democracy attained by the great religious bodies of the sixteenth and seventeenth centuries. There is always danger when a pyramid is placed on its apex.

We have found various conditions that seem to have retarded the growth of democracy in the household. Several questions remain to be raised even though they cannot be definitely answered. What does democracy in the household really mean? How far is it probable that the history of democracy in the household will parallel the history of political and industrial democracy? How far may we look for deviations from that history? What can the household itself do to facilitate its own progress? What social and intellectual conditions are conducive to its growth?

It is possible that among the outward manifestations of democracy in the household may be counted the possession of a checkbook by the wife. It may mean the opportunity for the wife to engage in some remunerative occupation, even though the husband may feel that such a course may reflect on his own ability to "support his family." It may mean the right of the daughter to decide for herself the question of occupation as well as the question of marriage. It may mean the right of the daughters, the right even of an only daughter, to leave home and follow a regular occupation. There is no more pathetic sight than that of the eager, enthusiastic young woman, fired with a holy zeal to do her part in the world's work, yet compelled by parental desires, by family traditions, by social custom, to live a life of inactivity and dependence on others. The father who refuses to support his son in idleness, but compels his daughter to remain in idleness is certainly a stumbling-block in the path of household democracy. All the birds are pushed from the nest and made to try their wings; it is only in the human family that even any part of it, least of all a large part of it, is kept in voluntary or involuntary inactivity. Democracy in the household may mean the equal claims of the boy and the girl to a college education and to professional or technical training. It may mean the equal right of all members of the household to make his or her special contribution to the sum total of human welfare. It may mean freeing the household from its deadly blight of "parasitism" so graphically described by Olive Schreiner in *Woman and Labor*. Democracy in the household, in its external manifestations, may mean all of this and more than all of this.

It may be asked how far it is probable that the history of democracy in the household will repeat the history of democracy elsewhere. We probably cannot look for a close parallel. Our political democracy and our industrial democracy have been in large part secured through legislation. But social democracy can never be secured, nor on the other hand can its progress be stayed, by legislation — sumptuary laws have never made a stable social aristocracy, nor have civil-rights bills brought about social democracy. We can create by law neither a social aristocracy nor a social democracy. Louis XVIII when confronted with the task of creating a new nobility found many willing to be dukes and earls but few willing to be anything else; Jefferson, "with his mind as well as his body clothed with French ideas," promulgated, as president, certain "rules of etiquette" that were to abolish all class distinctions, set aside all official precedence, and secure absolute social democracy. A democratic millenium was proclaimed, but the immediate result was a social upheaval and almost international warfare. While we may tolerate and even favor a natural aristocracy or a natural democracy, an artificial aristocracy or an artificial democracy throws us into spasms of rage. In nearly every community there is a natural gravitation, even without building restrictions or reservations, toward the same part of the town of houses of approximately the same rental or the same value. But a vigorous protest is made if a tenement house is put up in close proximity to detached houses, less probably because the tenement house may seem to bring democracy than because it is out of harmony with its surroundings. A sense of harmony and of eternal fitness is not incompatible with democracy.

The household can itself do much to promote democracy within its own boundaries. It is probable that a greater measure of democracy prevails in households where there is union instead of separation between the money-earning and the money-spending functions. Democracy is probably greater in households where at least one woman connected with it has a visible means of support. There may be less restlessness under routine, when in times of discouragement the household employee counts the number of dishes she washes after every meal and multiplies this by the number of meals served in a year and this by the total number of years she has spent in household employments, if her employer is able to match or perhaps to cap her tale of woe with the number of books she has handled as a librarian, the number of music lessons she has given, the number of children she has taught, the number of columns of copy she has sent to the daily newspaper. The total result seems less appalling to the houseworker and the isolation of her occupation seems less evident when she realizes how much she has in common with others, and that a great part of the work we all do is constant repetition — the bookkeeper is constantly adding figures, the bank teller is receiving and paying out money, the clerk measures off cloth, the trolley conductor rings up fares, and the ticket chopper mechanically empties his ticket box — and that our physical life seems but a constant repetition of sleeping, dressing, breakfasting, lunching, dining, and retiring.

Democracy is perhaps greater in households where at least one woman in it works for someone else. Many workers are restless under a "boss" and there is a somewhat universal ambition "to set up in business for oneself." This ambition is seldom realized, but the postponement of its realization makes a common bond between the houseworker who wants "a home of her own" but cannot have it and the stenographer, the cashier, the teacher, each of whom may also dream of a business of her own.

Greater appreciation of the artistic possibilities of the kitchen might bring about a greater measure of household democracy, as well as the remembrance of birthdays and anniversaries with flowers, cake, and confectionery rather than with more prosaic gifts. More idealism and more imagination in the household make for greater democracy.

The spirit of democracy is greater in households that are free from nagging and from minute directions given capable workers about how work is to be done. "The only way you can keep your hands on the business is to keep them off," said the president of a great industry to an overconscientious, fretful manager, and the lesson is not without application in the household.

Some progress toward democracy would be made could we cease to confuse democracy with paternalism, and could we recognize the real nature of paternalism. Democracy grows out of relationships that are mutually active and constructive, while paternalism compels one side of the relationship to be passive and receptive. With all its benevolence of aspect and of demeanor, paternalism is often but the guise of an uncontrolled love of power and of authority that seeks an outlet for itself rather than the real welfare of the object of its apparent solicitude. Democracy and paternalism are mutually exclusive, as are also democracy and love of authority.

Democracy might enter our households sooner did we but realize more fully the nature of the problems that lie beneath the surface. We have taken the settlement into the crowded city slums, into the lonely mountain district, into the black belt of the South, but rarely have we become settlement workers in the field that lies nearest — our own homes. Socialism has entered legislative halls, the factory, the office, and the shop, but the social spirit has not always entered every part of the home. Unity of purpose and unity of action in the household can come only as we remember with Kipling,

> For the strength of the pack is the wolf,
> And the strength of the wolf is the pack.

And if once more we ask, What social and intellectual conditions are conducive to the development of democracy within the household? we come once more to our starting-point, "The Kingdom of God is within you."

Monarchy and Democracy in Education

It is a truism that since the day of Plato's *Republic* no subject has had such widespread discussion as has that of the proper form of government. It is equally a truism that if imitation is the sincerest flattery, the hundreds of written constitutions that have sprung up since 1789 attest the belief that America has successfully put into practical form the theories of democracy. Yet a minority has always questioned whether democracy is after all the panacea for political evils, and recent writers like Mr. Lecky, have but given expression to a somewhat widespread feeling of uncertainty as to the permanent success of democratic institutions.

It is noteworthy, however, that the discussion of democracy has been confined to the field of politics, and that its adaptation to educational institutions, where presumably a high grade of intelligence, education, opportunity and experience seem to offer the greatest promise of success, is never publicly discussed, much less in this country practiced.[1]

It is equally anomalous that in Europe, with its tendency to monarchy in the state, there is found absolute democracy in the government of educational institutions, while America, democratic in the state, furnishes the most extreme illustration of absolute monarchy in the government of its educational institutions. It seems, if possible, even more strange that American college students have for years been going to European universities, and yet apparently have paid no attention to questions of educational organization. It can only be explained by the general lack of information and interest in the management of educational institutions.

The *Unpopular Review* is not a fitting place for the discussion of questions concerning the college, if frequent discussion means popularity: for the fashionable question in the serious periodical of the day is "What's the matter with the colleges?" But while there is absolute agreement that *something* is the matter, every diagnostician has his own explanation. Athletics, the curriculum, the classics, vocational training, and every part of the educational system unable to speak for itself, have been held responsible for the existing evils. It may, however, be sufficiently unpopular for a mere college professor to say that in his humble opinion at least one thing the matter with the college is its form of government, and that here is an interesting place in which to test democracy before abandoning it as hopeless. Certainly these opinions have been so unpopular as to lead many who honestly hold them to hesitate to state them. When they are stated, it is generally by those not within the academic pale.

One of the most serious evils in the situation is that it is impossible for those most concerned to meet and discuss it openly. More than one important article has come from a college professor, but it has been anonymous because it is out of the question for him to write freely of the position in which he is placed. If he openly questions the present system, he is called "a sorehead," "a knocker," and "a kicker." Every discussion of the administrative department of the university is interpreted as "an attack on the president." To publish a doubt of the wisdom of concentrating all authority in him is regarded as "attacking the administration." It is at least significant that in the great work on *University Control*[2] the opinions of two hundred and ninety-nine members of college faculties are anonymous, while a bare half-dozen are published under the names of men holding academic positions at the time of writing. Academic freedom is usually interpreted as meaning the right of speaking freely about matters and things in general, including the trusts, anarchy, socialism, prohibition, the control of public utilities by municipal, state, or federal agencies, and kindred subjects, but never about academic organization. That freedom of expression for which Wycliffe and the Lollard movement stood in England, Luther in Germany, Calvin in France — albeit his ecclesiastical followers in this country may have wandered far from his ideas — that movement for freedom led in Europe by great university men, when it comes to discussion of educational organization has, by the irony of fate, been denied to their heirs in America to-day.

It is easy to trace the path by which monarchy in education has been reached. When education was largely controlled by the Church, students were educated by the Church and for the Church. Educational institutions, as a part of the Church, were governed as the Church was governed. Implicit obedience was given superiors, not as educators, but as members of the Church. We have inherited from mediæval times a condition of educational organization that was the natural outgrowth of this organization, but we have perpetuated it in an age when education is controlled by the State, which has itself become democratic. The result is a tug-o'-war between the monarchical organization of education and the democratic spirit that permeates the vast body of educators and educated.

It is also easy to see the immediate steps by which we have arrived at the present situation. The institution with which the writer is connected had fewer than two hundred regular college students when he first became a member of the faculty. It has shared in the enormous development of such institutions all over the country, and its students now number more than a thousand. Yet in all this time, the method of government has not changed. In the early days it was convenient for the president to decide every question, and this system has been continued, even though the student body has increased more than fivefold, and the instructing body in the same proportion. In spite of changed conditions everywhere, this plan has been perpetuated, and has often been legalized by boards of trustees.

Thus, by both remote and immediate inheritance, education, in its organization, has arrived at absolute monarchy, with all its attending evils — evils that affect the university as a whole and all of its separate and individual parts.

One obvious evil is the confusion everywhere found in the academic world between legislation and administration. The normal plan in a political democracy — an administrative body — is reversed in education. The legislative and the executive departments may be combined, and the executive made responsible to the legislative, as in England, or they may be independent, as in America; but it is only in an absolute monarchy that the administrative body both legislates and administers its own legislation. The university has thus allied itself with absolute monarchy rather than with democracy.

Another element of confusion is found in the anomalous conditions of citizenship. Educational citizenship within a faculty attaches to the position, not to the individual. A man is appointed to a professorship in a faculty, and *ipso facto* he acquires full citizenship in that body, with power to vote immediately on every question submitted to it. Yet the faculty may list as "instructors" no small proportion of its members who have been connected with it many years, yet they have no share in the government of the institution. They are in a state of indeterminate probation, and are often never admitted to the privileges of full citizenship in the governing body.

Confusion also grows out of the application to the government of the university of the unit vote long ago abandoned in the federal government. In the New England Confederation, the experiment was tried of giving equal representation to each colony, regardless of its population. This proved unsatisfactory, and subsequent plans of union attempted to square the circle by increasing the number of representatives, but giving each colony only one vote. After this in its turn proved ill-advised, the whole system was thrown overboard, and a "one man, one vote" principle adopted. In college legislation has either theory or experience shown any necessity for reverting to an antiquated political custom, and requiring that the unit rule shall prevail and each department have one vote but only one vote?

The most disturbing factor in the situation is that all questions concerning the actual government in a university are decided, not by the faculty itself, but by an external board of trustees; that this body, rather than the faculty, is ultimately and legally responsible for all legislation affecting the university; and that it transfers this responsibility to the president of the institution whom it itself appoints. If it is suggested that the faculty is the natural legislative body in an educational institution, and that this body should determine all matters of educational policy, objections are immediately interposed.

The first objection is the alleged incompetence of a faculty to legislate. But it may well be asked how often matters of genuine legislation are even submitted to it. Some years ago a university president was elected, and the special correspondent of a great metropolitan daily sent it a two-column account of his probable policy. "All over America," he writes, "the question is being asked: 'What are President X's views? What is he likely to do with the elective courses? What with requirements for admission? What with the different departments of the University, re-modelling the scheme which now runs through each in a confused way? What with university extension? The compulsory chapel, and the college pastorate questions, and the complicated problems of undergraduate and general intercollegiate athletics?' " Yet every one of these questions represented as being asked "all over America" concerns not the administrative office of a university president, but the legislative department of the institution. Whether a faculty is or is not a failure as a legislative body can be only a matter of conjecture until the experiment has had a fair trial.

A variant of this objection is that "college faculties can not do business." To this it may be said parenthetically that a faculty has little opportunity except to fritter away its time, when a college president refuses to submit an agenda to it, and thus enable it to do its business in a business-like way. But every great university numbers among its faculty those who have from time to time been asked to render service to the state or to the community, and this service has been rendered in an acceptable, even a distinguished, manner. In the fields of diplomacy, finance, organized philanthropy, municipal affairs, the college professor is everywhere being requisitioned by the state as a consulting expert, or asked to render it temporary active service. Yet many of these prophets are without honor in their own country, in that no opportunity is ever given them to suggest improvements in the business administration of their own institutions or to confer officially on educational policy with the representatives of other faculties. Thus the powers of the faculty are being atrophied through lack of use, while the college, in the midst of abundance, suffers from poverty of nourishment.

It is also urged that faculties are not interested in general educational policies, since each member is primarily concerned with his own special department. This too is a matter of conjecture until the statement has been tested by experience. It may, however, readily be granted that not all members of every faculty are interested in educational legislation. But this is true in the state, and yet it is not used as an argument either for disfranchising voters or for refusing them the franchise. Rather, is every voter urged to do his political duty, and vote, and every alien urged to take out his naturalization papers, and as speedily as may be become a voting citizen.

The fear has also been expressed that if faculties were given increased legislative powers, the result would be confusion in the consideration of educational problems. This fear in its turn seems certainly not well grounded. It is seldom expressed with reference to the political system, yet if danger exists anywhere, it is assuredly there, and not in the college world. What education needs above everything else is all the wisdom that can be contributed to it by the experience, intelligence, observation, and theory of every person connected with it. The result would assuredly be, not confusion, but enlightenment. A recent examination of the academic career of the members of a single college faculty shows that they have been connected either as students or officers with nearly two hundred different institutions in this country or in Europe. This history is doubtless repeated in every other institution, showing what a wealth of academic experience and knowledge the college has never yet turned to account. It is generally believed that the great work of the trained mind is to utilize the forces of nature and make them do its bidding, to harness fire, water, air, electricity, and to reap the advantages of the power multiplied by these means. But no effort is made to utilize the educational forces that lie dormant in a college faculty, and to multiply a hundredfold the educational forces now used. The question may at least be raised whether some fraction of the confusion found in the educational system may not be due to the failure to bring to bear upon it the clarifying power of college and university faculties. Investigation has found an outlet in every field except that of education itself.

The fear was once expressed by Edward Thring lest in any scheme for the organization of education "the skilled workman engaged in the highest kind of skilled work should be deliberately and securely put under the amateur in perpetuity."[3] This fear is not unwarranted in its application to America. As long as college and university trustees are for the most part chosen from business interests, they naturally assume that college officers must "want something" in the way of personal advantage when they discuss the disadvantages of the present system of academic government. They do not understand that what college officers wish is not personal gain, but simply freedom of opportunity to serve the college to the limit of their powers, and that this opportunity must include a controlling voice in the educational legislation of the institutions with which they are connected, and in the formulation of the laws governing their own actions as legislating bodies. The members of college faculties seem justified in thinking that they are now deprived of all the broadening and deepening influences that come from sharing the responsibilities of the larger affairs of education. They are parts of a machine irresponsible for its final results: the planning, the direction, the thinking are all done by the administrative head. Were the duties of a college professor such as those of a letter carrier, a policeman, a snow shoveler, a brick layer, or a day laborer, it would be a simple thing to regulate his hours of work, his pay, his vacation, and his uniform. But the more complex the duties of any person, the more difficult the regulation of them by an external authority. The more serviceable any person to any organization, the more must he have freedom of thought, judgment, and action.

The further questions also arise — Does a university officer sustain the same relation to the president, or the board of trustees, that a minister does to the ministry, or that a diplomatic officer does to his government, or to the government to which he is accredited? Are college officers to be paid employees, or to be co-operators in the government of the college? If the former, then certainly military discipline must prevail. Men in high business or financial circles do not allow their employees to go about openly discussing or criticizing the way they conduct their business. But if college officers are to be co-operators in determining the educational policy of the institution with which they are connected, what is needed is not keeping them under army discipline, but the encouragement of frank discussion with them and by them of all matters pertaining to the welfare of the institution, and of education in all its largest aspects.

The situation may be confused by the custom of choosing the college president from the ranks of the clergy; the clergyman-president naturally believes that since his relations to his congregation have been those of an expert in theology to those who are ignorant of it, his relations to a college faculty must be similar. He forgets that he has to deal with those who are themselves experts, each in his own field, and that they are also presumably interested in the general field of education and acquainted with it.

It may be that college authorities intend to encourage college faculties to discuss with them questions of educational policy; but if so, the intention has not been made with sufficient emphasis to be clearly understood. "We are clerks in a dry goods store, the dean is the floor walker, and the president is the proprietor," is the way the situation has been put by a well-known university professor. The college professor sometimes feels that while, before the law, a man is innocent until he is proved guilty, in the college world faculties are guilty until they can prove themselves innocent, and their normal attitude thus becomes one of defense against an unseen power.

The results of all this confusion between the legislative and the administrative departments in academic government are unfortunate for all concerned. Destructive criticism will always prevail, and will sap the vitality of any institution that denies to its members the right of constructive action, while external government leads to the spirit and attitude of externalism — the members of the teaching body of a college rarely say "we," but refer politely to the institution with which they are connected as "the college." The impression is sometimes carried away from an educational assembly, that the profession of teaching has not attracted many brilliant college graduates. Will mediocre men continue to seek the teaching profession, while men of independence of judgment and character continue to shun a profession which offers little scope for their abilities? "What science and practical life alike need, is not narrow men, but broad men sharpened to a point," writes President Butler, and this admirably expresses the great need in education — a need difficult to be met as long as present conditions remain. It is a grave question whether the college professor is to continue an automaton or to become an initial force.

The chief administrative officer of the college has come to be considered the college; in his own eyes, and in the eye of the public, he *is* the college; he is the only person considered competent or authorized to represent it; and it is his view that is to prevail in all matters of educational policy.

Now with the college president as an individual, the college professor has no quarrel. He often counts him among his warmest friends, and his personal relations with him are often cordial and even intimate. But this is quite compatible with a strong and conscientious belief based on a study of facts and conditions, that the organization of the college presidency is an anomaly in a democratic state. The college professor may perhaps recognize the justice of the administration of the president *per se*, even when it takes such extreme form as regulations that members of a faculty are not permitted to invite anyone to speak to their classes without authorization from the president; that they cannot be absent from a class without getting permission from the president; that sudden illness, accident, or unforeseen emergency that has involved absence must be reported; when the president gives permission to accept an invitation to lecture at another university but with the proviso that it does not involve absence from class, or that the request be not repeated during the academic year, or with the reminder that a professor's first duty is to his own college; when it is the president who passes on the propriety of a professor's wearing a golf suit in the lecture room, and who sometimes decides the question of wearing caps and gowns on commencement day. The objection of the college professor lies less in the nature of the rules and regulations prescribed than in the manner of the prescription. He sometimes wonders why he could not be trusted to legislate on some of these questions, and why it is so difficult for the president to realize that a professor may take an active interest in educational affairs, without having his eye on the presidency.

The professor realizes that the president is not always to be blamed for present conditions — often he is himself the victim of a system he has had no part in creating, and forces that he cannot control apparently compel him to perpetuate it. Yet blame must be attached to him for defending it, and for refusing to discuss with his colleagues the possibility of modifying it. He seems equally remiss in not presenting the whole question of college government to the board of trustees, and pointing out to them the incongruities and anomalies of the present situation. The professor realizes that the president has a hard time of it — Does he not hear it at every educational convention? — but he always wonders if it is inevitable. He sometimes remembers an illustrated lecture given by the representative of a great manufacturing company, showing its organization and workings. One slide represented in graphic form its early organization; it was a pyramid trying to maintain stable equilibrium on its apex, and the apex was the president supporting on his shoulders the solid mass of the employees. Another slide represented the same pyramid on its base, and the apex, in its natural position, was the smiling face of the president. Underneath was the legend "It pays." If the organization of a great business enterprise has gained in strength and stability, and has found that "it pays" in dollars and cents as well as in comfort and peace of mind, to have the responsibility for conducting it shared by all connected with it, would not a similar organization "pay" the college? As a result of recent outbreaks on Blackwell's Island, the Commissioner of Corrections went among the inmates to learn the causes of their grievances, and with the same end in view called to the office a half-dozen of the most intelligent convicts, and invited them to state all their complaints. It is not on record that a college president or board of trustees has talked over causes of dissatisfaction with educational conditions, or has invited the members of the faculty to state their views. Is it possible that some pointers on academic government may be gained from a method employed in a modern penal institution?

It is conceivable that such a plan might also pay in dollars and cents. In one college it took nine years to get a requisition signed for a small improvement needed to relieve the officers working in the building from undue anxiety for the care of the property; and the total cost involved was six dollars. During these nine years the college treasurer was on record as saying that it cost three thousand dollars a year to enforce the compulsory attendance at chapel prescribed by the board of trustees. Would some conference between trustees, president, and faculty have resulted in a better showing on the treasurer's books?

If the present system has entailed endless confusion in the relations between the legislative and the administrative departments of the college, it has resulted in equally anomalous conditions in the administrative department itself. Some years ago, when a gentleman distinguished in the educational field was chosen president of a university, a member of another faculty remarked, "It seems a great misfortune, does it not, that he should be made president: he has done so much for education, and now of course he will have to give up all that work."

Nor are members of college faculties alone in thinking that the office of president is overweighted. At the time of the election of a certain university president, the alumni of the institution put themselves on record as believing "that the presidential prerogative has increased, is increasing, and ought to be diminished." In this opinion, probably the majority of every faculty in every college and university in the country would concur.

Many college professors are restive not only because "the presidential prerogative has increased," but also because they are called on to expend much mental and physical energy in preserving the prerogative. The offense of *lèse-majesté* has become almost as criminal in the educational as in the political world. They are restive because the presidential office is overweighted, and the result as regards the administration is to develop that most pernicious of all forms of government—a bureaucracy. They are restive because of their inability to remedy conditions not of their own making. Some of these are financial, and a college instructor once put the matter thus: "Our president has created conditions whereby we have an annual deficit of about $20,000. This deficit is met by the chairman of the board of trustees, and the president must stand in with him. The faculty are in a hole — they must hang on to the president, and he must hang on to the board of trustees, and they must hang on to their chairman, and trust him to pull everybody out." Some of these conditions are educational. Wisdom seems to be attached to the office of president, rather than to the individual filling it. A man may be made president because he is known to be a good businessman and an able executive officer, and *ipso facto* he becomes an expert on all educational questions. Progress in all educational matter must be halted while the excellent executive is familiarizing himself with the ABC of education, and perhaps in time learning how large the subject is.

Many professors are discouraged because, while the same tendency towards autocratic government has been seen in the political world, the reaction against it is already noted. The power of the speaker of the House of Representatives that gained the title of "czar" for one incumbent has already been modified by the rules of the House. But the college professor sees nothing on the educational horizon that portends a change for the better. Every week he reads somewhere the well-known account of the first official meeting between a president of Harvard University and his faculty. When changes were proposed, and some of the faculty reasoned why these things must be, the president replied, "Because, gentlemen, you have a new president." The professor always wonders if anything like it ever happens when a university acquires a new member of the faculty; he wonders why this vivid description of professors rubbing their eyes in amazement at the statement of their new master should give such pleasure to the press and to the public; and he wonders if the spirit of it has not blossomed in the most recent authoritative statement of the place of the university president as it is understood by the president himself.[4]

The professor is discouraged because, although, in the present organization of the educational system, a president is considered necessary, the supply of presidents never equals the demand. So varied and numerous are the qualifications insisted upon, that when a person is found approaching the desired standard, he is sought for every vacancy. Several well-known professors have for a number of years been "mentioned" in connection with every presidency vacant, and as a society belle is said to boast of the number of desirable offers of marriage she has refused, so the professor, or more often his wife, makes known the number of presidencies that he has declined. The professor wonders why one or more of our great universities, in this age of vocational training, does not establish a training school for presidents. But this in its turn leads to the query how the supply of students in such a school could be maintained.

The professor is discouraged because of the difficulty of "getting at things." The question of college government involves the relation of the boards of control to the president and the faculty, the relation of the president to the faculty, on the one hand, and to the student body on the other, with the result that the president becomes the official medium of communication between the governing body and the faculty. This triangular arrangement can but be productive of lack of harmony and of constant misunderstandings; and its evils fall upon trustees, president, faculty, students, and alumni. The trustees nominally exercise an authority that is virtually given over to the president, the office of president is overweighted, the faculty are left without responsibility, as are the students in their turn, and the alumni are often in ignorance of what the policy of the college is, while everybody is exhorted to be "loyal to the college" without any clear understanding of what loyalty to the college means, or even indeed just what "the college" means. He sometimes wonders if the Duke of York's gardener was anticipating present academic conditions in America, when he instructed his servants,

> Go, bind thou up yond dangling apricocks,
> Which, like unruly children, make their sire
> Stoop with oppression of their prodigal weight;
> Give some supportance to the bending twigs.
> Go thou, and like an executioner
> Cut off the heads of too-fast growing sprays,
> That look too lofty in our commonwealth;
> All must be even in our government.

Yet after all 'tis a good world, my masters! The professor is not wholly downcast. If he does not know by name, without consulting the catalogue, a third of the members of the board of trustees that controls his academic destiny; if he does not know by sight a fourth of them, and if he has never exchanged comments on the weather with more than a fifth of them, he at least hopes that the sixth of the board who may chance, through the college catalogue, to know of his connection with the institution may not feel unkindly toward him. He can only plead in extenuation of his rashness in suggesting a more democratic form of academic government, his strong conviction that only as *all* parts of the educational structure are strengthened can the structure approach perfection and serve the end for which it has been erected.

Research for Women

For more than sixty years women have been receiving degrees from adequately equipped and amply endowed colleges. The question may well be
asked what have they done during this long period to advance the outposts
of knowledge, what contributions have they made through research to the
sum total of human learning, what discoveries have they made in the fields
of natural science or of the humanities? The answer to the triple question
must be that as yet the net result is not impressive, but the explanation is
almost self-evident. Women were long discouraged from undertaking even
college work. They were told that their health was not equal to it, and then
that their minds were not equal to it, while it was many years before the
subject of research work for them was even broached.

These dismal fears were not realized. The health of women was not only
not shattered by college training but their health and their stature were
vastly improved. A homely but significant illustration of it is found in the
standard height of the kitchen sink. In 1901, this was thirty inches and no
plumber would risk his professional reputation by adding a single inch to it.
To-day the standard height is thirty-six inches.

The next fear was that the minds of women would be wrecked by the
fearsome strain college training would put upon them. This fear also proved
groundless, for thousands of women quickly entered not only the special
colleges for women where the courses were the same as those arranged in
colleges for men, but they also entered the co-educational colleges and
universities where they worked side by side with men. Neither type of college
noticeably increased the number of mental degenerates. When woman had
shown that neither physical nor mental health had deteriorated as a result
of opening the college door to them, the last academic stronghold that
remained to be taken was that of research. "The health of women would
break down" — but it had not. "The minds of women would break down" —
but they had not. These facts were recognized as self-evident. But research
was "somehow different" — women simply had not the ability to do it and it
was useless to argue the question — "*they could not do it.*" As late as 1880,
Francis Parkman probably believed that he had settled the question when
he wrote: "A small number of women have spent their time for several
decades in ceaseless demands for suffrage, but they have lost their best
argument in failing to show that they are prepared to use the franchise when
they have got it. A single sound and useful contribution to one side or the
other of any question of current politics — the tariff, specie payments, the
silver bill, civil-service reform, railroad monopoly, capital and labor, or half a

score of other matters — would have done more for their cause than years of empty agitation."[1] When women had achieved the impossible and through research had made their contributions to public questions, a breach was made in the last defense against the intellectual progress of women.

But this outpost has not fallen so easily. Women in large numbers have entered the field and proved their ability to do so, but the obstacle today is the tendency to prescribe arbitrary limitations to their work — to stake off certain portions of knowledge and assign them to women while other parts of the field are preempted by men; to protest against joint occupation of any part of the territory and to decide for women what part is to be their share.

This division into "man's work" and "woman's work" seems in reality a survival of an ecclesiastical conception of society, but extensive research into the subject is necessary before definite conclusions can be drawn. Such research would doubtless bring to light many important and interesting revelations in regard to the origin and history of "woman's work," but until this has been undertaken on an extensive scale it is idle to speculate who sowed the seed of this conception of the mechanical distribution of work appropriate to men and to women. That it persists today is evident by an article in a leading monthly, for September 1926, that says: "All women, whatever their training, whatever their ultimate ambition, should receive instruction in the art of homemaking as a matter of course. It should be assumed by our educators that every woman will marry and have a family."[2]

It is at this point that women have rebelled, not openly but through a restlessness that affects their lives and the lives of others like an irritating rash. In the last analysis all men are tillers of the soil, fishers, or hunters, or are engaged in some form of food production. Yet division of labor has carried the major proportion of men far afield into other forms of occupation and the decision of the special form to be taken up is made by the individual man. Women are conscious that not all women are adapted by nature for an exclusively domestic life and they are restless because the individual decision is not permitted them as is the case with men. Arbitrary decisions in regard to their careers made by others than the individuals immediately concerned are displeasing to men and women alike.

Today research is in the air and the active, alert, inquiring minds of women are not only asking what it means, but they are answering their own question in the time-honored fashion of successful experimentation with the dangerous thing.

But the term is often used loosely to cover a multitude of approximately similar processes and it is necessary to differentiate it from other words erroneously considered synonymous with it. Its nearest of kin is investigation. But investigation means inquiry into all that has previously been done; it implies taking stock of progress; it denotes an inventory of what has already been accumulated; it looks backward in an effort to make a complete survey of the field already tilled. Research begins at the point where investigation stops; it is based on knowledge of what has already been done; it uses investigation as a fulcrum to pry into the unknown; it looks forward and surveys what is yet to be done.

Scholarship and research are also confused. Scholarship represents the accumulation of knowledge that has resulted from wide reading and from acquaintance with what others have done; it is a passive condition, not an active force; it represents attainment rather than achievement; it is negative rather than positive, receptive rather than creative. Investigation presents a point of departure for research; scholarship represents a broad level plane affording rest, peace, and refreshment; both are amicably related to research though not to be identified with it.

Authority and research are sometimes used interchangeably since the upholders of authority maintain that it is based on research. But authority and research are antagonistic, mutually repellent, principles of work. Authority is complete in itself; it has reached the ultimate known and knowable; it brooks no questioning; its decisions are final, and it is an active force only in so far as it resists all efforts at change either slight or revolutionary. The utterances of authority are always *ex cathedra*. Between authority and research there can be no sympathy, no affiliation, no community of purpose or of action, no mutual understanding. Authority is as adamant in maintaining its position, while research is constantly shifting its place as new points of view are opened up. Research co-operates with investigation and with scholarship, it recognizes the place each has in the realm of knowledge, but it leaves authority far behind in its venturesome voyages of exploration and discovery.

Research again must be differentiated from production. It is the day of production, and the word and the idea it represents are constantly before us. Mass production is the goal of modern efficiency and the academic world can not fail to be affected by it. It is generally believed that appointments are often not made to educational positions because certain persons considered for vacancies "have not produced enough" — the standard of mass production rightly applied to the manufacture of automobiles is applied to the product of the individual human mind, and unless it has similar results to show, it is regarded as ineffective. But mechanical production results in endless repetition, and repetition results in multiplying advantages for all — all benefit by production as the field is extended. In things of the mind, however, production by the individual does not necessarily mean additions to knowledge. It does usually mean saying the same thing over and over again in treadmill fashion without thereby adding anything to what has previously been known. The writer of a successful textbook in any subject may be induced by his publishers to produce another textbook, and presto, the thing is done. Verbal changes, the expansion of a few paragraphs, the selection of a new title — and production has been effected. The technical publications that reach librarians, school and college officials, and dealers in books repeatedly contain warnings against mass production of this character. With production that makes no contribution to human knowledge research has nothing in common.

But research in its own turn is susceptible of varying interpretations. It may mean the discovery and the use of wholly new, or previously unknown, classes of material, or it may mean the discovery of new meaning in familiar material. In history it is generally interpreted as meaning the discovery of new material. It has meant, for example, the opening up of the great field of archaeology that almost literally, it may be said, did not exist a hundred years ago. It may mean the prolonged search for material known once to exist but feared to be irrevocably destroyed, as the lost ten books of Livy. It may mean the quest for isolated, fragmentary scraps of information in fields where little is known and where every item retrieved is priceless, as where Mr. and Mrs. C. W. Wallace examined more than five million documents in England and on the Continent in the hope of finding new facts relating to Shakespeare the man.

For all these and similar lines of research in the humanities there is needed command of time, opportunity to work in great treasure houses of material, as the New York Public Library, the British Museum, or the Bibliothèque Nationale, or the many highly specialized private collections, ability to travel extensively, command of foreign languages, and other less imperative but otherwise advantageous qualifications.

These opportunities for research have in America usually been the accompaniments of academic positions. Education is so organized that every college or university instructor is expected both to teach and to do research work. Theoretically both are on an equality, but since promotion and increase in salary usually depend on research rather than on teaching ability, however much such an intention may be disclaimed by academic authorities, the weight of interest tends to be thrown on the side of research. Unfortunately, this assumption that all persons in the academic world are equally well adapted to the two functions of research and teaching seems unsound. Some have little or no interest in research, and greatly prefer the teaching side; others have little or no interest in teaching but are greatly absorbed in research; some prefer to combine teaching and research, believing that each reacts favorably on the other. Some of the partial failures in college faculties can be explained by this attempt to standardize all college instructors and to expect equal interest and success in both lines. A more perfect understanding of individual abilities and tastes of members of college faculties would make it possible to fit the round peg into the round hole more effectively than is sometimes now the case.

Research in American universities was stimulated by the opening of Johns Hopkins in 1876 and since that time it has been developed by leaps and bounds until now every great university in the country has its graduate school. These schools are organized with members of their faculties carrying on research work in addition to teaching, with fellowships held by advanced students, and with other students just entering on graduate work. To these graduate schools women are now usually admitted — to some freely, to others somewhat grudgingly, to a few not at all.

But the graduate schools have their own problems, especially for women. The usual route to a professorship lies for men through the fellowship and the graduate school. But since these posts are practically as yet closed to women, except in the colleges for women where they may be also filled by men, the graduate school with its fellowships presented the *ultima thule* for them professionally. Happily, the door closed to roads that lead to academic promotion does not deter them from their continued quest for truth through independent research. Some of the most important historical work in this country has been done by men and women who have never held an academic position, as is illustrated by the contributions made by Ruth Putnam and Henry Osborn Taylor. The somewhat arbitrary arrangement, tacitly understood yet not down in black and white, by which practically all persons holding college or university positions are expected to do research for publication often fails to secure the best results as far as research is concerned. No artificial external pressure can make a person succeed in fields where his personal interest is not enlisted.

But this sudden demand for research found colleges and universities entirely unable to meet it. The result has been the foundation of literally hundreds of special funds for research in various fields. In the department of natural science alone a somewhat recent report shows that in 1920 there were five hundred and sixty-five funds that had been established, and that more than twenty-two million dollars a year were annually available for research.[3] Astounding as this sum seems to the ordinary mind, it has been pointed out that this is only a small fraction of what is expended in private research or by government agencies — an amount estimated at two hundred million dollars annually.[4]

The funds given for research in the humanities and kindred subjects number more than a score, but those given for research in natural science are far more extensive in number and in amount.

These funds, irrespective of the field in which they are to be used, all have a general family resemblance, both as regards their ultimate object and also as regards the organization of the special board through whom the object is to be sought. Their common object is the advancement of the outposts of knowledge, either in the field of the humanities, or of pure science, or of applied science, or of extending to the uttermost parts of the earth the knowledge of these results. It is almost impossible to conceive of a field where some form of research is not now being carried on or some new agency being arranged to secure the widest possible distribution of the results already reached.

Research may find its objective point in any or all of the countless fields that may immediately concern the humanities. It may apply its powers and facilities to the manifold phases of applied natural science where human welfare is promoted, as the multifarious questions concerning individual and public health. It may find its goal in the domain of pure science and make the proud boast that its discoveries will never be of the slightest use to any one. Whatever the field chosen, the ultimate result must be the attainment of the knowledge that all science is one.

Research may have as its aim the promotion of the welfare of a single race, as the Negro; or the occupational advancement of the Jews; or a better mutual understanding between the Scandinavians and the Americans; or an increase in the appreciation of the learning of a single country, as France; or it may aim to foster a general international fellowship and good-will through the discovery and abolition of causes of discord. The result of these forms of research may be the discovery that humanity is one.

Again research may encourage advancement in the field of music, or it may promote the pictorial or the descriptive arts — to find in turn that art is one, whatever the medium of expression chosen by men.

Research may seek the best methods of distributing its results and thus promote education from the pre-school age through the professional schools; it may discover how the best result may be attained in agricultural, or in business, or in industrial education; it may seek the basic unity in all languages and thereby hasten research in every field through shortening the period required for assimilating alien tongues. It may thus show that it is as important to expedite the distribution of the results of research as it is to secure the new enlightenment to be passed on to others. The General Educational Board alone distributed during the first twenty years of its organization, from 1902 to 1922, the enormous sum of $116,727,895. A considerable number of other funds have been established directly to promote education and thus to encourage research as well as to distribute the results attained through it.

The question naturally arises, How far is it possible for women to share in these opportunities for research? As has been suggested incidentally in another connection, these opportunities are as yet somewhat restricted and the explanation is not far to seek. One lies in part in the conventional tendencies of women themselves. They have been encouraged to accept the sheltered life as a necessary requirement of their assumed physical and mental weakness, their inexperience, and their ignorance of practical life. If they have rejected protection, they have gone to the opposite extreme and effaced themselves in their desire to serve others. Here they meet on common ground with one type of men who say with evident pride, "We like to feel that some one is dependent on us." The restricted opportunities for women are also explained by the undoubted desire of many men to preserve the last stronghold for themselves. A somewhat recent inquiry in regard to openings for women in a co-educational university evoked the reply,

"Give me a man and a woman equally well trained and I will take the man every time." That this feeling adverse towards the entrance of women into the fields held by men is somewhat general is recognized in the recent report of the Women's Bureau, U.S. Department of Labor, on the "Effects of Applied Research upon the Employment Opportunities of American Women."[5] The Bulletin shows "that applied research has not only prepared the way for the employment of more women in industry, but that the preliminary research itself may be carried on in large part by women."[6] But the Bulletin recognizes that "the intangible and invisible but effective bar of custom is still up in many of the institutions having excellent research facilities. Women are barred not by regulations but by the tenacity of the tacit assumption that creative research facilities and training 'are designed for men.' " Yet it believes that "a firm seriously vexed with a manufacturing difficulty is not likely to refuse to employ the successful researcher because such a worker happens to be a woman," but that "if the door of opportunity which leads from the research laboratories of universities and colleges to responsible and desirable positions in industry and commerce is to be accessible to women, the laboratories must be open to women in fact as well as in theory." The observation and experience of many women will substantiate its conclusion that "while industry and commerce have for many years employed women in routine processes, very grudgingly have women been permitted — except in times of national emergency — to share the responsible or technical positions afforded by the Nation's business."

In the extensive development of plans for research and the enormous increase in facilities for carrying it on, it does not seem possible to deny indefinitely the ability of women to carry on research or to ignore what they have already done. It is equally impossible to believe that in active constructive research the field open to women will indefinitely be restricted to research concerning women and children. Research is indeed abundantly needed in these directions, but many persons have never been convinced that a Chinese wall separates the interests of men and women or that arbitrary palisades can deter women from entering the promised land.

But all research funds have their complementary business organization through which research is conducted and it may be asked what part is taken by women, or rather, is allotted to them in this office organization. Here too a compromise seems to have been reached, though one not altogether satisfactory to women with a natural gift for organization. No woman has as yet been made president of a board for carrying on research, but occasionally two positions on such boards are filled by women, "the vice-presidency where there is nothing to do and the secretaryship where there is everything to do."

Not all of these boards that have been considered can be strictly said to have been organized to promote research pure and simple. The General Education Board, for example, was formed to centralize and co-ordinate the gifts to education made by its founder. During its first twenty years, from 1902 to 1922, it had appropriated for education, as has been seen, funds in excess of $116,000,000. Other funds have also been expressly given to promote education. But education is an intermediary stage between negative ignorance and positive research — it takes stock of what has been already accumulated through investigation and it learns the elementary technique of research that may later be developed into advanced research. Education as regards the individual often proves abortive — many buds are adventitious in the field of education as well as in nature — but unquestionably a large proportion of the expenditure on education ultimately flowers into research.

It seems unfortunate that the opportunities for research for women have been so restricted since not only are more workers needed in the field, but women as well as men need the training in methods of work that are applicable everywhere. For the term "scientific method" that has been preempted by the naturalists should be regarded as all-inclusive in its application. What are the characteristics demanded by and for research? The basis must be an inquiring mind, while observation, accuracy, comparison, judgment, patience, perseverance, the complementary powers of analysis and synthesis, the gift of creative imagination, are all called into requisition. Every desirable mental characteristic is demanded whether the subject of research lies in the field of nature or of man. And these characteristics are not monopolized by either men or women.

Considering research in its widest application, what special need have women for entering the field?

Women need a knowledge of the methods used in research and experience in their practical application because such knowledge is everywhere demanded of all workers. Improvement in methods of work keeps pace with the discovery of new fields to be explored and all persons must be equipped with chart and compass who are to voyage afield. It is impossible to think of the attainment of mental maturity unless it is accompanied by some form of personal responsibility and no more fruitful field for its exercise can be found than is afforded by research. The excellent phrase of Charles Oman that "every trained specialist owes his stone to the cairn" must be felt by women to be as applicable to themselves as it is to men.

But women with their restricted opportunities need especially such equipment, and its possession may save many from lives of selfishness or from unhappy married life. An interest in research provides an outlet for the activities of women when a time of leisure in domestic life has come, — it might lessen the number of spoiled grandchildren if grandmothers had their own definite work and interests.

The attempt has been made to differentiate research from other terms that are often confused with it, such as *investigation, scholarship, authority*, and *production*; to indicate the wide extent of the opportunities opening out for the higher forms of research that depend on great libraries, laboratories, and museums, or on the fitting out of great expeditions to uncover forgotten cities, to explore the uttermost parts of the earth; to suggest the royal endowments that have made such research possible for men; and to point out the undefined but none the less very real limitation put on the entrance of women in these fields. This is the form of research that seeks for new or previously unknown materials, that ferrets out new elements in the realm of nature or new combinations of previously known elements, or roams the heavens for new worlds, or penetrates the realm of nature to find the secret of life; that with manuscript or book, microscope or telescope enables us to enter other worlds in time or in space. This is the conventional interpretation of research.

But it has already been suggested that the term *research* may be made elastic enough to include the discovery of new meanings in familiar material. The physical eye sees nothing distinctly when objects are held close to it and immediately in front of it, and the mental eye may discern nothing of interest or importance in the familiar objects of everyday life. But as the physical eye may become accustomed to darkness and may be able to distinguish objects invisible to those dependent on the glare of noonday for clear vision, so the mental eye may easily discover worldwide, time-old records in the humble everyday concerns of common human affairs. Housework, for example, stands as the typical drudgery for women, and its virtues are extolled especially by those who have themselves taken no active part in it although profiting by the work of others. Dishwashing connotes drudgery in concentrated form and yet it well illustrates the discrepancy between assumed and actual conditions. Magazines and newspaper columns are filled with directions for dishwashing that hark back to a time when water was pulled up from a cistern by means of a pail, it was heated in a kettle hanging from a fireplace crane, it was carried into an adjoining room where the dishes were washed, and the waste water then carried out of the house by the same hand that had pulled it up from the cistern. But to-day when conditions are entirely different, when enameled sinks, running water, instantaneous hot water, waste water pipes, and sewage systems, have entirely changed conditions, the same directions for dishwashing are repeated as were given a hundred years ago. Listen to a recent authority: "Glass must be washed first, then the silver, then the dishes; after these wash the pans, and last of all the kettles." Can this mean anything except that water is precious, and that one dishpan, probably only partly full, must serve for washing everything used in the preparation and consumption of a meal? The mental and the physical eye are assuredly out of focus when such directions are both given and obeyed. The homely illustration may suggest that undiscovered fields, if not for research, at least for investigation, lie all about us. Elementary investigation may show that while the general principles governing life may be retained throughout many centuries, the means of applying them are changing. One of the fundamental principles has, perhaps unconsciously, been conservation. The conservation of heat was a principle applied in baking in hot ashes or in a Dutch oven, and it is seen to-day in the more convenient form of the fireless cooker and the covered gas range. Conservation of energy was once found in the large kitchen where all domestic processes were carried on by members of the household and where the family life was maintained. Today conservation of energy reverses the process; the kitchen has been reduced in size to the smallest possible compass, and the family has transferred its gathering place to the living room. Conservation of expense once led to making within the home itself all articles used by the family. But to-day conservation of expense is found in buying many articles made without the home, even in bringing them to the home from remote distances.

Division of labor was once applied within the home where every member of the household had his own particular "chores" to do. The expanding walls of the home to-day has applied division of labor to the world itself.

No more fruitful field for investigation and even for research can be found than is afforded by the house and home. But this by no means solves the problem of research for women. Incredible as it seems to the orthodox, many women are not at all domestic in their tastes. This was convincingly shown a few years ago by Ralph Barton Perry when he pointed out that it is men who are predominantly domestic, that the reason they do not go to church more regularly is not because they have little interest in religion but because Sunday is practically the only day in the week that gives an outlet for their domestic tastes; that women often attend church not because they are specially religious but because church services afford a respite from excessive domesticity. The question of research for women is altogether different from that involved in the placid assumption that their interests are bounded by the walls of their home.

If then women are equipped for research and have an interest in it, and either do or do not wish to confine their research to domestic affairs, opportunity, even if as yet somewhat restricted, is theirs.

But many women adequately prepared for research are so situated as to be personally unable to take advantage of opportunity, and a sheaf of questions naturally arises as to what, if anything, can be done under such circumstances.

What opportunities for research are open to women in homes where division of labor has freed a part of their time? What can be done by maiden aunts or by grandmothers who do not enjoy leading superfluous lives in the homes of others? What can be done at home by the non-domestic woman? What can be done by women who are on part-time remunerative work? Can anything be done by women whose homes are in small villages remote from great centers where libraries, laboratories, and museums are found? What can be done by those who are physically handicapped? Are there any openings for women whose domestic life has been materially changed by the marriage of children or by the loss of husband? What can be done by mentally and physically alert women whose presence is needed in the home but who still have command of their own time?

A few general lines of research may be suggested that will illustrate the open door that swings both inward and outward. They all presuppose a knowledge of the principles of general research and an acquaintance with the technique of a special form of research, for research can not be "picked up" at will by those whose chief qualification for it is their desire to carry it on.

No field of study and research is more inviting than that of words and at least parts of it seem open to women equipped for research but handicapped by personal conditions for giving full time to it. Notable contributions to the study of words and of language have been made by distinguished scholars, but much yet remains to be done, as in the study of foreign words fully adopted into the American language; the translation of foreign proper names; proper names that have become common nouns; the characteristics of regional language; the differences in language of different social classes; the persistence of incorrect language in intelligent and educated classes; changing conditions recorded in the titles of books and of musical compositions; the changes in theology as recorded in the transformation of hymnals, — these are but suggestions of the infinite variety of changes that almost unnoticed come into language and remain as records of changing human thought and interests.

The mail catalogue is a fruitful field for the study of domestic and economic conditions nowhere else so faithfully recorded. The full page, double page and quadruple page advertisements of great department stores in any great city are mines of information showing how well all sides of modern life can be reconstructed from this source alone. The collective advertisements of any contemporary metropolitan daily may be compared during a series of weeks with the social theories and practices recorded in great works of literature of an earlier period, as in Dickens, Thackeray, George Eliot, or Victor Hugo — no more striking contrasts can be found than such a study discloses.

Political life is not fully revealed in headlines, — a study of postage stamps is rich in possibilities. Material for it is available in the press accounts of auction sales of stamps and of exhibitions and loan collections. Catalogues of dealers are for most purposes as valuable as the collections themselves. The interests of the collector and of the student of history are widely different, yet both use identical materials. The student of history finds in these diminutive delicate bits of paper records of political revolutions, suppressed rebellions, hero worship, royal successions, chauvinism, international comity, and descriptive scenes commemorating important events in the history of nations.

Children's games often seem foolish, meaningless, and incomprehensible, yet in many of them are found records going back as far as human history can be traced. String figures, like the universal cat's cradle, have been located in every part of the world and Mrs. Caroline Furness Jayne discovered in her elaborate study of the subject that the most complicated of them all are found among the tribes considered the least civilized. Children's toys, battered and broken though they be, contain important records of passing fads and fancies, as well as of the permanent characteristics and interests of children and of those that are fostered in them by their elders. Careful research work concerning the games and toys of children in the past and the present, in every part of the world, could not fail to contribute much to a better understanding of children.

The catalogues of book publishers, of dealers in second-hand or rare books, of auction sales of collections about to be dispersed, are all source material affording opportunity for research. The catalogues of art collections to be disposed of at auction are equally enlightening.

Fashion magazines and women's magazines are often held up to scorn by the pseudo-intelligentsia and they are triumphantly shown as illustrating the dictum as old as Rome, *varium et mutabile semper femina*. Yet they afford equal ammunition for those who defend the thesis of the eternally feminine. Changing fashions always seem amusing illustrations of the bad taste of our ancestors. Is there not a wide field for research in the comprehensive subject of fashions for both men and women, fashions not only in dress, but in foods, in furniture and in all household furnishings, in amusements, in sports, in means of locomotion, in private and public architecture — in every thought of the human mind that has been given concrete form? The last word in regard to woman's place in the world has not yet been said!

Sufficient illustrations have been given to indicate that in the single field of everyday life there is abundant opportunity for research that may be carried on by those who do not have access to large collections of books or of other source material. Much of the material needed may be had for the asking, as many varieties of catalogues — art catalogues of auction sales are sold and they are often expensive. The newspaper is always at hand and its resources as a field of investigation are limitless. Books can usually be borrowed from state libraries or the Library of Congress through loans arranged by the public librarian. The attic, the rummage sale, the second-hand book shop, the auction room, even our own habitations as well as those of our neighbors and friends are all filled with treasures for the inquiring mind. The biographer of Pasteur says of one of his experiments, "Pasteur had entered the realm of the infinitely small that he made his own." Women are often restless because they find themselves in the realm of the infinitely small. But the realm of the infinitely large lies all about us and it may be entered by the door of our own homes.

It may be said that research belongs to the university and that only women who have had university training as differentiated from college training are equipped for carrying it on. But this is an assumption that has no foundation in reality. Research is a method of work whose principles are everywhere applicable and it must be learned in college rather than deferred to a later, perhaps never-to-be-known, experience. In the colleges for women it is especially necessary to emphasize the importance of research, since the conviction has been so deep-seated and so widespread that women are not fitted to do research.

It is of interest to note what the attitude of Vassar College has been towards research. When its *Prospectus* was issued, in May, 1865, the word "research" had probably not been heard in any American educational institution. In all universities members of faculties were carrying on research, but to the students it probably seemed far removed from their own academic experience. It was more than ten years after the opening of Vassar College before Johns Hopkins University opened — for men — and through its graduate school made research a household word.

But while the word "research" does not appear in the *Prospectus* of 1865, the rose is there under another name and it smells as sweet as though it were called a rose. The *Prospectus* (p. 27) fully describes the Astronomical Observatory and then adds this special paragraph: "These valuable instruments will be placed for use in the hands of an American lady-observer, who enjoys a well-earned celebrity at home and abroad for her scientific attainment and discoveries, and who will also act in the College as its Professor of Astronomy." Valuable instruments were to be placed "for use" in the hands of an observer whose discoveries had already made her celebrated, and by inference was now to have the opportunity of making still further discoveries. What is "scientific attainment" but passive scholarship, and "discovery" but active research? Is it not clear that Maria Mitchell was expected first of all to give part of her time to the use in the Astronomical Observatory of the astronomical apparatus, "all of the most approved manufacture," while she was "also" to "act in the College as its Professor of Astronomy"? Could happier expression have been given in 1865 to what must then have been the novel idea of uniting research in the Observatory with teaching in the College? Thus did Vassar College, even before it opened its doors to students, announce perhaps unconsciously its educational creed that the advancement of the boundaries of knowledge was one function of the college, even of the woman's college. It must be a cause for satisfaction on the part of all who rejoice in what Vassar College has from its earliest days contributed to the advancement of knowledge to know that more than one fund has been established to assure to the College the facilities for research, the means for making the facilities for research available, and for publishing the results of research.

Suggestions for the Year's Study
History I
Vassar College

Take these hints as suggestions, not as instructions, and improve on them as you grow in experience.

Historical genius consists in an unlimited capacity for taking pains.

I. What the student brings to the first year of college work in history.
    History.
        One year's work.
            what has been studied —
                Ancient history to 800 A. D.
            how it has been studied —
                study of a single text with collateral reading,
                some practice in note-book work,
                some training in re-constructing the past through the use of illustrative material.
    Language.
        English,
        a fair command of Latin,
        a fair reading knowledge of two of the three languages — French, German, or Greek.
    Mathematics.
        ability to reason.
    Science.
        ability to observe.
II. What the student should gain from Course I in History.
    From the subject studied:
        a bird's-eye view of Western Europe,
        an appreciation of historical developments,
        an understanding of the unity and continuity of history,
        historical perspective,
        a background for work in other subjects.
    From the study of the subject:
        ability to use books,
            to analyze material,

Vassar College History Department, 1905.

to vivify history,

to understand the difference between reading history and studying history,

to appreciate the difference between history and historical record,

to understand what the historian does in writing history,

to connect the present with the past and the past with the present. "The roots of the present lie deep in the past, and nothing in the past is dead to the man who would learn how the present comes to be what it is." — *Stubbs*.

III. Material with which the student works.

Books, maps, charts, diagrams, genealogical tables, photographs, and similar reproductions of works of art.

IV. Material that should be owned by every student.

1. Books.

James Harvey Robinson.

History of Western Europe, price, $1.60.

Readings in European History, 2. vols., price, $1.50 each.

Earle W. Dow,

Atlas of European History, price, $1.50.

2. Accessories.

History pads .05 each.

Heavy manilla envelopes, two for .01

Suggestive Lists for Summer Reading, price, .25.

Small globes may be obtained, if desires, price, .10.

V. The college library.

1. Description.

Consult *Handbook*; also, pamphlet, *The Thompson Memorial Library Building*.

2. History.

Wood, F. A. *The Evolution of the Library*.

3. The building — meaning of

Exterior form.

Interior,

west window,

printers' marks in windows,

college seals,

tapestries.

General plan —

location of

card catalogue,

works on history,

basement,

floor,

> gallery,
>   seminary room,
>   drawing tables.
> 4. Plan.
>   [omitted]
> 5. The card catalogue.
>   Types of card catalogues.
>   Consult *Handbook*, p. 3.
>   Meaning of
>   blue cards,
>   red edged cards,
>   cross reference cards,
>   series cards.
>   Analysis of specimen card;

---

940 **Robinson, James Harvey,** 1863–
R562   An introduction to the history of western Europe, by
James Harvey Robinson. . . Boston and London, Ginn &
company, 1903.

xi p., 1 l., 714 p. front., illus., pl., maps. 19 ½^{cm}.

In two parts. Part one was first published in 1902.
"List of books": p. 689–690.

The Library has 3 other copies

Subject entries: Europe — Hist.   3-6172

Library of Congress, no.   D103.R67.   Copyright.

VI. General steps in studying any history.
   Analysis of the book with reference to, —
   1. *Author* — nationality, residence, education, occupation, politics,
      religion, personal characteristics.
   2. *General form* — title-page, copyright, contents, chapter headings,
      head-lines, side-lines, margins, signature, body of work, foot-notes,
      illustrations, maps, charts, diagrams, genealogical tables,
      appendices, index.
   3. *Structure* — sentence, paragraph, chapter, book. "Every good book
      can be summed up in a single sentence."
   4. *Contents.*
   5. *Authoritativeness.*

VII. First steps in studying Robinson's History of Western Europe.
    1. Study the points VI, 1–2 above.
    2. Read the Table of Contents.
    3. Read the Preface, — what purpose does it serve?
    4. Consult the bibliography at the end of each chapter and
       underscore,
          with ink, all books owned,
          with pencil, all books accessible in the Library and elsewhere.
VIII. Suggestions for preparation of work.

A. Reading.

1. Read an entire chapter to gain a general view of the subject and note the relation of the sub-divisions to the main topic.

2. Supplement this by reading the same subject in a more detailed work, such as one of the volumes in *The Periods of European History* series, Emerton's *Mediaeval Europe*, or Bémont and Monod's *Medieval Europe*.

3. Vivify the subject by reading the corresponding selections in Robinson's *Readings*, the University of Pennsylvania *Translations and Reprints*, Henderson's *Select Documents*, or other primary sources.

4. Read such authorities as will serve to bring together and interpret the important lines of thought, as Adams' *Civilization During the Middle Ages*, Taylor's *Classical Heritage of the Middle Ages*, or Bryce's *Holy Roman Empire*.

5. Read some work of poetry or fiction bearing on the period. Consult *Suggestive Lists for Summer Reading*.

"Historical events and movements are frequently fixed in the memory by the perusal of books which may be inaccurate in themselves, especially as to details, but which, nevertheless, leave a permanent and reasonably correct impression on the mind of the reader." — Channing and Hart, *Guide to American History*, p. 135.

6. Study some work of art illustrating the subject, as Dürer's Charlemagne, Chapu's Joan of Arc, photographs of cathedrals, etc.

7. Aim to make all general reading and study of art bear on college work.

B. Notes from Reading.

1. *Note-taking.* Place the main headings above the red line of the "History pad." These will usually be derived from the authorities used. Take the notes under these main headings in analytical form, following in the subdivision the authority used. Make them as brief as possible, using catch words and abbreviations, but do not sacrifice clearness. Do not put more than one topic on a slip. At the bottom of each page of notes, indicate the authority, or authorities, in a footnote giving the author, the title of the books when necessary, the volume and the page.

2. *Preservation of notes.* Preserve the notes in envelopes, or by attaching

them to cardboards with elastic bands, or by fastening them together with clips.

3. *Bibliography.* Make a bibliography in card catalogue form of all authorities used on any one piece of work. Each card or slip should include

    a. name of the author in directory form,

    b. title of the book,

    c. if the work has more than one volume, the number of volumes in the set,

    d. place and date of publication,

    e. brief estimate of the value of the book for the purpose used.

4. *Supplementary bibliography.* This may include the titles of books not used in connection with the work but desirable to preserve for future use. These titles should be distinguished from those under 3, above, by the use of an asterisk.

5. *Analytical Outline.* After the completion of the notes from reading, an analytical outline should be made based on the material contained in the notes. This outline may consist of the main topics and sub-topics.

C. Notes from Lectures and Class Discussions.

Take the notes of the lecture and discussion in such a way as to indicate the chief divisions and subdivisions of the subject as presented. This may be done by leaving a left hand margin, by underlining the main headings, and by indenting the subdivisions. By means of catch words, phrases, and brief sentences, get as clear and concise a statement as possible of the new points given, noting especially the relation and importance of events as emphasized. Whenever an authority is cited, or a reference, or a suggestion for reading given, make a marginal note of it. The best notes are the most intelligible notes.

X. Explanation of the chart.

The writer who today brings before the public a new history must be prepared to find his every statement met by the question, "What is your authority?" The challenge that in one form or another meets the historian at every step on his way is, "What is the basis of your conclusion?" "How do you know?" If at any point he fails to meet the challenge, his entire work falls to the ground unsupported.

From the child who asks for a "true story" to the mature reader and student of history the demand is universal that story-teller and historian alike shall give an absolutely faithful portrayal. Consciously or unconsciously the reader of to-day looks with disfavor on "Froudacity"; on history written solely for effect; on superficial, inaccurate work; on formless, jellyfish histories written to please everybody; on "safe" histories that like "safe" candidates are offered, the one to find purchasers, the other to find votes.

If therefore the historian cannot show that his authority is unimpeachable, that the evidence he produces is absolutely trustworthy, that those upon whose authority he is forced to rely have had an eye single for the truth, his work justly fails in creditability in the view alike of readers and of scholars.

This demand for evidence, made today of every historian, is the explanation of the wealth of bibliographical material that accompanies every history, of the elaborate foot-notes through which the author substantiates his statements, of the change in the preface from apologies for literary shortcomings to statements concerning the writer's indebtedness to fellow-historians. The historian exhausts every means at his command to show the authoritativeness of his work; this is the alpha and omega of his historical creed.

If then we turn to the most recent works worthy to be called history, we are able to lay bare the evidence on which they are based and to penetrate to the very substratum of the authority on which they rest. It is the purpose of the accompanying chart to show how this may be done. Mr. Robinson's work has been selected for the illustration because it is the most recent of the manuals in general use, and because through preface, foot-notes, bibliographical lists, maps, and illustrations it invites the most thorough examination of the sources of its authority.

The historian classes the authorities he uses under the two main heads — secondary and primary. The term *secondary authorities* does not mean that these are of secondary importance; nor does it mean that they are second rate in character, for they are often more valuable than so-called primary authorities, since the work of a distinguished historian can usually be accepted at its face value, while primary authorities must be tested by every known canon of historical criticism before they can be accepted by the historian. The best secondary authorities are based on original sources and on other secondary authorities that are unimpeachable. They deal with certain periods of phases of history so well and so exhaustively that they have become authoritative. It is impossible for any historian to investigate from the sources alone any period of history, however limited it may be, and he therefore avails himself of the work done by others.

If we examine the "History of Western Europe," we may class the secondary authorities on which it is based under the heads *Manuals* and *Exhaustive Works,* and each of these again under the heads *General* and *Special.* If we examine a general manual, like Adams's "European History," we shall find that it in its turn is based in part on secondary authorities such as certain well-accepted works of reference, especially those by French and German scholars, and certain English classics, like Gibbon, which in their turn are based in part on secondary and in part on primary authorities. But Adams's handbook also is in large measure based directly on primary authorities both literary and monumental, as is indicated by the chart. If we turn to Henderson's history, a manual dealing with a special period, we have the

CHART ILLUSTRATING
ROBINSON'S HISTORY OF WESTERN EUROPE

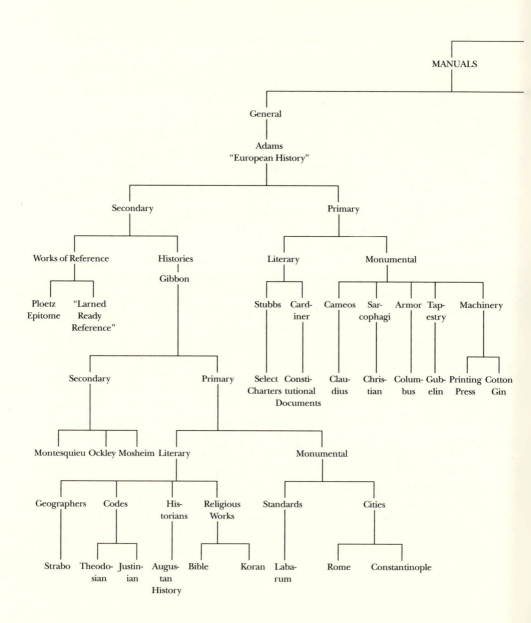

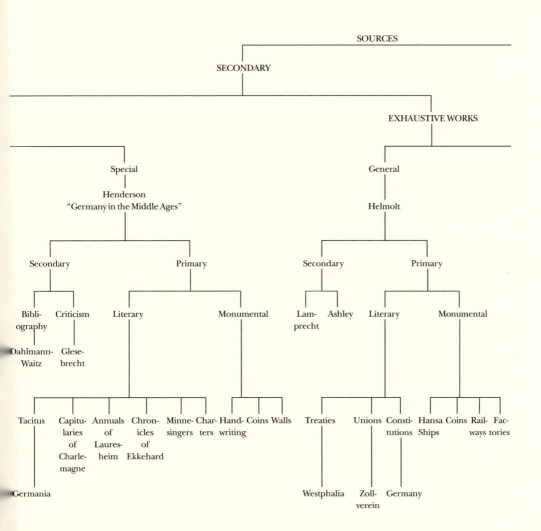

(continued)

CHART ILLUSTRATING
ROBINSON'S HISTORY OF WESTERN EUROPE (Continued)

SOURCES

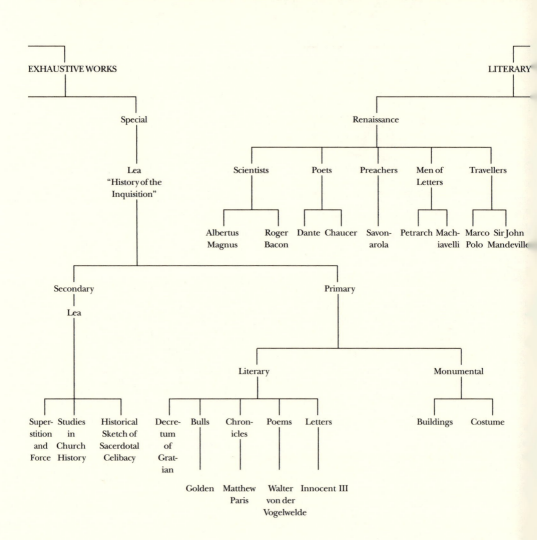

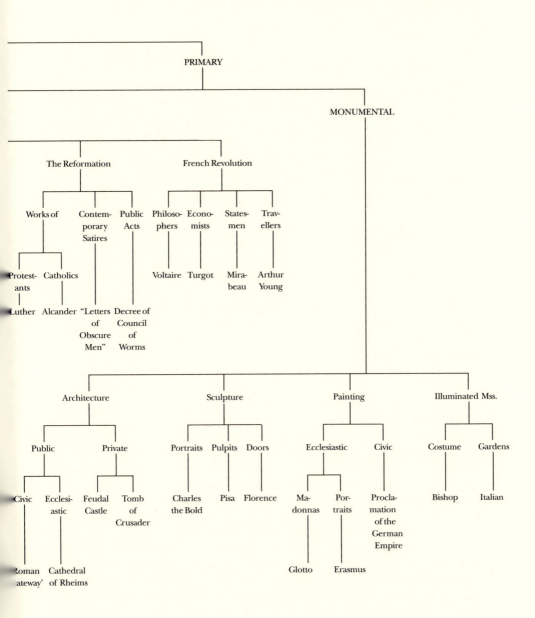

PRIMARY

MONUMENTAL

The Reformation

French Revolution

Works of   Contem-   Public
            porary   Acts
            Satires

Philoso-   Econo-   States-   Trav-
phers   mists   men   ellers

Protest-   Catholics
ants

Voltaire   Turgot   Mira-   Arthur
                      beau   Young

Luther   Alcander   "Letters   Decree of
                      of   Council
                      Obscure   of
                      Men"   Worms

Architecture

Sculpture

Painting

Illuminated Mss.

Public   Private

Portraits   Pulpits   Doors

Ecclesiastic   Civic

Costume   Gardens

Civic   Ecclesi-   Feudal   Tomb
         astic   Castle   of
                               Crusader

Charles   Pisa   Florence
the Bold

Ma-   Por-   Procla-
donnas   traits mation
                   of the
                   German
                   Empire

Bishop   Italian

Roman   Cathedral
Gateway' of Rheims

Glotto   Erasmus

same result, — a basis of secondary and primary authorities; the same principle holds with reference to exhaustive works like those of Helmolt and, to some extent, of Mr. Henry C. Lea.

If now we turn to the class of primary authorities, we shall include in it all those contemporary records of a period whose authenticity has been investigated by the author himself. These records may be classed as literary and monumental.

The homely phrase "everything is grist that comes to the mill" well characterizes the vast amount of seemingly heterogeneous literary material that the historian must sift and analyze before he is ready to combine contemporaneous records into an orderly history that shall give a true picture of the past. Constitutions, charters, laws, proclamations, decrees, papal bulls, treaties, statistical tables, are all examined as to their authenticity and importance. The works of contemporaneous historians, of chroniclers, biographers, geographers, travelers, linguists, men of letters, economists, scientists, theologians, statesmen, and philosophers, are eagerly studied for the conscious records of the time. The historian searches poems, dramas, satires, essays, novels, letters, diaries, journals, memoirs, sermons, hymns, songs, for the unconscious records of the period. He searches newspapers, magazines, and a mass of ephemeral literature and tests its value as historical material by a study of the laws affecting freedom of the press. Everything in printed or in manuscript form that bears on the period studied is summoned before the bar and the testimony given is accepted or rejected in accordance with the laws of historical evidence.

But the historian does not rely alone on the record written with the pen. He has come to realize that this constitutes but one part of the evidence that must be examined and weighed before he can write the history of a given period. The records left by nature through geological formations and anthropological changes; the record left by spoken and written language, by existing forms, ceremonies, and rituals, the original meaning of which has long since passed away; the records left by architecture, painting, and sculpture, by coins, medals, and seals, by armor and heraldic emblems, by rugs and tapestries, by wood carving and wood inlaying — all these infinitely varying forms of the monumental record must be examined and tested before the historian is ready to portray the past.

If now we turn to the chart, it will be evident that the "History of Western Europe" is based not only upon reliable secondary authorities but also in part on original records both literary and monumental. The works of scientists, poets, preachers, travelers, philosophers, and statesmen, constitutions, laws, treaties, decrees, and papal bulls — every variety of literary material has been placed under requisition. Sites of towns, city walls, construction and plans of buildings, portraits of individuals made by pen, brush, and chisel, cartoons and caricatures, costumes and jewels, household furniture and arrangement of gardens and hedges, inventions and machinery—every form of material expression of the activity of human thought has directly or indirectly been examined.

It is obviously impossible to indicate on the chart more than a fraction of the very large number of authorities on which the "History of Western Europe" is based. A sufficient number is given, however, to show that every historian, as differentiated from a compiler of text-books, bases his work in the last analysis on contemporaneous records and that he is prepared to answer fully and satisfactorily the searching question asked with reference to every statement made, "What is the authority?"

XI. Classification of histories as to
    1. Scope, —
      General, as *Helmolt,*
      Special, as *Henderson,*
      Monograph, as *Jusserand.*
    2. Content,
      Political, as *Gardiner,*
      Ecclesiastical, as *Alzog,*
      Economic, as *Ashley,*
      Military, as *Mahan,*
      Social, as *Traill.*

XII. Definitions.
    Make a list of all technical terms found in history reading and give each its proper definition, as *bull, charter, code, dispensation, fief, indulgence, peace, treaty.*

XIII. Helps.
    1. Bibliographies.
      Make use of bibliographical lists, such as those found in Robinson and other recent histories, and in the college library catalogue.
    2. Works of reference.
      "A reference book is a book which is to be consulted for definite points of information rather than read through, and is arranged with explicit reference to ease in finding specific facts." — *E. C. Richardson.*
      a. General.
      Kroeger, A. B. *Guide to the Study of Reference Books.*
      Plœtz, Carl. *Epitome of Ancient, Mediaeval, and Modern History.*
      b. Dictionaries.
      Murray, J. A. H. *New English Dictionary of Historical Principles.* vols. 1–5.
      The Century Dictionary. 6 vols.

   c. Encyclopædias.
     Encyclopædia Britannica. 25 vols.
     Larousse, P. A. *Grand dictionnaire universel du xixᵉ siècle.* 17 vols.
     Meyer, H. J. *Konversations-lexicon.* 21 vols.
     Consult Kroeger, p. 12, outlined paragraphs, for suggestions as to
     the use of encyclopædias.
   d. Periodicals.
     Poole's *Index to Periodical Literature.* 6 vols. and annual supplements.
     New York Daily Tribune. Index.
   e. Year Books.
     Hazell's Annual.
     Statesman's Year-Book.
     World Almanac.
     Minerva; Jahrbuch der gelehrten Welt.
   f. Autobiographical.
     Who's Who? (England.)
     Who's Who in America?
     Qui êtes-vous?
     Wer ist's?
   g. Biographical.
     The Century Dictionary of Names.
     Stephen, Leslie. *Dictionary of National Biography.* 63 vols.
     Cyclopædia of American Biography. 7 vols.
   h. Ecclesiastical.
     Addis, W. E., and Arnold, Thomas, *A Catholic Dictionary containing
     some Account of the Doctrine, Ceremonies, Councils, and Religious Orders
     of the Catholic Church.*
     The Catholic Encyclopædia. 15 vols.
     The Jewish Encyclopædia. 12 vols.
     McClintock, J. and Strong, J. *Cyclopædia of Biblical, Theological, and
     Ecclesiastical Literature.* 10 vols. and supplement.
   i. Miscellaneous.
     Du Cange, *Glossarium Manuale ad Scriptores mediae et infimae
     Latinitatis, etc.*
     Lalor, J. J. *Cyclopaedia of Political Science, Political Economy, and of the
     Political History of the United States* 3 vols.
     Low, S. J., and Pulling, F. S. *Dictionary of English History.*
     Palgrave, R. H. I. *Dictionary of Political Economy.* 3 vols.
     Sturgis, R. *Dictionary of Architecture and Building.* 3 vols.

XIV. The formation of a library.

   Every student should begin at once the collection of books that shall
   be the nucleus of a permanent library. The following lists are
   suggested for history:

Course I. Medieval History.

List 1.

This list is indispensable.

Robinson, J. H., *Western Europe* $1.60

————— *Readings*, vol. I........................... 1.50

Dow, E. W., *Atlas of European History*...................... <u>1.50</u>

*$4.60

List 2.

This list adds three important secondary authorities.

Add to List 1 .... $4.60

Adams, G. B., *Civilization in Western Europe.*................. 2.50

Bryce, J., *Holy Roman Empire* .... .60

Cheyney, E. P., *Short History of England*..................... <u>1.40</u>

*$9.10

List 3.

This list suggests as an alternative to List 2, one secondary authority and several inexpensive sources.

Add to List 1 .... $4.60

Bémont and Monod, *Medieval Europe.*..................... 1.60

University of Pennsylvania, *Translations and Reprints* ....

    Early Germans............................ .25

    Notitia Signitatum .... .25

    Laws of Charles the Great...................... .25

    Ordeals .... .25

    First Four Councils .... .25

    Early Christian Persecutions .... .25

    Letters of the Crusaders .... .25

    Urban and the Crusaders...................... .15

    Life of St. Columban .... .25

    Monastic Tales............................ .15

    Mediaeval Student .... <u>.15</u>

*$8.65

List 4.

This list adds two important collections of sources.

Add to List 3 .... $8.65

Colby, C. W., *Sources of English History.*.................... 2.00

Henderson, E. F., *Historical Documents of the Middle Ages*....... <u>1.50</u>

*$12.15

List 5.

This list adds important collections of sources on special subjects.

Add to List 4 .... $12.15

Remaining numbers of *Translations and Reprints* 3.00

Robinson, J. H. and Rolfe, H. W., *Petrarch* 1.50

Whitcomb, M., *Source Book of the German Renaissance.* 75
— — — — — — *Source Book of the Italian Renaissance* 75
                                                                  *18.15

* The list price is given. The books can be purchased at a discount —
often of 20 per cent.

Course II. Modern History.

List 1.
This list is indispensable.

Robinson, J. H., *Western Europe.* . . . . $ 1.60
—————— *Readings*, vol. II 1.50
Dow, E. W. *Atlas of European History.* 1.50
                                                                  *$4.60

List 2.
This list adds two important secondary authorities.

Add to List 1 . . . . $ 4.60
Johnson, A. H., *Europe in the Sixteenth Century* 1.75
Hassall A., *The Balance of Power* 1.75
                                                                  *$8.10

List 3.
This list adds two other important secondary authorities.

Add to List 2 . . . . $ 8.10
Wakeman, H. O., *European History 1598–1715* 1.40
Robinson, J. H., and Beard, C. A., *Development of Modern Europe,*
2 vols. 3.00
                                                                  *$12.50

List 4.
*This list suggests as an alternative to List 3 several brief works on special
periods.*

Add to List 2 . . . . $ 8.10
Seebohm, F., *Protestant Revolution* 1.00
Creighton, M., *Age of Elizabeth* 1.00
Gardiner, S. R., *Puritan Revolution.* 1.00
—————— *Thirty Years' War.* 1.00
Airy, O., *English Restoration* 1.00
Longman, F., *Frederick the Great* 1.00
                                                                  *14.10

List 5.
This list add two somewhat full histories of the period covered.

Add to List 4 . . . . $14.10
Grant, A. J., *French Monarchy*, 2 vols. 2.25
Fisher, G. P., *History of the Reformation.* 2.50
                                                                  *18.85

*List price. Nearly all the books named can be obtained at a discount of 20 per cent.

XV. What is History.

History has formed the subject of many interesting essays. The following are a few of them.

1. The nature of history.
Birrell, A., *Obiter Dicta, Second Series.*
Harrison, Frederic, *The Meaning of History.*
Morrison, J. C., Article *History* in Encyclopædia Britannica.
Robinson, J. H., *History.*

2. The study of history.
Channing and Hart, *Guide to American History.* (The suggestions given, while intended specially for American history, are of universal application.)
Hart, A. B., *American History Told by Contemporaries.* 4 vols. (The introductions are of general value.)
Committee of Seven, *The Study of History in Schools.*

3. Historical fiction.
Consult the titles in *Suggestive Lists for Summer Reading.*

XVI. Definitions of History.

Find, copy, compare, study, and discuss the various definitions that have been given of history. Consult, for example, Emerson, Carlyle, Macaulay, Freeman, Shelley, Matthew Arnold and others.

Historical Practice

For Salmon, the great subject of history was history itself. Her foundation course at Vassar College started with the question of how we know what we know, and students were sent to repositories of historical knowledge to puzzle out answers. Increasing the places they were sent looked less and less traditional: not just to books but to the library building itself, not just to buildings and monuments but to the backyard; they were asked to read newspapers and even laundry lists in historical terms. To show how history was built up by generations of observers of the past, Salmon distributed a kind of genealogical chart to her students that showed the sources used by their textbook, James Harvey Robinson's *Introduction to the History of Western Europe* (1903), as if to remind them of the fact that even the apparently authoritative work they were called on to read was, like every other work of history, an accumulated man-made edifice. Most important, history was not a neutral accumulation of sources; history was always and inevitably read from the present; and history was always being rewritten.

As if to demonstrate the possibility of approaching historical material in different ways, Salmon herself practiced many forms of history over her career. Her earliest work, on the appointing powers of the president, employed congressional and constitutional and legal printed sources; her book on domestic service employed statistical methods for the collection of data, a technique she returned to with a study on vacation reading among Vassar students. Her sources were the objects around her, and her personal experiences became the trigger for historical investigation; her monumental two-volume study of the newspaper probed the value of these so-called impure sources. Two volumes, both published posthumously though prepared partially under her direction, summarize her thoughts as they developed over her lifetime. *Why Is History Rewritten?* (1929) examines the role of the present in relation to how we view the past, and *Historical Material* (1933) poses the many ways that the world around us reveals the past.

One significant project did not come to fruition. After completing *Domestic Service* in the first years of the twentieth century, Salmon started collecting material for a book on historical museums. In letters home to friends, she refers to this as her *magnum opus*. Unfortunately, another book covering similar material, David Murray's *Museums: Their History and Their Use* (1904), put an end to the idea of a book, but her interest in the historical museum continued, and the 1911 proposal for a museum of Vassar was one product of the experience. The foundation of Vassar, as Salmon surely knew, had been undertaken with the provision of works of art designed to provide moral instruction. Her museum, influenced by her Scandinavian experiences, would have been a public forum for her new history with exhibits of historical photographs of the changing costumes of gymnasts, original plans of the buildings, original beds, washstands, and even a wall to show how the typical dormitory room was decorated.

History became the great unifying force in life, a force of almost theological power. History weaves together domestic service, the president's powers of appointment, the newspaper, and the backyard. It is everywhere.

The Historical Museum

Dr. David Murray tells us, as a result of his extensive researches into the literature of the subject, that the origin of the museum has been traced to Noah's Ark. This derivation seems to confuse the museum with the zoological garden, but it is at least certain that the museum is of great antiquity, as is indicated by its very name, and it has never known geographical limitations. Moreover, it has been most versatile in its usefulness. It antedates the orchestra as a drawing feature of coffee houses and restaurants, it precedes the public library as a convenient lounging place, it rivals the galleries of the Louvre as a refuge from inclement weather, it has anticipated the rummage sale as a harbor for discarded treasure, and it has supplied the lack of a local Madame Tussaud or Eden Musée as an available means of entertaining visiting guests.

It is not surprising that historians have long abjured the historical museum, not only because of this versatility, but also because the typical one has contained an Egyptian mummy, hairs from Noah's beard, the boots that Washington wore when he crossed the Delaware, and mermaids valued at one thousand pounds each. It has also been held in ill repute, because even today it is often managed by the same authorities that police a city and care for its pavements, more often in our country by patriotic societies ambitious to show the military achievements of America, while it is as a rule under the immediate supervision, not of trained curators, but of caretakers whose duties are fulfilled if the building is kept clean and the entrance fees scrupulously accounted for.

But historians who long abjured the use of all pictorial material because compilers filled their books with illustrations showing Columbus in the act of sighting land, and kodaks of the battle of Bunker Hill, have come to recognize the great serviceableness of such material not only as a valuable adjunct in vivifying the past, but also as one of the records on which the historical narrative is based. In a similar way the historical museum may justly lay claim to an honorable and dignified place in the field of historical research, and it must in future be reckoned with by every worker in that field.

It, indeed, ill behooves us to question the right of the historical museum to make this claim, when we realize how closely its history has paralleled the history of history itself. If a collection of miscellaneous relics once constituted a museum, so was a collection of miscellaneous facts and dates once considered history. If the museum once collected what was rare and abnormal rather than what was typical, so the historian once valued only those

Educational Review 4 (1911): 144–60.

facts that were little known. If the treasures of a museum were once arranged "to create surprise rather than to afford instruction" — the anatomical collection at Dresden was arranged like a pleasure garden — so the historian spiced his prosaic facts with romance in order to whet the appetites of his readers. If the historical museum still has its detractors, it may be recalled that scarcely thirty years ago Herbert Spencer found in history only descriptive sociology, that Alexander Bain considered that the study of history required so slender a mental equipment that it might well be eliminated from the curriculum, and that even today men like Sir John Richard Seeley have anticipated a time when history as a distinct subject will have been merged into its various component parts. If thru many fluctuations of purpose, plan, organization, and arrangement the historical museum has been late in coming into its own, it must be remembered that the historian was long in discovering a controlling principle that should guide his work.

The historical museum as it exists today represents an accretion of interests, since in its growth it has reflected contemporaneous interests. The medieval church, with its treasury of relics, constituted a museum of theology, the renaissance created a widespread interest in art collections, changes in method of warfare transferred the armor of the medieval knight from his person to the palace museum, the circumnavigation of the globe made the collection of curiosities a business as well as a passion, the development of interest in all questions of physical life demanded collections illustrating natural history. It is small wonder that the museum in its zeal to combine all these features became a collection

> Of unicorns and alligators,
> Elks, mermaids, witches, satyrs,
> And twenty other stranger matters.

Yet equally ambitious was Ordericus Vitalis, who purposed to write a history of what passed under his own observation, yet began his work with an account of the birth of Christ.

The fundamental questions therefore are, first, what constitutes an historical museum, and, second, how should such a museum be arranged. It is, perhaps, possible to reach a negative conclusion as to what constitutes an historical museum by considering the classes of museums already found. If these are classified according to the material nature of the exhibits, eliminating those that are obviously purely scientific, as botanical museums and museums of natural history, we find already existing museums illustrating the history of agriculture, anatomy, anthropology, architecture, art, coins, colonies, commerce, education, ethnology, household products, industry, music, phonology, and religion. If this seems a miscellaneous enumeration, it must be said that it is based on an examination of catalog lists given by Murray.

If, on the other hand, the classification is based on the material of which the exhibits are composed, we have collections of bronzes, plaster casts, china, glass, gold and silver, and ivory.

But if we consider the processes of creation, we have museums of wood carvings, mosaics, painting, sculpture, and tapestry.

If again the classification is based on the development of human life, we find museums showing the history of the aborigines, the museums of biography (for such may be termed museums associated with a single life, as the Goethe museum at Weimar, and the Carlyle collection in Chelsea), the museum of civic life, as the Carnavelet Palace, museums illustrating the development of royal life, as the Rosenberg of Copenhagen, the folks museums of Copenhagen and Stockholm, the museum of national life, as that at Nuremberg and Cambridge, the museum of social history, as that at Lund (which, however, does not differ from the folks museum of Copenhagen and Lyngby), the museum of ethnology, which, however, is rather comparative than historical, and the museums of the dead, as Westminster Abbey, St. Denis, Roskilde, and the Riddarholms-Kyrka of Stockholm.

It is obvious that no one of these classes, with the exception of the last, can be considered in itself an historical museum, altho a museum of music may be arranged to show the history of music as well as a comparative study of musical instruments, — a museum of religion may illustrate the history of religion as well as a comparative study of religion, and thus both correspond with a literary history or comparative study of music or religion.

If, on the positive side, the attempt is made to define an historical museum, it must be said that while it is always rash to attempt a definition, the reward of rashness is that the ill success in giving a satisfactory one induces someone else to formulate a better one. It may then, perhaps, be said that any museum may justly be called historical that shows the origin and continuity of human life and its accompanying material interests, and that illustrates development from simple into complex forms.

The principle on which exhibits should be classified must be determined by the object sought thru the museum.

The art museum ministers primarily to the idea of beauty, and its collections must be arranged in accordance with the principles of esthetics.

The crafts museum is concerned with all forms of handiwork, and the controlling principle of arrangement must be that of the nature of the materials employed. The worker in the precious metals, or in copper and bronze, or in leather or ivory, is specially concerned in studying the objects made from the particular medium in which he works.

The industrial museum represents the resourcefulness of the human mind in the direction of mechanical work and its exhibits must illustrate processes of manufacture. The student and the manufacturer are alike interested in the processes by which the silk of the cocoon is transformed into the woven piece, and the cotton boll into the bolt of cloth.

The mineralogical museum shows the natural resources of the world and the essential principle to be shown is the location of these resources. Where specific minerals have or have not been found is the important question illustrated by the museum for the benefit of the student and the capitalist.

The museum of natural history seeks to show the development of animal life, and it must represent the family life of animals in its natural habitat. The wild grouse, its nest and its food — the kingfisher and its prey — every form of animal life in its native field must be found in the museum of natural history under the same conditions as when found in nature. It is seldom possible for the student to traverse the world in search of them, — the mountain must be brought to Mahomet.

The museum of ethnology represents a cross-cut section of human life. The principle underlying it is that of comparison, and its collections must be so arranged as to show the environment of the various exhibits. A comparative study of the dwelling-huts of the Esquimaux and of the Fiji Islanders, of the religious ceremonies of the Laplanders and of the Patagonians, and similar comparative studies, is what the student wishes opportunity for in the ethnological museum.

The biographical museum seeks thru the preservation of personalia to make real the personality of one who has been a leading character of his time. It must seek, therefore, every object, it matters not how small or insignificant, that will make live again thru these material objects the one in whose honor the museum has been founded, and its object must therefore be sentimental rather than scientific.

These different illustrations have been given to show that no formal, definite law can be laid down for the classification and arrangement of all museums. The museum of the past in its effort to shelter every variety of object has in that very effort shut out all hope of becoming a genuine help in serious studies. A miscellaneous collection of words from many different languages would not be held to be literature. Even the introduction of words and phrases from a single foreign language into a work of literature is considered a mark of pedantry. But no incongruity has been felt when an Egyptian mummy has been given a place in an art museum or a collection of South American birds in a mineralogical museum, or when ethnological collections have been incorporated in a museum of natural history.

The underlying principle of arrangement in the historical museum must therefore be the chronological one. As history is thus written with the pen, so must history be written through a chronological arrangement of its material records.

The questions that arise in connection with the organization of an historical museum are more easily discust than answered and more easily answered in theory than carried out in concrete reality.

The site must be convenient and attractive, and afford opportunity for expansion. The building must be built around the collection rather than the collection moved into a building, and therefore it must represent appropriateness and harmony of ideas. A renaissance palace for housing collections illustrating pioneer life, a classic temple for New England life, and a Gothic cathedral for Southern life, are scarcely more extreme illustrations of possible inappropriateness than are some of the examples of buildings now used for historical museums. On the other hand, the magnificent collections of the Northern Museum at Stockholm seem most appropriately housed in a Swedish palace of sixteenth-century style; the ecclesiastical collections of the Christiania museum are found in a building erected on the model of an early Norwegian church; the ecclesiastical collections at Sevastopol are to be arranged in a building modeled on a Christian basilica; the Hôtel de Cluny is an ideal home for the great medieval collections of France, as is the Bargello for those of Italy.

The questions of maintenance is one of the most difficult of practical questions. The establishment and maintenance of museums must always be enormously expensive, and the problem is presented as to whether this expense should be met by national, state, or municipal appropriations; whether it should be borne by patriotic societies or educational institutions; whether the museum is justified in depending on the more precarious support of gifts, subscriptions, and entrance fees; whether it should be maintained wholly as a private or as a commercial enterprise — all of these plans with mutual modifications are in operation in different places.

The problem of maintenance has as its converse that of management. Should the museum be administered by civic, ecclesiastic, educational, or business representatives; should they be appointed, elected, or be self-perpetuating; should the position be honorary or carry with it an honorarium; should the position be permanent, or for a limited term; all of these various methods have also been tried.

The questions presented to the administration carry with them their own perplexities. Fundamental on the material side must be prosaic questions of entrance fees, free admission, or an equitable balancing of pay days and free days, special privileges to students and school children, the price of admission if fees are charged, and Sunday and holiday opening. Protection from fire and theft, and provision for guards and guides, must be considered.

But more important than questions of material care must be that of providing for the intellectual care. How can the caretaker be superseded by the curator? Thus far in the history of the historical museum, its curators have been self-trained — brilliant, original men, who have blazed their own way thru the wilderness. But unhappily the genius is rare, and with the extension of the museum, there must be an unfailing source of supply of trained curators. But the question of training is as yet an experimental one. Is the curator of the future to be prepared for his work in an American training-school, or by serving an apprenticeship in a great museum, or to be prepared by foreign travel, or thru visiting and studying the museums of

Europe, or by the theoretical training of the university; if a special school for training curators is to be established, shall it be in connection with a university, or non-academic as is for the most part the library school, or could provision be made for an extension of the classical school at Athens or at Rome?

The qualifications demanded of a curator are as varied as those sought in a clergyman's wife. His position presupposes collections that must be augmented, and he must steer between the Scylla of extravagance and the Charybdis of letting desirable specimens slip through his hands. He must be able to answer the classic question, "If England wishes to sell the Elgin marbles, what price shall be offered?" and he must be a Sherlock Holmes in detecting possible fraud and imposition in the articles offered for sale.

If the museum is to serve the ends of research, the curator must plan for a museum library, and maps, charts, descriptive labels, catalog of exhibits must all be furnished. If, on the other hand, the museum is to serve an educational end, and an intelligent interest in the museum created and ministered to, the curator must provide for lectureships, the loan of specimens, visiting classes, frequent change of exhibits, a not too easy scheme of passage from room to room, resting-places for the faint in mind or body, and encouragement at every turn to lay aside indifference and apathy.

Whatever the object to be served by the museum, the curator is at all times beset by difficulties he alone can deal with. Not only must he collect, classify, and arrange the specimens of the museum, having in mind the needs of the two quite different classes — students and casual visitors — but he must keep constantly in mind the material care of the museum. The specimens must be preserved from injury from moth, mold, dampness, heat, and cold; appropriate colors and textures must be selected for the background of walls and display cases; the effect of light, as regards the fading or discoloration of specimens, must be considered; the arrangement of doors and windows, side or ceiling lighting, the best form of artificial lighting — all of these problems must be decided after prolonged and often costly experiments. The question of the repair and the restoration of specimens is a rock on which a curator may be shipwrecked.

The position of curator of a museum, like that of the librarian, was once the refuge of the decayed scholar and gentleman. Today, and it will be still more true tomorrow, the position is demanding the highest form of trained, expert service.

If the question is asked where we may find the ideal conditions of the historical museum most nearly realized, the answer is — in Scandinavia. Denmark, Sweden, and Norway differ somewhat in the details of their museum policy, but the three countries must be considered parts of one whole, and their great national museums must be looked upon as containing the records of a more or less unified Scandinavian life.

The first claim of Scandinavia to an important position in the history of museums rests on the fact that Sweden was the first country in Europe to collect its own antiquities, and its first efforts in this direction date back to 1666.

Its second claim is based on the admirable legislation which guards its archeological treasures. In Sweden all excavations belong to the government, and no barrow can be excavated without the permission of representatives of the government. If for any reason the owner of the land where a barrow is found wishes to have it removed, he must obtain permission from the government before it can be done. The government conducts the excavation, takes what is found within the barrow, and leaves to the owner the surface of the soil. The greater part of the treasures in the national museum of Sweden have come from government excavations and the government knows definitely where these have been found, how they have been found, and what has been found.

Undoubtedly the greatest contribution to the science of museum arrangement was made by the Danish archeologist and curator — Thompson. He did not originate the terms *stone age, bronze age, iron age,* but he was the first curator to arrange in a museum prehistoric archeological specimens in accordance with this principle of development. When this scheme of classification was applied to the seemingly heterogeneous collections in the Copenhagen museum, chaos became order, and general information was transformed into a science.

The result of this early interest in the monumental remains of its past and the jealous care with which they have been guarded has been the formation of a small but admirably equipped body of trained Scandinavian archeologists and curators who rank today among the foremost in the field.

The greatest contribution that in recent years Scandinavia has made to museum science has been that of the open-air museum. This is a museum that "not only illustrates and perpetuates the houses of bygone ages with all that they contained, but it should revive and commemorate ancient types and customs and functions."

This unique form of museum has not yet been developed outside of Scandinavia, while here are already found at least five — two in Sweden, in Stockholm and Lund; two in Norway, in Christiania and near Lillehammer; and one in Denmark, at Lyngby, near Copenhagen. The open-air museum is for the most part the complement of the indoors museum, if one may use the descriptive phrase. The great Northern Museum in Stockholm has its complement in the open-air museum called Skansen, the Danish Folks Museum in Copenhagen is supplemented by the open-air museum of Lyngby, the national historical museum of Norway has its open-air counterpart in Bygdö, a suburb of Christiania; the museums at Lund and near Lillehammer are local rather than national.

The origin of the open-air museum is in doubt. Did the idea come from Copenhagen, where Dr. Bernhard Olsen started the Danish Folks Museum, with the affiliated open-air museum at Lyngby; or was it from Stockholm, where Dr. Arthur Hazelius began in a small private way the collection that has developed into the great Northern Museum, with its out-of-doors complement at Skansen, or was it from Christiania, where King Oscar II set up two peasants' houses, which have formed the nucleus of the open-air museum in its suburb of Bygdö; or was it from certain wealthy merchants who saved several old buildings from destruction; or was it from a far-sighted dentist who began collecting the treasures from Gudbrandsdal, or is it possible that the idea developed contemporaneously in several widely separated localities? Certain it is that the historical museum has been established on a far more extensive scale in Scandinavia than anywhere else in the world, and nowhere else is found at all the out-of-doors museum.

It is in Stockholm that this form of museum has been brought to the highest stage of perfection. Its Northern Museum is the finest in the world, it is adequately housed in a building of magnificent proportions erected on the plan of a Swedish palace of the sixteenth century, and it contains illustrations of every form of normal Scandinavian life. But its unique feature is its open-air complement known as Skansen. This is an extensive landed property of about seventy acres, situated directly opposite the Northern Museum. Its natural configuration is varied and attractive, and from many points gives a survey of Stockholm and its environments. Here has been collected a remarkable series of buildings gathered from every part of Sweden, taken down and erected here to give an epitome of Swedish life. It is, indeed, "a picture book of the past, on the leaves of which are illustrated the homes, the surroundings, the belongings, the whole life of former generations," and it thus seems to realize the ambitions of its founders and to be "an image in miniature of the great fatherland." Not only does the collection represent the houses of nearly every class and station in Sweden, with all their exterior surroundings and interior furnishings, but the natural resources of the country are represented. The products of mines and quarries, lumber camps, and fishing stations, with all the accompanying machinery, are found here. All native birds and animals are found in large wire inclosures, on the outside of which are framed pictures of the occupants, with the common name and the scientific name, so that every specimen can be instantly identified. The inclosures are made to conform in every respect to the material conditions in which the animals and birds are found, and thus they can be studied in their native habitat. In a similar way all flowers and shrubs, savory herbs, and all medicinal herbs native to Sweden or cultivated there are found in Skansen.

But the great desire of Dr. Hazelius was to reproduce the daily life of the people. This is reached thru the revival at Skansen of Swedish music, Swedish games, Swedish dances, Swedish amusements, Swedish story-telling — every form of national self-expression. Swedish restaurants provide national dishes, while waiters in national dress are in attendance.

Skansen, perfect as it seems to others, is as yet incomplete, when measured by the ideals of its founder. When completed, if it is ever possible or wise to think of it as such, it will be "an image in miniature of the great fatherland," a concentration within a limited area of all that characterizes Sweden.

The great advantages that Skansen has over other open-air museums are first of all its central location, with its commanding view of Stockholm and the vicinity, its own inherent attractiveness, and its accessibility from every point of the city. It has also apparently unfailing financial support, and the interest of the Swedish nation has been enlisted in its behalf, altho it is under a board of managers and not under official government direction. This national interest that has been created in its work and in its ideals is today its most important and valuable asset.

The open-air museum of Stockholm was begun under great difficulties and discouragements, and it was brought to its present state of success only thru the persistent energy of Dr. Hazelius. His confidence in its ultimate success was unfailing, and this confidence triumphed over ridicule and well-meant warnings of friends not to persist in so chimerical a scheme. Without financial support, he became "the greatest beggar in Sweden," and the Northern Museum and Skansen today have an ample annual budget. The great monument of Arthur Hazelius is Skansen itself. It is, too, the last resting-place of his body, and the spot where it lies, in a remote part of the estate, is marked by a rough-hewn granite slab, containing only the name, with date of his birth and death, and the large circle in which it stands is a mass of the wild flowers native to Sweden.

Lund, the location of the other open-air museum in Sweden, is more easily reached from Copenhagen, being scarcely more than two hours distant by steamer and railway. Its culture museum contain a mass of somewhat ill-arranged articles that illustrate provincial life, while its open-air complement, containing only half a dozen buildings, seems small in comparison with Skansen. But there are evidences of enlargement and reorganization in progress, and, with apparently large resources to draw upon, its future is most promising. Its great advantage is its immediate proximity to the technical art school, and the opportunity it is consequently able to offer to students of art and those who draw their inspiration from the past.

The Folks Museum of Copenhagen, with its open-air counterpart at Lyngby, and the Historical Museum of Christiania, with its open-air counterpart at Bygdö, are similar in purpose to those of Sweden.

Scandinavia has thus made a great and permanent contribution to museum science, in that she has been the first to collect her own antiquities, adequate legislation controls all excavations made, its trained curators, like Montelius of Stockholm, are of world-wide reputation, its open-air museums are a unique development from the conventional indoors museum, and its collections represent what it usual, typical, and normal rather than what is rare, abnormal, and eccentric.

All of these various contributions made by Scandinavia are perhaps but illustrations of one great fundamental principle — that the historical museum should have something to say, and should say it. It must represent an idea and not be a miscellaneous collection of incongruous objects — *de omnibus rebus et quibusdam aliis.*

"As historians," says a recent writer, "we have perhaps learned how to read the past, but we have not yet learned how to see it." It is the great glory of Scandinavia not only that she has learned to see her own past, and has taught others to see it, but that she has no copyright on the plan. What she has done we may do and should do. It has been an axiom in America that we have nothing to learn from the effete monarchies of the old world. It has been a corresponding axiom in Europe that America had no history. But in an age that asks for proof in regard to William Tell's apple, and questions the finality of the nebular hypothesis, even an axiom may be brought before the bar of the investigator and compelled to prove its claim to axiomity. While, therefore, we have ourselves half believed that we have no history, we have at the same time defended ourselves most vigorously from the charge, and we have insisted that the inculcation of patriotism should be the objective point in the study and teaching of our national history. If this, indeed, is to be our objective point, it is at least an open question whether that end is not better attained by a study of great historical museums that preserve the material remains of a native past, than by saluting the flag on set occasions, and by disturbing the peace on the Fourth of July. If our history is to show the development from simple into complex forms of life, surely the historical museum, better than any other instrumentality, shows this development.

The combined product that we call our public national life may have its component parts made known thru the museum. Much that has been distinctive in our life has already past away, and much is quickly passing. The New England schoolhouse, the Southern plantation, the early manor house, the frontiersman's log cabin, the lumber camp, the sodhouse, the adobe hut, these are but suggestions of what should be preserved if in the future we are to realize our past aright. Inventions have changed our domestic life. The individual open fire in the center of the hut has developed on one side into the electric range for purposes of cooking, and on the other side into the central heating company for supplying heat; the pine knot has grown into the incandescent light, and the individual lantern into the municipal system for lighting city streets; the household cistern and pump has developed into municipal water works; the huge iron pot and the brass caldron of the fireplace crane have given place to the enamel saucepan and the chafing-dish; the bed of boughs has become a hair mattress, and from the sod floor has sprung the metal bedstead; the household churn has been transformed into the community creamery, and the domestic spinning-wheel develops into the woolen factory. This material side of our domestic life must become only a tradition unless its records are preserved for the future thru the historical museum.

A more recent interest in our past concerns the different ethnic elements that have entered into our national life. Here also it must be the historical museum that is to preserve for us the material remains of the foreign influences that have gone to make the America of today — it is in the historical museum that we must seek the English furniture, the Dutch household objects, the French china, the German toys, the Swiss embroideries, the Italian lace, the Swedish textiles, and all other material remains that have been distinctively national, but now make part of American life.

The historical museum is again a distinct educational force. The majority of persons are interested in all processes and advantage is taken of this interest by commercial houses, which display in shop windows as advertisements the successive stages in the making of hats, the weaving of rugs, or the manufacture of ribbon. Everywhere there is the keenest interest in the study of origins. The child digs up the seed he has planted, and the cutting he has set out, with the eager hope of the biologist that he will discover the mystery of life. He takes apart the clock and the sewing-machine to discover the secret of its motion, and the manufacturer, often in advance of the educator, recognizes the commercial possibility of this desire and makes clocks specially arranged for being taken apart and put together again. It is the historical museum that is the most effective agency for ministering to this all but universal desire to understand origins. It has, indeed, its dangers as an educational agent. Great works of literature have often lost their meaning when used as a vehicle for studying indirect discourse or grammatical construction, or for passing college entrance examinations. Should a similar fate await the Parthenon and the Forum, we might well deprecate the movement towards making the museum a part of our educational system. The danger may seem imminent when high school pupils are asked to compare the height and the width of the Arch of Constantine, to note the faults of certain collections, to pass judgment on the respective merits of the Venus of Milo and the Venus de Medici, and to state what is the most beautiful fragment of the Parthenon. Yet this use of the museum belongs to a false system of education, and ought not to militate against its advantages when used in connection with a reasonable system of education.

If the historical museum is to be a genuine educational force, the important question arises as to the best principle to be followed in preserving the material remains that show the beginnings of our national life. It is here again that Scandinavia has shown us that a museum gains in value when its exhibits are shown as far as possible in their natural environment. A book loses no value when transferred from one place to another; museum directors have in the past acted on the belief that the same principle has held true in the case of monumental records of a past life. But today we are coming to realize that often the most valuable service that can be performed by the governing body of an historical museum, is, not in bringing together specimens from the uttermost part of the earth, but in leaving articles where they were found, and as they were found. Not infrequently single objects are of little or no value for purposes of study, since a number of articles of the same class are needed for comparison. The Egyptian obelisk in Central Park is an object of curiosity and perhaps serves serious study to the same extent as would Bunker Hill monument if taken down and set up on the Desert of Sahara. But the book is complete in itself, while the various specimens in a museum, altho each individual article is complete in itself, are but single words that must be placed in conjunction with other specimens — words to form the specimen sentences, as these specimen sentences must in their turn be combined into the specimen book, the museum. The museum thus becomes what Huxley has defined it to be — "A consultative library of objects." The museum as it is for the most part found today exists because of the passion for collecting that knows no limitation of country, age, or sex. "Natural curiosities" and "natural rarities" have been brought together from every known clime and housed in buildings more or less suitable for their reception. We need today greater emphasis placed on the importance of preserving what is vital to our own national and local past, and preserving it amid its own natural surroundings. If every state could preserve *in situ* the material remains of the types of life and occupations once found within its boundaries, if our national government could preserve the material remains of our common national life, if what is expended on ephemeral expositions could be turned into the channel of permanent historical museums, it would seem that we should awaken to a greater appreciation of what it is that had gone to make America.

The historical museum with its complement, the open-air museum, is of today in Scandinavia. May its today soon come in America!

President Wilson as an Autophotographer by an Old Acquaintance

Daguerre's invention from its early days to its latest development in the kodak has met a wide-felt want. Portraiture, once a luxury of the rich, has been brought to every man's door and no individual is now unable to achieve the once impossible and "see himself as others see him." Yet the photograph, like all labor-saving devices, has certain inherent disadvantages. The very stage of perfection that it has reached has led to the atrophy of the power of observation, it has fostered confusion between the reality and its simulation, and it has led many to believe that in seeing the counterpart they have known the original. This confusion has in its turn been promoted by the illustrated press that through photograph, sketch, cartoon, caricature, and every known form of representation delights to set forth all public officials in every pose and attitude known to the craft. "It is the business of the photographer," as has been happily said, "to turn a politician into a statesman." The more successful the photographer is in this metamorphosis the greater is the danger of widespread intellectual myopia.

It is not the fault either of press or of photographer if a single person in America, or indeed in the newspaper-reading world, is not familiar with the features of President Wilson, and many apparently believe that in recognizing these external features they thereby know the man. Yet he has himself given a far truer photograph of the real man than has ever been revealed by camera, brush, or pencil. Oliver Wendell Holmes has said that six persons are always engaged in a conversation between John and Thomas — each as he thinks he is, each as the other thinks he is, and each as his Maker knows he is. But in the case of President Wilson at least two of these persons seem to have coalesced and in all conversations with John, the Woodrow Wilson as many Johns think he is and as they believe his Maker knows he is are identical.

What was the picture of Woodrow Wilson left years ago in the mind of one somewhat closely associated with him for many months? It was that of a man absorbingly interested in his own development and in his own career; disappointed that the American political system with its duplicate arrangement of congressional committees offered no inducement for an able man to enter public life as a career, since the limit of ambition was reached in attaining by slow stages the chairmanship of a committee and this eminence must be shared with more than a hundred other chairmen; the road to

Lucy Maynard Salmon Papers, 1919, Vassar College.

ambition apparently being blocked in this direction, dropping into the career of a college professor as the conventional occupation open to a university graduate; fulfilling punctiliously the requirements of the position, but finding in writing an outlet for his mental activities and temporary scope for his abilities; looking to Bagehot and to Burke as model literary statesmen who overtopped their generations and came into such rightful recognition of their genius that their fame is enduring; having a consuming desire for immortality and seeing the path opening to it through the production of literature; obsessed by the importance of acquiring a literary "style" as a means to this end — in a word, a courteous gentleman somewhat oblivious to the existence of other persons apart from the assistance they afforded him in his own mental and spiritual development.

What is the picture he has unconsciously drawn of himself in all of his published writings and in his public speeches? The picture is much the same both in general outlines and in details as that given through conversation. It is therefore open to every John to see the real man and to converse with the real Thomas whenever he reads anything whatsoever under the signature of Woodrow Wilson. Many books are in reality double in their character. They are usually read for their superficial content, but often the most interesting book is the one the author unconsciously writes in which he discloses his real self — his ambitions, his aspirations, and his attitude of mind toward his associates. Woodrow Wilson, whether writing "Mere Literature," "The Author Himself," "On Being Human," "When a Man Comes to Himself," or any article in the long list of literary and political works credited to him, has given the most perfect revelation of his personal characteristics it is possible for any writer to make. In all of his political writings he has drawn in clearest lines his own political ambitions, as he has described himself in whatever he has written of the literary achievements of others. It is this book of self-revelation that is of greater value than are the books that he ostensibly writes. Substitute the name of Woodrow Wilson for that of Burke or of Bagehot in the essays "A Literary Politician" and "The Interpreter of English Liberty," and apply to him the descriptions and characterizations he gives of these, the companions of his thoughts, and the picture is complete.

The picture of Burke as a boy leads him to recall that "other lads before and since have found big libraries all too small for them. What should arrest our attention is, the law of mind disclosed in the habits of such lads: the quick and various curiosity of original minds, and particularly of imaginative minds. They long for matter to expand themselves upon." His ideal plan of education is stated in "The Author Himself": "The rule for every man is, not to depend on the education which other men prepare for him, not even to consent to it; but to strive to see things as they are, and to be himself as he is. Defeat lies in self-surrender." He has a contempt politely expressed but not concealed for "specialist omniscience," for the modern critic who is "a leader of fashion," for "modern *literati*, sophisticated in all the fashions," for "our universities [that] are erected entirely for the service of the tractable mind," and he finds that "life is [the heart's] only university."

The matter of individuality is one that he has much at heart. It does not consist, he says in "The Author Himself," "in the use of the very personal pronoun *I*: it consists in tone, in method, in attitude, in point of view; it consists in saying things in such a way that you will yourself be recognized as a force in saying them." He finds that "The ability to see for one's self is attainable, not by mixing with crowds and ascertaining how they look at things, but by a certain aloofness and self-containment. The solitariness of some genius is not accidental; it is characteristic and essential. To the constructive imagination there are some immortal feats which are possible only in seclusion. The man must heed first and most of all the suggestions of his own spirit; and the world can be seen from windows overlooking the street better than from the street itself." "It is your direct, unhesitating, intent, headlong man," he says again, "who has his sources in the mountains, who digs deep channels for himself in the soil of his times and expands into the mighty river, to become a landmark forever." He finds that "learned investigation leads to many good things, but one of these is not great literature, because learned investigation commands, as the first condition of its success, the repression of individuality."

His point of view in regard to political affairs has not always been novel. Gamaliel Bradford for years advocated in the *Nation* the union of legislative and execu-departments in the interests of efficient government. *The State* is a work of industry, not of genius, and it might well have been written by many persons whose interests have run in that direction, but even in this compilation, for it is scarcely more than this, the same mental photograph is found.

The personal and the political sides of the shield seem indeed in the last analysis to be really the counterpart of each other. The advocacy of executive leadership of the legislative department provides a way for a single leader, while self-analysis and self-approbation point to Woodrow Wilson as the person best qualified to fill the position. His description of himself as having "a single track mind" tells the story. There is everywhere but a single track, Woodrow Wilson is the locomotive engineer and all others, having found a leader, are to be safely brought to the station, and thus to the development of the powers of the engineer. "And so men grow," he says in "When a Man Comes to Himself," "by having responsibility laid upon them, the burden of other people's business."

There have been certain delusions born of Woodrow Wilson's own opinions about himself from which there must be a rude awakening, if one takes the pains to read his published writings. One of these is that he is a believer in democracy. It must be granted that no two persons agree on what is meant by democracy, and that no one person would be willing to submit his own definition to the acid test, but there is a well-defined feeling that certain things go with a democratic society and that one of these is that the opportunity for education should be given to all. It seems otherwise, however, to President Wilson. "Our present plans for teaching everybody," he says in "Mere Literature," "involve certain unpleasant things quite inevitably. It is obvious that you cannot have universal education without restricting your teaching to such things as can be universally understood. It is plain that you cannot impart 'university methods' to thousands, or create 'investigators' by the score, unless you confine your university education to matters which dull men can investigate, your laboratory training to tasks which mere plodding diligence and submissive patience can compass." As regards its content, no more specious paragraph has ever been written. But its intrinsic value is great in the photograph it gives of the author's attitude towards universal education as a generally recognized accompaniment of democratic communities.

But it is a well-accepted belief that it is quite possible to advocate democracy as an abstract principle and yet be averse to the application of the principle to particular cases. Democracy is admirable as a political slogan, but translated into actual life it "involves certain unpleasant things quite inevitably." It may have its convenience as a social fiction, but he cites with evident approval the words of Bagehot when he speaks of "a patient sympathy, a kindly fellow feeling for the narrow intelligence necessarily induced by narrow circumstances." "We do not want our poetry from grammarians," he says in "On Being Human," "nor our tales from philologists nor our history from theorists—neither do we want our political economy from tradesmen nor our statesmanship from mere politicians, but from those who see more and care for more than these men see or care for." "It is a prerogative of every truly human being," he says in the essay "On Being Human," "to come out from the low estate of those who are merely gregarious and of the herd, and show his innate powers cultivated and yet unspoiled—sound, unmixed, free from imitation; showing that individualization without extravagance which is genuineness." This seems to indicate that his belief in democracy is at least a qualified one, in spite of many fervent apostrophes to it.

The other side of the shield of democracy with its education for all is the question of the teacher. With tiresome iteration, the opponents of President Wilson have referred to him as "the schoolmaster" and by the reference have intended to condemn him to a low intellectual and social plane. It is possible that some reconstruction is needed of the prevailing ideas of schoolmasters. Many teachers are not such if tested by the principles suggested by George Herbert Palmer, and holding the title of college professor does not in and of itself make men teachers. Two of the four tests named are "the aptitude for vicariousness" and "a readiness to be forgotten." These have certainly never been a part of the mental equipment of President

Wilson. The aptitude for vicariousness has never been his, and his inability to get the point of view of other persons explains in part why so many of his political appointments have been justly criticized. No man can know men so long as he is both center and circumference of a circle. Nor can "a readiness to be forgotten" be deemed a characteristic of a man who never forgets himself. "Must not all April Hopes," he asks, "exclude from their number the hope of immortality?" When then the terms "professor," "schoolmaster," "pedagogue," "teacher" are applied to him as explaining his shortcomings, it may in all truth be said that, tested by the principles of Professor Palmer, President Wilson has never been a teacher. No man belongs to any occupation so long as he lacks the essential characteristics of that class.

Much has been said of Woodrow Wilson as a master of the English language, and constant reference is made to him as "a matchless phrasemaker," as using "faultless diction," and it is said that "he uses the best diction," "his diction is superb," "his English is masterly." Yet to those who know his mental processes it must seem that the machinery of his English is always visible and its creaking is always audible. His "polished diction" seems smooth as glass and as difficult to grasp and to hold.

He once said in effect to an acquaintance that in writing a book it was necessary to tell readers in the beginning where they were to be taken, to tell them at the end where they had been taken, and in between to say the same thing over again a great many times. This principle is repeatedly exemplified in his own writings as is shown in three passages taken quite at random:

> It is very difficult indeed for a man, for a boy, who knows the Scripture ever to get away from it. It haunts him like an old song. It follows him like the memory of his mother. It reminds him like the word of an old and revered teacher. It forms part of the warp and woof of his life.

> The world has been going on. The world has a habit of going on. The world has a habit of leaving those behind who won't go with it. The world has always neglected stand-patters.

> I believe, for one, that you cannot tear up ancient rootages and safely plant the tree of liberty in soil which is not native to it. I believe that the ancient traditions of a people are its ballast; you cannot make a *tabula rasa* upon which to write a political program. You cannot take a new sheet of paper and determine what your life shall be to-morrow. You must knit the new into the old. You cannot put a new patch on an old garment without ruining it.

To anyone familiar with this habit of thought and who has frequently heard the elaboration of this belief, it becomes an interesting psychological fact that it seems difficult to write of "the master of English style" without unconsciously and almost inevitably falling into the same repetition.

It has been a rude awakening for many to have these personal characteristics so prominently displayed by a man in public life, to see old friends, ardent admirers, political rivals, new devotees, apparently used as stepping-stones to the achievement of greater things on the part of President Wilson, to realize that it is a question of "watchful waiting" where others are concerned, as in the case of Belgium and the *Lusitania*, but that it is a case of instant, vigorous action where his personal self-respect is involved as in his recent telegram to the head of the American Truth Society.

But the question after all is how far these personal characteristics affect the administration of public office. Is it possible for a man who is fundamentally self-conscious and whose ambitions center in his own career to be an admirable executive officer? The real question at issue at the present time, as far as it relates to President Wilson, is whether these personal inhibitions — so plain that he that runs may read — outweigh a praiseworthy desire to give the presidential office greater authority in the legislative department. Let the answer be read in his essay "When a Man Comes to Himself."

Our Greatest Historian: An Honor Not Yet Settled, but the Title of Great Historian Is Allowed to a Number of Americans

To the Editor of the New York Times:

The unasked question, Who is the greatest American historian? has been answered by anticipation within the past few days and answered quite differently. Many persons will agree with you in placing Motley at the head of the list, others will agree with The New Republic and its reviewer in crediting the late Professor Osgood with the position of honor, but still others are ready to defend vigorously the statement that all such ratings are utterly futile. As you have yourself said in regard to diagnosing literature, "all such positive and dogmatic ratings of book and authors are a vain thing under the sun."

What is meant by "the greatest historian" or "the greatest historical scholar"? If we consider history a branch of literature, then assuredly Motley and Parkman were "magnificent writers, at once lucid and elegant." If, however, we regard history as a part of "science [which] is a general name for human knowledge in its most definite and general shape, whatever may be the object of that knowledge," then the literary presentation of the results of scientific research are no longer the only standard by which the historian is judged and other names come to the front. To some historians the facile pen has been given, to others the gift for scientific research, but comparatively few have the double ability, as had the late Moses Coit Tyler, to carry on scientific historical research and to present the result of this research in artistic literary form.

But history takes on protean forms, and often our greatest historians have not written history at all or very little that can be classed as literature. No greater service to history has been given in this country than that of the late Charles Gross in his study, "The Bibliography of British Municipal History." The preparation of manuscripts for the use of the historian calls for extensive knowledge and for the very greatest skill in passing on their authenticity and in rendering them available for the use of scholars. Thus the work of great editors like W. C. Ford, J. F. Jameson, V. H. Paltsits, and the late R. G. Thwaites has been of immeasurable advantage to the historian, and recognition of this has been given in the election of at least two great editors to the Presidency of the American Historical Association.

Editing in its turn has assumed various forms, and the late Justin Winsor — in his "Memorial History of Boston" and later in his "Narrative and

New York Times, March 7, 1926.

Critical History of America," the latter published in eight portly volumes and of inestimable value to every student of American history—may well rank as one of our greatest historians. Mr. Winsor may rank as such on at least four different counts. Not only was he great as an editor in his skill in selecting his assistants in this truly monumental work and in securing their hearty cooperation, but his unrivaled bibliographical knowledge of the sources of American history has made every student of the subject his debtor. He was also at the head of cartographers in this country, and he added a new form of history in introducing the cooperative method of work. This was an innovation, but its success has been proved by its extensive adoption. In addition it may be said that Mr. Winsor's contributions to historical literature were numerous and noteworthy. It will be a gratification to many to know that he served as the third President of the American Historical Association.

Again, the greatest historian may be the one who is able to add great collections of historical material to previous resources. The collection of sources for the study of the French Revolution made by Andrew D. White was, for example, so important that it served as an inducement for H. Morse Stephens to come to this country from England and to fill the chair of Modern History at Cornell University. President White's collections that are now a part of the great library of Cornell are among the most valuable resources available for the historian in this country. It may be noted that Andrew D. White was the first President of the American Historical Association. H. Morse Stephens also was elected President of the American Historical Association after he had accepted a professorship in the University of California, where he later served as custodian of the great H. H. Bancroft library of material for the study of the history of the Pacific Coast.

It is quite true that H. H. Bancroft himself, in his written history, lacked the graces of a literary style, but none the less he must be counted as among the greatest of our historians in that "he collected an enormous amount of highly valuable and trustworthy material for the use of others." He, with many others, illustrates admirably the statement that it is not necessary to write history in pleasing literary form in order to be a great historian.

The greatest historian may be the one who, like the late H. C. Lea, opens up previously unexplored fields through the use of sources not generally familiar. Mr. Lea also became President of the American Historical Association.

Again, the greatest historian may be he who gives historians a new and veritably great idea—an idea like the lens of the telescope or the microscope transforms an unknown world into reality, that like the acquisition of a new language opens the mind to new stores of learning, or that like the flash of lightning makes darkness visible. The literary output of F. J. Turner has been comparatively small, and it is thus in striking contrast to that of other historians who have already achieved a personal five-foot shelf. But the question may at least be raised whether any historian in this country has more profoundly influenced the thinking of his fellow-historians than did Mr. Turner in his slender pamphlet of thirty-four pages on "The Significance of the Frontier in American History." It is gratifying to note the appreciation of the great contribution made by Mr. Turner to historical thought as seen in his election to the Presidency of the American Historical Association, and that his presidential address was on "Social Forces in American History."

This by no means exhausts the types of great historians who have made their contribution to the cause of history in this country and who have been content "to add their stone to the cairn" without thought of ribbons, badges, medals, keys, or office either high or low. The late Edward G. Bourne almost revolutionized the use of certain forms of historical material conventionally used in writing American history through his critical acumen in dealing with the sources of accepted traditions, attributions of authorship, and obscure narrations of hypothetical events. A. R. Haase has worked out classifications of different but kindred varieties of sources, and these have clarified previously unintelligible relationships and done much to bring order out of chaos for the often-bewildered historian. F. G. Davenport has located in foreign archives and libraries a wealth of official material, the publication of which has already done much to reconstruct our ideas of America's relation to Europe. The eventual publication of other material of the same character must affect advantageously our foreign relationships through the knowledge gained of what these relationships have already been. The publication of B. F. Stevens's "Facsimiles of Manuscripts in European Archives Relating to America" has had great influence in creating a better understanding between England and America.

All this is but saying that history has many facets. To ask who is the greatest historian America has produced is much like asking, to use homely comparisons, which is more valuable, a watch or a cane; which is more useful, a hat or a pair of shoes; which is better, a peach or an apple. It all depends! And it may be "news," in the newspaper's use of that word, to know that not only has America produced her share of really great historians but that it has had so many that it has been impossible for them all to fill the honorable office of President of the American Historical Association.

Lucy M. Salmon
Poughkeepsie, N.Y., Feb. 25, 1926

Many Claimants for an Honor — in America

If the problems of history are illustrated by an examination of the wide range of those that have arisen in the case of a single country like England, so they may also be illustrated in the single concrete case in America, as they are disclosed in the history of the origin of the American Constitution. Interest in this document has of necessity varied from generation to generation, owing in part to the increasing stability of the nation. During the early period after its adoption, the chief interest centered around the question, "Will it work?" The Federalist party answered emphatically, "Yes," but qualified the statement with the reservation that the leadership of the Federalists was necessary to its success. When the leadership passed to the Democratic Republican party and the machinery of government worked as smoothly as it had previously done, the period of testing the constitution practically closed. Interest in the constitution shifted to the discussion of the question, "What does the constitution mean?" and its interpretation occupied the foreground. At the close of the Civil War, the constitution had successfully withstood every test that could be applied to it, both on the side of the foreign policy and of the domestic policy of the nation. The interpretation given it by the great constitutional lawyers and jurists of the pre-war period had been practically accepted and therefore for the first time leisure was afforded for the consideration of the question, "What was its origin?"

The time for such consideration was fully come. Already public opinion was crystallizing along quite different lines and mutually contradictory explanations were at hand, all made with an appearance of finality such as seemed to preclude further discussion. Gladstone had proclaimed in pontifical tones that "As the British Constitution is the most subtle organism which has proceeded from progressive history, so the American Constitution is the most wonderful work ever struck off at a given time by the brain and purpose of man."

This dictum was assuredly not the result of any profound study of the origin of the American Constitution, as Gladstone was himself the first to admit, but it is an interesting record of the acceptance by the theological mind of the "special creation" and "spontaneous generation" theories then under fire in the field of natural history. It was, however, apparently fully accepted by historians as well as by the general public. But even at the time the "special creation" theory was enunciated, it was being disposed of by Von Holst who submitted, apparently from a contemporary authority, that

Why Is History Rewritten? (New York: Oxford University Press, 1929), 134–61. Copyright 1929 by Oxford University Press, Inc. Used by permission of Oxford University Press, Inc.

"the Constitution had been extorted from the grinding necessities of a reluctant people."

Another statement as to its origin may be called "the inspiration" theory. This is illustrated by a version of the situation given early in the Civil War. An anonymous writer, in discussing "Loyalty," in the *North American Review* for January 1862, explains that "Such a government we regard as more than the expression of calm wisdom and lofty patriotism. It has its distinctly providential element. It was God's saving gift to a distracted and imperiled people. It was his creative fiat over a weltering chaos: 'Let a nation be born in a day.' "

The danger of passing judgment on origins without full knowledge of a situation is again illustrated by a somewhat recent account of the Philadelphia Convention given by a distinguished clergyman-editor. He states: "In 1787 a little over three million people, living along the Atlantic Coast, desired a new organic law for the republic. They selected, after due debate, representative men from the different sections of the country. These representative men met and debated the provisions for the new organic law. The debates were open and public. The debaters not only discussed the provisions of this new organic law in constitutional convention, but upon the platform and through the press presented them to the people of the various States. The American people made for themselves the Constitution under which they were to live." But it has long been a matter of common knowledge that the Philadelphia Convention sat behind closed doors, that its debates were not "open and public," but that on the contrary every precaution was taken to prevent any information concerning its deliberations from leaking out; that the debaters did not at the time present the provisions of the new organic law to the people of the various states upon the platform and through the press; and that it was not until after the Philadelphia Convention had adjourned *sine die* and the question of the ratification of the Constitution by the States was to be decided, that Hamilton, Madison, and Jay began through the press to explain the provisions of the new organic law proposed.

All these different impressionistic accounts of the origin and adoption of the constitution reflect little the actual conditions. But they are interesting records of the ease with which history is written alike by the learned and the ignorant. They are in part explained by the almost complete lack of knowledge on the part of the general public of the work of the Philadelphia Convention, and the consequent opportunity given for allowing free rein to the imagination. "One hundred per cent Americanism" has always been popular and the belief in "a chosen people" has had a long ancestry.

The first departures from these assumed but popularly accepted versions of the origin of the constitution were at first timidly made by historians, but they rested on a more substantial foundation than inspiration. Changing views of the relation between England and her colonies began to come in and in 1884 Edward Channing wrote that "the constitutional history of

Massachusetts and Virginia before their settlement is one history — the continuous history of the English people." This was assuredly giving a firmer foundation to our constitution than that of a special creation or the inspirational theory, and with the dying out of the old animosity toward England, the theory of the English origin of the American Constitution came into vogue. Douglas Campbell was probably in part correct in saying that "most American authors, and all Englishmen who have written of America, set out with the theory that the people of the United States are an English race, and that their institutions, when not original, are derived from England." His own work was written to combat this idea, but the result was not history, but a case of special pleading. The effort was made to show that the Pilgrims, after a residence of eleven years in Holland, had transferred to America, where their settlements were practically confined to New England, everything that was admirable in the institutions of Holland, while everything in America open to adverse criticism was a base residuum left from an unworthy English connection. This theory has found acceptance among those wishing to do honor to "brave little Holland," but the book remains, in the words of a distinguished American historian, the late H. L. Osgood, "one of the most pretentious, but least substantial, of all the works ever written on early American history."

But discussions in regard to the origin of the English Constitution itself were already coming up. Violent controversies, as has been seen, had been waged around the questions of its indebtedness to Germanic institutions; the contributions made to it by the Romans as a result of their five hundred years of occupation of Britain; the possible, or probable, or indisputable, survivals from the Celtic tenure of the island. The Germanic origin advocated by Edward A. Freeman for a time held the field and is well stated by one of his disciples, H. B. Adams, when he says, "The Constitution of England is not written at all; it is simply a rich but sturdy growth of popular institutions, derived originally from the forests of Germany and transplanted across the sea." If this lineage of the English Constitution was accepted, it followed that all who accepted the theory of the English origin of the American Constitution naturally transferred to it the same Germanic origin, and Mr. Adams goes on to say, "What is thus maintained and acknowledged concerning our Saxon forefathers, may likewise be urged concerning the Pilgrim fathers. They were merely one branch of the great Teutonic race, a single offshoot from the tree of liberty which takes deep hold upon all the past."

This theory was in turn quickly assumed to be the final word in regard to the origin of the American Constitution. "Our institutions," says one writer, "are essentially Teutonic, and the channels through which the ancient influences have made themselves felt in the Constitution are conceded to be predominantly Colonial and English." Freeman himself had presumably uttered the final word when he wrote Hannis Taylor, who had sent him a copy of his *Origin and Growth of the English Constitution*, "The conception of your book, taking American history as part of English, and English as part of general Teutonic, is indeed just what it should be."

It must be self-evident that these theories in regard to the source of the American Constitution are but hypotheses that rest on a very insecure basis. But the reasons are perhaps understandable. Our direct, contemporaneous knowledge of the transactions of the Philadelphia Convention is extremely limited, not only because of the secrecy attending its sessions, but also because of the long delay in publishing both the official and the unofficial records that had been kept. The nearly sixty years that elapsed before all the most important records and notes of the Convention were published was a period long enough to permit ignorance to indulge in vain imaginings and baseless theories. Moreover, when the contemporaneous material was published, it was not easily available, and had it been so, it seems probable that the desires of the time ran in the direction of effusive speculation rather than in that of hard consuming study. Another long period elapsed before such study was undertaken, so that it was practically more than a hundred years before the tools were at hand, and use was made of them; only thus could productive scholarship give an authoritative version of the work of the Federal Convention of 1787.

The most exhaustive study is that made by Max Farrand entitled *The Records of the Federal Convention of 1787*, published in three volumes, in 1911.[1] It takes up the work of the Convention day by day as recorded by its official secretary, William Jackson, and supplemented by the notes of the various members present. This edition of the *Records* forms the basis of the editor's work, *The Framing of the Constitution of the United States*, — "a brief presentation of what took place in the federal convention." A third work by Max Farrand, *The Fathers of the Constitution*, is a less technical, more popular account of the Convention and of its historical setting. These collectively form the most important single series of exhaustive studies made of the Federal Convention, and it is now for the first time possible to study it at first hand.[2]

This long delay in the publication of the essential records of the Convention needs explanation. The official secretary of the Convention deposited his papers with Washington, who had then turned them over to the Department of State, and it was not until 1818 that Congress by resolution ordered their publication. The task of editing them was entrusted to John Quincy Adams, as Secretary of State. He found it an extremely difficult one, since the papers were "no better than the daily minutes from which the regular journal ought to have been, but never was, made out." But with the help of others who could supply him with important documents, he was able to rescue from "their disorderly state" the records of the secretary and "with all these papers suitably arranged, a correct and tolerably clear view of the proceedings of the Convention (might) be presented." The volume was printed in 1819—with the mistakes inevitable when the editing had necessarily been done without compass or chart.

It is always an agreeable task to write history in "the past potential subjunctive" and in this matter it is especially easy to realize how much more dependable would be our knowledge of the Convention had its official secretary, " a Major Jackson," as described by Madison, been selected for his fitness for the post rather than through political influence;[3] had he not "burned all the loose scraps of paper which belong[ed] to the Convention; had the minutes been written out at once; and had the journal been published immediately—as late as 1799 Madison questioned the expediency of doing it even then. As it is, it seems remarkable than even John Quincy Adams was able to do as well as he did. It is at least a matter for congratulation that Major Jackson did not add still greater confusion by adopting the advice of Timothy Pickering who, forty years after the adjournment of the Convention, urged him to prepare "those speeches in the General Convention which formed the Constitution of the U. States, of which you took abbreviated notes, and which yourself alone can write out at full length."

There were other regrettable delays, and these too need explanation. A long period elapsed before the publication of the notes of the debates taken by Madison, "evidently regarded by his fellow-delegates to the Convention as a semi-official reporter of their proceedings." He had been frequently urged to publish them, but before all else he was cautious, and he naturally demurred. In 1799, he had felt that it was "a problem what turn might be given to the impression on the public mind" were the official records to be published. In 1821, in a confidential letter to Thomas Ritchie he acknowledged the truth of the general belief that he had "materials for a pretty ample view of what passed in that Assembly," and that he had not intended that "they should for ever remain under the veil of secrecy," but "of the time when it might be not improper for them to see the light" he "had formed no particular determination." In general it had appeared to him "that is might be best to let the work be a posthumous one," that at least "its publication should be delayed till the Constitution should be well settled by practice, & till a knowledge of the controversial part of the proceedings of its framers could be turned to no improper account." These, with many other fine-spun reasons, seemed to him to justify the postponement of the publication, but it is his purpose, he writes, to arrange his material and when that is done, he will be better able to decide on the question of publication. But even in 1827, he still felt that the publication of what he had preserved might be "most delicate" and that it should be deferred until "the living obstacles" should be removed—"of the lamps still burning, none can now be far from the Socket." His own lamp burned out in 1836, and four years later his *Papers* were published.

The excessive caution of Madison had seemed to him warranted by the conditions of his time, but to-day the delay of more than fifty years in the appearance of his material seems much to be regretted. Not only had this delay given opportunity for a lessening interest in the affairs of the Convention, but Max Farrand has shown the weak spots in the report of Madison as published. Through a comparison of the official records published in 1819 with the Madison *Papers*, he makes it evident that after this record was made available, Madison corrected his own report by it, and thus was sometimes led into error. It was a time of little knowledge of textual criticism and presumably of even less general interest in it. Madison accepted the *Journal* as authoritative and thereby detracted somewhat from the value of his own more carefully kept reports; the value of the *Journal* would assuredly have been greater had the secretary of the Convention been better qualified for his position, and Madison's account would probably have had greater value had he had more confidence in his own version and less in that of the official secretary. But even so, with the publication of the Madison *Papers*— "more than half of this work was given over to his notes of the debates in the Federal Convention" — "at once all other records paled into insignificance."

There are thus available for the study of the origin of the Federal Constitution several different classes of contemporaneous material. To follow somewhat the classification of Max Farrand they are first, the official record of the Convention; second, the unofficial report of Madison; third, the notes of members, other than Madison, taken during the Convention but published subsequently; fourth, supplementary material; fifth, the documents of the Committee of Detail; sixth, the drafts of the Constitution printed for the use of the delegates when the work of the Convention was practically finished; and seventh, the work known collectively as Elliot's *Debates*— which was not published in complete form until during the years from 1827 to 1845, but, "in spite of its imperfections, (it) is the great storehouse of American constitutional history. It is almost impossible to exaggerate its importance."

Of these classes only the third and the fourth need additional explanation. The third class, — notes of members, excluding those of Madison, who may justly be considered in a class by himself— comprises those taken by Robert Yates, Rufus King, James McHenry, William Pierce, William Patterson, Alexander Hamilton, Charles Pinckney, and George Mason. The value of these notes considered collectively is well stated by Max Farrand when he says: "In view of the fact that the *Journal* is so imperfect and not altogether reliable, and that Madison made so many changes in his manuscript, all other records of the Convention take on a new importance. Formerly they have been regarded only in so far as they might supplement our information; now it is seen that they may be of service also in determining what the action really was in doubtful cases."

Individually, these notes of members may be fairly well illustrated by referring to those of two of them. Robert Yates was a member from New York and, with his colleague, John Lansing, Jr., left the Convention because he felt that in view of his instructions he could not continue his attendance. His credentials definitely stated that the delegates from New York were appointed "for the sole and express purpose of revising the Articles of Confederation." When, therefore, the Convention deliberately put aside the Articles and framed a constitution *de novo* he withdrew. This withdrawal and his pamphlet entitled *Secret Proceedings and Debates of the Convention*, published in Albany in 1821, probably explain his opposition in the State Convention of New York to the ratification of the Federal Constitution.[4] William Pierce was a delegate from Georgia. His somewhat informal notes remain; a part is in manuscript, a part was published in the *Savannah Georgian* in 1828, and a letter giving his general impressions of the Convention was printed in the *Georgia Gazette* in 1788. In the main, the *Notes* are less an account of the work of the Convention than a characterization of the appearance and the personality of the various delegates to it.

A fourth class of contemporary documents has been called by Max Farrand "supplementary material." A collection of this could not be made exhaustive, he explains, "without covering practically all of the material, printed and unprinted, on American history since 1787." But he has selected from "the more obvious and accessible sources" such material as has an immediate bearing on the subject since this "throws not a little light upon the work of the Convention, and in particular upon the parts taken by individual delegates, and upon opinions and personalities." The enormous amount now available fills nearly the entire third volume of the *Records* and is in itself indicative of the indebtedness of students to the keen insight and tireless activity of the editor.

Other forms of important supplementary material have been included in an elaborate series of papers by J. F. Jameson called collectively, "Studies in the History of the Federal Convention of 1787." Specially noteworthy was the skill shown in reconstructing the draft presented by Charles Pinckney — a reconstruction confirmed by the subsequent discovery of a large part of the original text of his long-lost plan.

It is also possible to class as supplementary material the important bibliographical work of P. L. Ford. This includes an invaluable *Bibliography and Reference List of the History and Literature relating to the Adoption of the Constitution of the United States*, 1787–8. It contains one hundred and forty-one titles of works contemporary in origin, though a few were not published until some years after the formation of the Constitution. It also contains lists of histories of the Constitution; printed documentary sources; a list of seventy-six contemporaneous newspapers, published in all the thirteen states, that discussed the Constitution; lists of drafts and plans presented or proposed; a bibliography of the biographies of the members attending the Convention; lists of contemporaneous partisan pamphlets for and against the Constitution; together with a bibliography of the contests over ratification carried on in all the states, and a list of the accounts of the celebrations held in honor of the ratification.

This elaborate bibliography and reference list of sixty-one pages ought in itself alone to settle definitely the inspirational theory of the origin of the Constitution, but the work is continued by *A List of the Members of the Federal Convention of 1787*. In this, the author was able not only to extend the list of members as it had been previously given, but also to add much valuable information in regard to their attitude towards the Constitution and its ratification. Still other important contributions to the subject were made by Mr. Ford in his *Pamphlets on the Constitution of the United States, Published during its Discussion by the People 1787–1788*; and a volume of *Essays on the Constitution of the United States, Published during its Discussion by the People*, 1787–1788. These essays were written by prominent citizens and appeared in the newspapers during and soon after the meeting of the Philadelphia Convention.

All of this invaluable bibliographical material gives a substantial, impressive foundation for such a study of the Constitution as must controvert all the off-hand hypotheses assumed in regard to its origin. But this is only the beginning of the material which is now available. New and carefully edited editions of the works of Franklin, Hamilton, Jay, King, Madison, Mason, G. Morris, and Washington have placed in the hands of all who wish enlightenment authoritative collections of the papers of men who took a leading part in the Convention.

Madison was apparently the guiding spirit of the Convention, and it is interesting to know that as soon as he realized that the disintegration of the Articles of Confederation was inevitable, he wrote Jefferson, then in France, and gave him carte blanche to purchase for him "whatever may throw light on the general constitution and droit publique of the several confederacies which have existed"[5] — he has observed in a catalogue "several pieces on the Dutch, the German, and the Helvetic." Thus with the help of Jefferson and a study of the catalogues, Madison brought together a remarkable collection of material on the history of federal government, "probably the most complete in the country at that time," since his library contained all the great classics on government and politics, as well as the important works of the current years and works in all languages. From this material, in preparation for the Philadelphia Convention, "he drew up a careful analysis of the constitution of the Lycian League, the Achaean League, Amphictyonic Council, Swiss Confederation, Germanic Empire, and the United Netherlands." In his very careful study of Madison's library, E. G. Bourne has shown not only the special use Madison made of this material for the Convention itself, but also how much he drew upon it in the subsequent struggle to secure the ratification of the Constitution by the States. Thus for Madison, "all his study of the history of Federal government confirmed his diagnosis of the existing evils. Permanent peace, prosperity, and development could not be obtained under any type of confederacy known to history."

The profound and exhaustive studies made by Madison alone seem effectively to dispose of the Gladstonian "special creation" theory of the origin of the Federal Constitution, as well as of the providential origin theories.

The English, the Germanic, and the Dutch origin of the Constitution have seemed at first blush to have a more solid foundation, but these have in turn been shown to be scarcely less specious than the inspirational and special creation theories. All alike have been overthrown by the careful studies made by scholars of the document itself and of the history of the colonies before its adoption, and by the development of other branches of knowledge.

One explanation of its progressive origin may be found in the influence on all thought of the modern theory of evolution. The interest in the study of evolution in the world of nature has led to the study of developments in all other fields. Applying this to the study of the Constitution and to the conditions under which it was developed, at least three natural sources for it can be found. In the Convention and in the discussion of the ratification by the States, Madison had been unalterably opposed to the idea of a confederacy, since his study of the history of every European confederacy known had shown him that all had fallen a prey to dissension and disintegration, that their evils were obvious, and that these evils were irremediable.

But an additional reason was at hand for rejecting every plan of union based on the confederate idea. This was that in America itself the confederate idea had been in operation, in one form or another, for nearly a hundred and fifty years and that during all this period the tendency had, probably unconsciously but none the less surely and inevitably, been away from a confederacy and in the direction of "a still more perfect union." In the very beginning the colonies along the Atlantic Coast were confronted by "a situation, not a theory." This was the fact of their isolation in the new world, far removed from the mother country, and their consequent danger from foreign foes and from the Indians. This led them to draw more closely together and to form one after another a series of brief, imperfect, sometimes only theoretical unions, that have collectively been called "early impulses to national unity."

These "impulses," however, took on very concrete forms. As early as 1643, scarcely more than twenty years after the first New England colony had been settled, four of the eight New England colonies united to form the New England Confederation that lasted in effect for twenty, and in name for forty, years. The immediate occasion for its formation was, in the words of the document itself, that "whereas by our settling, by a wise providence of God, we are further dispersed upon the sea coasts and rivers than was at first intended, so that we can not, according to our desire, with convenience communicate in one government and jurisdiction: and whereas we live encompassed with people of several nations and strange languages, which hereafter may prove injurious to us or our posterity; and for as much as the natives have formerly committed sundry insolences and outrages upon several plantations of the English, and have of late combined themselves against us, and seeing by reason of the sad distractions in England, (which they have heard of), and by which they know we are hindered both from that humble way of seeking advice, and reaping those comfortable fruits of protection, which at other times we might well expect; we therefore do conceive it our bounden duty, without delay, to enter into a present consociation amongst ourselves for mutual help and strength in all future concernments." Thus was formed the association of Massachusetts Bay, Plymouth, Connecticut, and New Haven, known by those forming it as the United Colonies of New England. But it is significant that the union was incomplete, since the other four New England colonies were not invited to join it. Governor Winthrop of Massachusetts Bay explained that the jurisdictions of Sir Ferdinando Gorges beyond the Pascataqua "were not received nor called into the confederation, because they ran a different course from us both in their ministry and civil administration; for they had lately made Agamenticus (a poor village) a corporation, and had made a taylor their mayor, and had entertained one Hull, an excommunicated person and very contentious, for their minister." As for the Providence Plantations and Rhode Island, Governor Bradford of Plymouth had already written Governor Bellingham of Massachusetts, "Concerning the Islanders, we have no conversing with them, nor desire to have, further than necessity or humanity may require."

The New England Confederation thus took shape consisting of four small colonies, similar, though not identical, in their political and ecclesiastical organization. An analysis of the Articles that cemented this union shows very clearly that both the confederate and the national ideas were found in them, but the confederate idea occupied the foreground; it was an inorganic union with only the germs of nationality present. Every precaution was taken to prevent any colony from having any advantage over any other — the meeting place of the Commissioners was to be migratory; the chairman of the meeting was to be selected by the Commissioners, but was to be "invested with no such power or respect, as by which he shall hinder the propounding or progress of any business, or in any way cast the scales otherwise than in the preceding article is agreed"; the local government of each colony was to be preserved; colonial boundary lines were to remain unchanged; two colonies were not to unite without the consent of the others; the colonies were to have equal representation, irrespective of size, population, or wealth, though the burdens of war, both in men and in expense, were to be borne proportionately, not equally; there was to be no executive head and no judicial department, and fugitives from service and from justice were to be delivered up under carefully regulated provisions. The Confederacy was a purely defensive alliance, and scarcely even a grudging recognition was given of their mutual concerns apart from this single idea of defense. It served a temporary purpose, it inevitably languished, and it finally disintegrated with the union of Connecticut and New Haven under a common charter.

But the New England Confederation had in the very fact of its formation made a distinct contribution to the future formation of the more perfect union. Penn's Plan of Union in 1697, although a union on paper only, was a definite advance over its predecessor. It had a constructive purpose — it was to be formed that it "may be made more useful both to the Crowne and one another's peace and safety with an universall concurrence," and one of the specific ways named for accomplishing this was "to prevent or cure injuries in point of commerce." It was to be a union of all the colonies, not of an exclusive few; it provided for the germ of an executive department in the person of the King's Commissioner, and since he would probably be the Governor of New York, New York was, for that reason as well as for its central location, suggested as the permanent meeting place.

Penn's Plan of Union was similar to the New England Confederation in that it provided for a legislative department of one house, for equal representation of all the colonies, for annual meetings of the legislature, and for the return of fugitives from justice. It was to be a union still based on the confederate idea, but the germs of nationality were beginning to show life. The Plan existed only on paper, but it represents a definite development over the New England Confederation. It was followed by several other plans suggested both by the colonies and by England "looking toward some kind of a defensive union among the English colonies against the aggressions of the French," but the only one that was constructively worked out was the Albany Plan of 1754 largely formulated by Franklin.

The Albany Plan in turn marked a still greater development in political thought over that of its predecessors. It provided for a Grand Council to be chosen by the legislatures of the several colonies, the number from each to range from two to seven and to be determined by the proportion of the contribution made to the general treasury by each colony. The term of office was fixed at three years, sessions were to be held annually, and the members were to receive a stated per diem wage and also mileage. A genuine executive department was constituted with a President-General, appointed by the Crown, whose assent to all acts of the Grand Council was necessary and who was to execute all laws. The President-General, with the advice of the Grand Council, was to have power to make treaties with the Indians, to declare war against them, to make peace with them, and to purchase land from them; to make and to govern new settlements; to raise and equip troops; to levy taxes; and to make appropriations.

It is at once apparent that the Albany Plan provided for a genuine union of all the colonies, with a legislative department having enlarged constructive powers, and for an independent executive also having expanding constructive powers, while the local colonial element was duly recognized and maintained. The Albany Plan records still a conflict between the principles of nationality and of confederation, but the contest was turning in favor of nationality. But unhappily, the plan, while accepted by all the members of the Albany Conference, was voted down by every colonial assembly, in some, without even being discussed. It was opposed by some because the President-General was to be appointed by the Crown and was given so much authority. The Board of Trade on its part sent it to the King without recommendation and thereby rejected it; probably it disapproved the extensive powers proposed for the legislative body of the united colonies — Franklin himself had said that the plan was not altogether to his mind. Later, after talking it over with Governor Shirley of Massachusetts, his conclusion was that "the different and contrary reasons of dislike to my plan make me suspect that it was really the true medium; and I am still of the opinion it would have been happy for both sides of the water if it had been adopted." Both the colonies and England were clearly afraid to take a step in advance and thereby endanger the position already held.

The Stamp Act Congress of 1765 formulated no plan for a permanent theoretical union, but, in the very act of assembling, it achieved an actual temporary union. The tendencies towards a union of all the colonies were slowly maturing. The idea had been given actual concrete form in the New England Confederation and it had grown with every succeeding plan of union proposed. It had been fostered by a common nationality, common traditions, political institutions, and literature; by distance from England and by the exclusion of France from the continent; and by the common dangers from the Indians and the French. But mutual jealousies and lack of a common cause held the balance even between the tendencies towards and away from permanent union, — the separation from England finally turned the scale in favor of union.

But the question then arose, Under which flag, confederacy or nationality? For there was no thought of continuing a separate independent existence on the part of the thirteen colonies. At the very time that the Continental Congress appointed a committee to report concerning the advisability of recommending independence from England, it also appointed another committee to present a plan of union to be considered if the decision for separation was made. The Articles of Confederation were the result of the deliberations of this second committee. The character of the document is indicated by its name. In spite of a very obvious advance over previous forms of union that had been carried into effect or proposed, the Articles of Confederation were destined to be the last plan as yet made in this country that embraced all the States, and that was founded on the confederate idea.

The States endured them impatiently for a brief period and then discarded them for the Constitution that embodied the progressive idea of nationality.

Was the Constitution "struck off at a given time by the brain and purpose of man"? Assuredly not! For a century and a half, the colonies had experimented with the opposing principles of confederacy and of nationality, and the result alike of experiment, theory, and conditions had ultimately been in favor of nationality.

But experience in union had not been the only influence at work that had determined the nature of the Constitution. Out of the charters under which the colonies had been settled, the colonists had worked out their local governments that were adapted to their own special needs, even their own special whims. When the separation from England was effected, the Continental Congress recommended to the colonies that they should form state constitutions — a simple matter since the charters were at hand and with a few verbal changes they blossomed out into ready-to-wear state constitutions. When the Federal Constitution was under consideration in the Philadelphia Convention, all the thirteen states had their own individual constitutions, comprising legislative, executive, and judicial departments. Their local legislative bodies might have one or two houses, these houses might bear any name the particular State chose to give, the members might be elected in any way agreeable to the State, and have any length of term, as well as any qualifications deemed suitable, and also be assigned such special or collective functions as seemed desirable to the citizens. The chief state executive might be a governor, a president, or a president and an executive council; he might have a term of one, two, or three years; he might be chosen by direct or indirect election; and his powers were such as the States chose to give him. In a similar way the judicial department in each state was such as the State had chosen for itself. The States had also had their own bills of rights; in eleven, freedom of religion had been guaranteed; in nine, freedom of the press; in seven, freedom of the right of petition; in five, freedom from quartering of troops; each and every personal right guaranteed had presumably grown out of some conspicuous violation of that right in the past or from some insistent advocacy of it.

All of these provisions of the state constitutions found in 1787 had been matters of evolution, — they had grown out of the early charters granted by the Crown to the chartered companies. Since these were intermediary steps in the development of the constitution, it is necessary to consider them briefly, especially the relations between the chartered companies and the settlers who came out under their auspices.

The theory of the ownership of newly discovered or conquered territory has always been a simple one, — it belongs to the Crown to be disposed of according to his own best judgment. But the difficulties of administering remote lands by the king in person have been insuperable, and since the early years of the seventeenth century a general process of development has been followed.

The first stage has been the exaggerated reports of the wealth of the country brought back by the first discoverers and adventurers — reports industriously circulated by friends and neighbors, reproduced in current drama and poem and finally reaching fabulous proportions.

It is but natural that the second step has been the formation of a stock company to exploit the new lands. Since the king himself has been unable to take immediate advantage of the reputed wealth laid at his feet, he has given an attentive ear to those who have asked the privilege of exploiting the new fields in his name. Thus the chartered company has been formed — a small group of men have subscribed stock and received a general charter of incorporation from the crown. The charter has secured certain privileges to the authority granting it, while conferring still greater ones on those receiving it. Thus have been formed all the great chartered companies of the past three hundred years. Nor has this manner of developing a new country been peculiar to any one nation. England, Holland, France, and Denmark, all chartered companies to trade with the East Indies during the seventeenth century. The English Crown chartered the London Company with a dual organization entitling it to trade in Virginia and in Plymouth; the States of Holland chartered the Dutch West India Company to trade in America; Sweden incorporated the South Company to develop its possessions on the Delaware; Spain granted the Chartered Company of Seville a monopoly of the American trade. Country after country has begun in a similar way the development of its newly acquired lands. Trade has come first, but settlements have followed hard in the wake.

The objects of the colonists sent out under the chartered companies were various, — they came for religious freedom, or for political freedom, or for personal wealth, or to escape from adverse economic or social conditions at home. But the object of the chartered company has everywhere and at all times, irrespective of time, place, or nationality, been the same, — it has been to seek wealth for itself primarily through trade, while the settlement of the territory has been a secondary consideration.

The Chartered Company, with trade as its primary object, has not concerned itself too closely with the character of the colonists settling under its protection and it has cared little about the objects that have led the colonists to seek a new home. It has sent out vagrants, debtors, and criminals, as well as political refugees and religious zealots; it has encouraged gentlemen of leisure and others of no occupation, as well as men skilled in various forms of industry. Is it strange that the Chartered Company has never been successful as a colonizer?

Yet we must remember the difficulties that have beset the Chartered Company. Its task has been a twofold one. It has had in the first place to secure as many privileges for itself as could be wrested from the Crown. These have generally concerned the right of governing the colony, freedom of trade, a definitely stated share of the mineral wealth of the colony, and similar privileges.

But the task of the Chartered Company was but half accomplished when it had secured a definite statement under the great seal of its own relation to the Crown. There remained the even harder task of arranging the inducement to be held out to prospective colonists. In some cases, as in Virginia, settlers were induced to come out through the offer of passage money to be redeemed by service. Others, as in Plymouth, were offered a part of the proceeds of the venture. The Georgia Company promised freedom from past debts. Massachusetts Bay held out the promise of freedom from the forms of religious worship established in England. The Dutch West India Company offered large tracts of land. But in every case the Company reserved for itself directly, and for the Crown indirectly, the internal and external management of the colony established under its patronage.

The colony might, as in Virginia, elect representatives to a colonial assembly, but it was the Chartered Company that gave the privilege. It might choose its own executive officers, but this favor was due to the Chartered Company. If religious freedom was assured, it was at the hand of the Company. If the "concessions and agreements" virtually gave to the colonists the absolute right of self-government, it was the result of a self-denying ordinance on the part of the body standing as an intermediary between the Crown and the colonists. Thus it was to a chartered trading company that Virginia and New England had been granted; Maryland, the Carolinas, and Pennsylvania had served to balance her cash account with various English capitalists; New York and New Jersey had been won from her most formidable rival. Feudalism was resuscitated and given a new lease of life in the proprietary grants of Maryland and Pennsylvania; absolutism set its mark on the early royal provincial governments of Virginia and the Carolinas, while the principles of the purest democracy received sanction within limited circles in New England. The instincts of the colonists brought order out of the political chaos and made in each State something of a miniature copy of the English government. Theories yielded to the necessities of practical conditions and inherited traditions proved stronger than abstract plans.

It was assuredly to the credit of the members of the Philadelphia Convention that they did not undertake the creation of a new constitution, as the French were attempting to do at practically the same time, but that they took the material at hand and made an application of it to the enlarging conditions of the new nation. This material was, as has been seen, their own experiences in forming their own colonial governments under the provisions of the colonial charters granted them and the transformation of these colonial governments into state governments, when they acted on the advice given them by the Continental Congress; the tentative plans of union that covered nearly one hundred and fifty years prior to the meeting of the

Philadelphia Convention; and their general familiarity with the English Constitution and English political procedure. These three lines of development converged in 1787 and the Federal Constitution resulted. If into that document there went the experience of European countries that had experimented with the confederate idea as that idea had filtered to the Convention through Madison's studies made in preparation for its convening; if some acquaintance with French political theories and French political philosophy had permeated the Convention through the correspondence of Jefferson, then representing the country in France, with Madison, the guiding genius of the Convention; if a brief residence in Holland of five score Pilgrims had introduced them to political methods and customs foreign to English habits—all of these exotic conditions and theories were but as a perfume that permeated the document but in no way affected its fundamental nature, modified its stature, or changed materially its tendencies. In the reasoned words of George William Curtis, "Our Constitution is not an inspiration but an application."

Notes

Introduction

1. Frank Lyman to Lucy Maynard Salmon, December 19, 1907, Lucy Maynard Salmon Papers, Vassar College, Special Collections, box 5.2.

2. For details of Salmon's life we rely on Louise Fargo Brown, *Apostle of Democracy: The Life of Lucy Maynard Salmon* (New York: Macmillan, 1943), and on the extensive Salmon papers in the Vassar College Special Collections.

3. Brown, *Apostle of Democracy*, 50.

4. Salmon to Edith Rickert, June 22, 1910, Salmon Papers, box 49.3.

5. Salmon to R. S. Baker, January 6, 1926, Salmon Papers, box 58.18. On women as college and university students see Helen Lefkowitz Horowitz, *Campus Life: Undergraduate Cultures from the End of the Eighteenth Century to the Present* (Chicago: University of Chicago Press, 1988); Helen Lefkowitz Horowitz, *Alma Mater: Design and Experience in the Women's Colleges from Their Nineteenth-Century Beginnings to the 1930s* (New York: Knopf, 1984); Lynn D. Gordon, *Gender and Higher Education in the Progressive Era* (New Haven: Yale University Press, 1990); and Barbara Miller Solomon, *In the Company of Educated Women: A History of Women and Higher Education in America* (New Haven: Yale University Press, 1985). On M. Carey Thomas of Bryn Mawr, on whom Salmon had decided opinions, see Helen Lefkowitz Horowitz, *The Power and the Passion of M. Carey Thomas* (New York: Knopf, 1994), and Marjorie Housepian Dobkin, *The Making of a Feminist: Early Journals and Letters of M. Carey Thomas* (Kent, Ohio: Kent State University Press, 1979).

6. Salmon, "History of the Appointing Power of the President," *American Historical Association Papers* 1 (1884): 291–419.

7. Quoted in a letter from Thomas Updegraff, House of Representatives, January 9, 1984, Salmon Papers, box 47.29. The review in *Harper's* is quoted in Brown, *Apostle*, 98.

8. Salmon, "History of the Appointing Power of the President," 403.

9. Salmon, "History of the Appointing Power of the President," 403.

10. On the American Association of University Women see Susan Levine, *Degrees of Equality: the American Association of University Women and the Challenge of Twentieth-Century Feminism* (Philadelphia: Temple University Press, 1995).

On women in the American Historical Association at the time see Jacqueline Goggin, "Challenging Sexual Discrimination in the Historical Profession: Women Historians and the American Historical Association, 1890–1940," *American Historical Review*, 97, no. 3 (June 1992): 769–802. On Salmon's relationship with the Committee of Seven and the American Historical Association, see Salmon Papers, which include many letters from leaders of the profession. See Peter Novick, *That Noble Dream: The "Objectivity" Question and the American Historical Association* (Cambridge: Cambridge University Press, 1988).

11. Caroline Ware, public discussion, Evalyn A. Clark Conference, October 12, 1984. Among the various works on the reform spirit of the times, see Kathryn Kish Sklar, *Florence Kelley and the Nation's Work: The Rise of Women's Political Culture, 1830–1900* (New Haven: Yale University Press, 1995); Eileen Yeo, *The Contest for Social Science: Relations and Representations of Gender and Class* (London: Rivers Oram, 1996); Ellen Fitzpatrick, *Endless Crusade: Women Social Scientists and Progressive Reform* (New York: Oxford University Press, 1990); Evelyn Brooks Higgenbotham, *Righteous Discontent: The Women's Movement in the Black Baptist Church, 1880–1920* (Cambridge: Harvard University Press, 1993); Martin Bulmer, Kevin Bales, and Kathryn Kish Sklar, eds., *The Social Survey in Historical Perspective* (Cambridge: Cambridge University Press, 1991).

12. Unsigned, *Nation*, April 1, 1897, 250. See the reviews of the first edition by Roland P. Falker in *Annals of the American Academy of Political and Social Sciences* 10 (1897): 112–13; C. R. Henderson in *American Journal of Sociology* 3 (1897–98): 114–15; M. Simiand in *Année Sociologique* 2 (1897–98): 484–86; Marion Talbot in *Journal of Political Economy* 5 (1896–97): 397–99.

13. A bone-headed reviewer in the *Nation* concluded his review by pompously restating this position: "Upon the whole, when we review the prodigious improvement in the condition of the serving class that has taken place within the space of a few generations, we may well feel that the problem of domestic service, from the point of view either of mistress or of servant, has lost most of its terrors, and may be left to work itself out under the influence of mutual forbearance and good will."

14. Salmon, *Domestic Service*, 169.

15. Salmon, *Domestic Service*, 186–93. In this respect her conclusions were at odds with the proposals of the noted Vassar graduate Ellen Swallow Richards, whose sponsorship of cooperative kitchens was well known. See Caroline L. Hunt, *The Life of Ellen H. Richards, 1842–1911* (Washington, D.C.: American Home Economics Association, 1958), 121–31.

16. Talbot, *Journal of Political Economy* 5 (1896–97): 399. Talbot was dean of women at the University of Chicago.

17. On the transformations in household service, see Faye Dudden, *Serving Women: Household Service in Nineteenth-Century America* (Middletown, Conn.: Wesleyan University Press, 1983).

18. Andrew Dickson White, a leading scientific historian, was not immune from the hysteria surrounding the subject. In a letter to Salmon, complimenting her on the work, he went on to demonstrate how feverish interpretation of the problems of household help might be. "I have a strong suspicion that the lack of household aid is one of the causes why such great numbers of American women are to be found in our lunatic asylums and in the ranks of chronic invalidism." White to Salmon, May 1, 1897, Salmon Papers, box 47.30. For the variety of solutions to the "servant problem," see Dolores Hayden, *The Grand Domestic Revolution: A History of Feminist Designs for American Homes, Neighborhoods, and Cities* (Cambridge: MIT Press, 1981).

19. *Evening Transcript*, September 11, 1897, Salmon Papers, box 49.

20. Letter from Harriet M. Scott, Pasadena, California, January 22, 1902, Salmon Papers, box 47.27. Another admirer was Andrew Dickson White at Cornell University, who wrote May 1, 1897: "You are not quite so much a stranger to me or to Mrs. White as you may suppose, for we have lately been reading with especial interest your book on the great 'help' question. It seems to me excellent, and I hope that, what-

ever other fields you may enter, you will not neglect this in which you have done so well," Salmon Papers, box 47.30.

21. Salmon to Adelaide Underhill, August 5, 1900, Salmon Papers, box 45.15.

On the tenor of life among faculty at women's colleges see Patricia Palmieri, *In Adamless Eden: The Community of Women Faculty at Wellesley* (New Haven: Yale University Press, 1995); on the lives of single women, Martha Vicinus, *Independent Women: Work and Community for Single Women, 1850–1920* (Chicago: University of Chicago Press, 1985); on women intellectuals of Salmon's time, Rosalind Rosenberg, *Beyond Separate Spheres: Intellectual Roots of Modern Feminism* (New Haven: Yale University Press, 1982).

22. This account is constructed from Salmon's letters to Underhill between 1898 and 1900, Salmon Papers, box 45. Not all letters to Underhill are in this file. Some were extracted by Louise Fargo Brown for her biography and are either filed elsewhere in the collection or are missing.

23. Salmon to Underhill, March 9, 1899, quoted in Brown, *Apostle of Democracy*, 153.

24. Salmon to Underhill, August 5, 1900, Salmon Papers, box 45.15.

25. Salmon to Underhill, March 17, 1900, Salmon Papers, box 45.15.

26. Salmon to Underhill, August 23, 1900, quoted in Brown, *Apostle of Democracy*, 180.

27. For one understanding of an object-based epistemology, see Steven Conn, *Museums and American Intellectual Life, 1876–1926* (Chicago: University of Chicago Press, 1998), 3–31. We thank Karen Lucic for this reference.

28. Salmon to Underhill, January 1, 1903, June 1904, December 23, 1904, Salmon Papers, box 45.18.

29. "Housekeeping," 1901, manuscript in Salmon Papers, box 58.45.

30. Lucy Maynard Salmon, "Philosophy, Art, and Sense for the Kitchen," *Craftsman* 10 (1906): 811–17, later published as "Our Kitchen," in *Progress in the Household* (Boston, 1906).

31. Frank Lloyd Wright, "The Art and Craft of the Machine," lecture of March 1901 at Hull House, Chicago. Reprinted in *Frank Lloyd Wright: Writings and Buildings*, ed. Edgar Kaufmann and Ben Raeburn (New York: Meridian, 1960), 55–73.

32. Salmon to Mercer Kendig, January 14, 1914, Salmon Papers, box 4.7.

33. Lucy Maynard Salmon, "College Government," *Vassar Miscellany* 24 (1895): 159.

34. Lucy Maynard Salmon, "Lydia Booth," *Vassar Miscellany* 25 (1896): 159.

35. James Monroe Taylor to Salmon, December 12, 1900, Salmon Papers, box 9.1.

36. Salmon, "The Environment of Vassar College. History," *Vassar Miscellany*, May 1970, 385–90.

37. Violet Barbour to Salmon, September 5, 1914, Salmon Papers, box 5.11.

38. "Training and Observation Through the Study of History," lecture, Salmon Papers, box 56.6.

39. See Salmon Papers, boxes 54–56 (laundry lists).

40. These testimonials were presented at the Evalyn A. Clark symposium at Vassar College in October 12, 1985. See also Beatrice Bishop Berle, *A Life in Two Worlds* (New York: Walker, 1983). Historian J. B. Ross also testified to Salmon's teaching methods in several interviews in 1986.

41. Louise Fargo Brown published a series of examination papers, 1907–26, in *Apostle of Democracy*, 279–92.

42. Gertrude Mason to Salmon, quoted in Brown, *Apostle of Democracy*, 213 (original not found in archives).

43. Both were reprinted posthumously in her book *Historical Material* (New York: Oxford University Press, 1933).

44. An interesting comparison is James Russell Lowell's "My Garden Acquaintance" (1869) in which the approach to nature is mediated by a book (Gilbert White's *Natural History of Selborne*). Lowell, "My Garden Acquaintance," in *The Complete Writings of James Russell Lowell*, 16 vols. (Cambridge: Riverside Press, 1904), 1: 259–90.

45. John Ruskin, *The Nature of Gothic* (London: George Allen, 1892), 6–7; Wright, "The Art and Craft of the Machine."

46. See Sigmund Freud, *Civilization and Its Discontent*, 16–17.

47. J. B. Jackson, *Discovering the Vernacular Landscape* (New Haven: Yale University Press, 1984).

48. Quoted in Brown, *Apostle of Democracy*, 69.

49. Ruskin, *The Nature of Gothic*, 53.

50. "The variety of historical evidence is nearly infinite. Everything that a man says or writes, everything that he makes, everything he touches can and ought to teach us about him." Marc Bloch, *The Historian's Craft* (New York: Vintage Books, 1953), 66. See also Gaston Bachelard, *La Poétique de l'espace*, 4th ed. (Paris: Quadrige, 1989).

51. See, for example, the section of *Leaves of Grass* entitled "Faces," though it has the fragmented quality of the stream-of-consciousness that one finds in the work of Gertrude Stein or James Joyce.

52. William James, "Pragmatism: A New Name for Some Old Ways of Thinking," in *Writings, 1902–1910*, ed. Bruce Kuklick (New York: Library of America, 1987), 495. We do not know whether Salmon read James, but the connection between her writings and pragmatism is suggestive. See Charlene Haddock Seigfried, *Reweaving the Social Fabric: Pragmatism and Feminism* (Chicago: University of Chicago Press, 1996). Seigfried does not mention Salmon.

53. Novick, *That Noble Dream*.

54. John Bach McMaster, *A History of the People of the United States from the Revolution to the Civil War* (New York: D. Appleton, 1884), 1:1. The series was promised in five volumes but ran to eight.

55. James Harvey Robinson, *The New History* (New York: Macmillan, 1912), 52. Robinson's essays had appeared starting at the turn of the century in journals. In book form, as *The New History*, they had considerable influence.

56. Robinson, *The New History*, 139. Such discussions in historical circles resonate much later in the history of architecture. See Sigfried Giedion, *Mechanization Takes Command: A Contribution to Anonymous History* (New York: Oxford University Press, 1948).

57. Robinson, *The New History*, 48. On "amateurism," see Bonnie G. Smith, "High Amateurism and the Panoramic Past," chap. 6 in *The Gender of History: Men, Women, and Historical Practice* (Cambridge: Harvard University Press, 1998).

58. Novick, *That Noble Dream*, chap. 4.

59. Robinson, *The New History*, 70.

60. Salmon, *Why Is History Rewritten?* (New York: Oxford University Press, 1929), 201.

61. Miscellaneous note, Salmon Papers, box 58.32.

62. This correspondence all appears in Salmon Papers, box 49.

63. Salmon, *The Newspaper and the Historian* (New York: Oxford University Press, 1923), v.

64. Salmon, *The Newspaper and Authority* (New York: Oxford University Press, 1923), v. For scientific history, association with the newspaper represented precisely what was wrong about earlier historical studies. The classicist Heinrich Nissen, for

example, in his study of Livy published in 1863 argued that "ancient historians had normally not worked like modern historians but like modern journalists." Quoted in Anthony Grafton, *The Footnote: A Curious History* (Cambridge: Harvard University Press, 1997), 58. In the early twentieth century, however, historians had become more interested in the newspaper as a source for historical writing, and in 1908 a session at the annual meeting of the American Historical Association was given over to the topic. Salmon, *Newspaper and the Historian*, xli.

65. Salmon, *Newspaper and the Historian*, 470.

66. On women and the press in nineteenth-century America, see Thomas C. Leonard, *News for All: America's Coming-of-Age with the Press* (New York: Oxford University Press, 1995), 21–31.

67. Brown, *Apostle of Democracy*, and Salmon Papers, which contain various folders on William and alcoholism.

68. Salmon, "A Museum of Vassar College," *Vassar Miscellany*, November 1911, 43–46. It is interesting to compare this proposal with the original "Report of the Committee on the Art Gallery of Vassar Female College, 1864," which foresaw a more conventional fine arts museum for Vassar that would be "the innermost shrine of purest incentive and most graceful refinement." This museum would be "an influence for good" that would "emanate to the boundaries of lofty culture everywhere" (xiii). Salmon remained interested in the idea of the history museum as revealed in her letter to the editor, entitled "Historical Museum Needed: Record of a Nation's Growth Should Be Preserved for All to See as Well as Read." *New York Times*, June 6, 1926.

69. Quoted in Conn, *Museums and American Intellectual Life*, 167.

70. See J. C. Dana, "The Little Red School House, an Exhibit and a Museum," *Museum* 1, no. 1 (1917): 4–7; on "the kitchen" see Alice W. Kendall, "A Year's Work of the Newark Museum Association," 20–26.

71. This interpretation, derived in part from Yve-Alain Bois and Rosalind E. Krauss, *Formless: A User's Guide* (New York: Zone Books, 1997), puts Salmon intellectually in line with such contemporaries as Marcel Duchamp.

72. Salmon to Underhill, March 17, 1900, Salmon Papers, box 45.15.

73. See especially Underhill's correspondence over these two volumes with editors at Oxford University Press, Salmon Papers, box 49.1. Widely reviewed, the books were also excerpted in *Reader's Digest*.

74. We have chosen not to deal with the issue of Lucy Salmon's influence at Vassar; there are others more specialized in the history of the college and its educational practices. Obviously her curricular innovations were evident in the offerings of the history department and practiced in the teaching methods of many of the members of that department. Despite the popularity of Salmon's methods, however, not all history faculty followed them, as her struggles with James Baldwin (hired 1897) reveal. For a discussion of these troubles, see Elizabeth A. Daniels, *Bridges to the World: Henry Noble MacCracken and Vassar College* (Clinton Corners, N.Y.: College Avenue Press, 1994), 59–63. In other departments the principles of direct observation pioneered by Salmon were notably influential. Laura Johnson Wylie (1855–1932), for example, viewed English literature within the context of social history and with her colleague and friend Gertrude Buck (d. 1921) encouraged students "to make use of observational sources in the laboratory of the world off-campus" (Daniels, *Bridges to the World*, 196). Helen Lockwood, too, was a student of Salmon and Wylie and followed many of Salmon's principles in instruction in the English department. Edith Rickert, a much-loved student of Salmon's (English) used many of her teaching methods. On Lockwood, see Alan Simpson, *Helen Lockwood's College Years, 1908–1912* (Poughkeepsie, N.Y.: Vassar College, 1977). On Rickert, see the preface by

Margaret Rickert to the collection of documents, *Chaucer's World* (New York: Columbia University Press, 1948) and many other publications. Evalyn A. Clark (b. 1903), though a student at Vassar while Salmon was still teaching there, did not take courses with her. When she returned to Vassar to teach, however, she became more familiar with Salmon's teaching methods, notably through her colleague and companion Mildred Campbell.

75. For this correspondence between Taylor and Salmon, see Salmon Papers, box 10.5.

Domestic Service Since the Colonial Period

1. A New England woman writes: "In several instances our 'help' was married from our parlor with my sisters for bridesmaids. I correspond with a woman doctor in Florida whose sister was our cook when I was a child, and who shared her sister's room at our home while she earned her education, alternating work in the cotton mills and going to school." This is but one illustration of hundreds that have doubtless come within the experience of most persons living in New England fifty years ago.

2. A visit to many New England burying grounds will illustrate this statement. It was doubtless a survival of the English custom. A curious and interesting collection of epitaphs of servants has been made by Arthur J. Munby, *Faithful Servants: Being Epitaphs and Obituaries Recording Their Names and Services* (London, 1876).

3. "Help, for I love our Yankee word, teaching, as it does, the true relation, and its being equally binding on master and servant." James Russell Lowell, *Letters of James Russell Lowell*, 2 vols., ed. Charles Eliot Norton (New York, 1894), 1:105.

4. Even Americans commented on it. John Watson writes: "One of the remarkable incidents of our republican principles of equality is the hirelings, who in times before the war of Independence were accustomed to accept the names of servants and to be drest according to their condition, will now no longer suffer the former appellation; and all affect the dress and the air, when abroad, of genteeler people than their business warrants. Those, therefore, who from affluence many have dependents, find it a constant subject of perplexity to manage their pride and assumption." — *Annals of Philadelphia* (Philadelphia, 1830), 165.

5. Harriet Martineau, *Autobiography*, 2 vols. (Boston, 1877), 1:331.

6. Harriet Martineau, *Society in America*, 2 vols. (New York, 1837), 2:248.

7. Ibid., 2:245.

8. Ibid., 2:254–55.

It is of interest to contrast this picture of service in America by an Englishwoman with one given a little earlier of service in England by an American. Elkanah Watson writes from London in 1782: "The servants attending upon my friend's table were neatly dressed, and extremely active and adroit in performing their offices, and glided about the room silent and attentive. Their silence was in striking contrast with the volubility of the French attendants, who, to my utter astonishment, I have often observed in France intermingling in the conversation of the table. Here, the servant, however cherished, is held at an awful distance. The English servant is generally an ignorant and servile being, who has no aspiration beyond his present condition." — Elkanah Watson, *Men and Times of the Revolution* (New York, 1857), 169.

9. Alexis De Tocqueville, *Democracy in America*, 2 vols. (New York, 1841), 2:194.

10. Francis J. Grund, *The Americans in Their Moral, Social, and Political Relations*, 2 vols. (Boston, 1837), 236–37.

Thomas Grattan also says, "The native Americans are the best servants in the country." — *Civilized America*, 2 vols. (London, 1859), 1:260.

11. William Cobbett, *A Year's Residence in the United States of America* (London, 1828), 201.

Charles Mackay also says that "service is called 'help,' to avoid wounding the susceptibility of free citizens." — *Life and Liberty in America*, 2 vols. (London, 1859), 1:42.

12. Frances E. M. Trollope, *Domestic Manners of the Americans*, 2 vols. (London, 1832), 1:73.

13. Michel Chevalier, *Society, Manners, and Politics in the United States* (Boston, 1839), 284.

14. He adds the interesting facts that cooks usually received $1.50 per week; chambermaids, $1.25; gardeners, $11 per month, and waiters $10 per month. — Samuel Breck, *Recollections*, ed. Horace E. Scudder (Philadelphia, 1877), 299–300.

15. Isabella Bird, *The Englishwoman in America* (London, 1856), 43, 214.

16. Grattan, *Civilized America*, 1:256–58.

17. Ibid., 1:259.

18. Ibid., 1:264.

19. Ibid., 1:269.

20. Madame Frances Wright D'Arusmont, *Views of Society and Manners in America, 1818–1820, by an Englishwoman* (New York, 1821), 338.

21. Ibid., 338–42.

22. U.S. Treasury Department, *Arrivals of Alien Passengers and Immigrants in the United States from 1820 to 1890* (Washington, D.C., 1893), 16, 23.

By the *Census of Massachusetts* for 1885 it is seen that 49 percent of all women in that state of foreign birth are Irish. *Census for 1885*, 4 vols. (Boston, 1887–88), 1:574–75.

23. Salmon, *Domestic Service*, 11.

24. Lowell says of the Irish immigration, "It is really we who have been paying the rents over there [in Ireland], for we have to pay higher wages for domestic service to meet the drain." — *Letters*, 2:336.

A racy discussion of the influence of the Irish cook in the American household is given by Mr. E. L. Godkin under the title "The Morals and Manners of the Kitchen," in Edwin Lawrence Godkin, *Reflections and Comments, 1865–1895* (New York, 1895), 2:336.

25. *Arrivals of Alien Passengers and Immigrants in the United States from 1820 to 1890*, 15, 22.

26. Women constituted 41.8 per cent of the total number of German immigrants arriving here during the twenty-two years ending June 30, 1890; the Irish forming 48.5 per cent. — Ibid., 11.

27. The United States Census for 1890 gives the number of domestic servants born in Ireland as 168,993; the number born in Germany was 95,007.

28. The number of Chinese in domestic service in 1890 was 16,439.

29. Francis A. Walker, *The Wages Question* (New York, 1886), 376–77.

30. An illustration of these various changes is seen in the case of one employee, who was born in Ireland, engaged in service in New York, and afterwards drifted to Minnesota, where the report was made.

31. This is indicated by the various definitions given in early dictionaries. It is a curious fact that *The New World of Words or General English Dictionary*, large quarto, 3d ed., London, 1671, does not contain the word *servant*. Phillips's *Universal English Dictionary*, London, 1720, has "*servant*, a man or woman who serves another." Bailey's *Dictionary*, London, 1721, 1737, and 1770, defines *servant* as "one who serves another." *The Royal Standard English Dictionary*, 1st American ed., Worcester, Massachusetts, 1788, "being the first work of the kind printed in America," defines *servant* as "one who serves." The second edition, Brookfield, 1804, has "*servant*, one who serves for wages."

Some interesting illustrations of this early use of the word are found in colonial literature. Thus Thomas Morton in his *New English Canaan* (Boston, 1883), 179, says, "In the month of June Anno Salutis, 1622, it was my chance to arrive in the parts of New England with thirty servants and provisions of all sorts fit for a plantation."

Governor Bradford in his *History of Plymouth*, 235–36, speaks of "Captaine Wolastone and with him 3. or 4. more of some eminencie, who brought with them a great many servants, with provisions & other implments fit for to begine a plantation." — William Bradford, *History of Plymouth Plantation* (Boston, 1856).

A "Narrative concerning the settlement of New England," 1630, says, "This yeare there went hence 6 shippes with 1000 people in them to the Massachusetts having sent two yeares before betweene 3 & 400 servants to provide howses and Corne against theire coming, to the charge of (at least) 10,000*l.*, these Servants through Idlenes & ill Government neglected both theire building & plantinge of Corne, soe that if those 6 Shippes had not arrived the plantation had ben broke & dissolved." — *Massachusetts Historical Society Proceedings*, 31 vols. (Boston, 1859–1896), 1860–62: 130–31.

The same use of the word is found a number of times in the list of the Mayflower passengers.

32. J. F. D. Smith says, "However, although I now call this man (a backwoodsman of the Alleghanies) my servant, yet he himself never would have submitted to such an appellation, although he most readily performed every menial office, and indeed every service I could desire." — *Tour in the United States*, 2 vols. (London, 1784), 1:356.

33. Fanny Kemble writes, "They have no idea, of course, of a white person performing any of the offices of a servant"; then follows an amusing account of her white maid's being taken for the master's wife, and her almost unavailing efforts to correct the mistake. — *Journal of a Residence in Georgia in 1838–39* (New York, 1864), 44–46.

34. An illustration of this change is seen in the different definitions given to the word. In the *Royal Standard English Dictionary*, 1813, a servant is "one who attends and obeys another, one in a state of subjection."

Johnson's *Dictionary*, London, 1818, gives "(1) One who attends another and acts at his command; the correlative of master. Used of man or woman. (2) One in a state of subjection."

Richardson's *New Dictionary of the English Language*, London, 1838, defines *servant* as the correlative of *master*.

The American usage was practically the same. The first edition of Webster, 1828, gives "(1) Servant, a person, male or female, that attends another for the purpose of performing menial offices for him, or who is employed by another for such offices, or for other labor, and is subject to his command. *Servant* differs from *slave*, as the servant's subjection to a master is voluntary, the slave's is not. Every slave is a servant, but every servant is not a slave."

Worcester, 1860, says of *servant*: "(1) One who serves, whether male or female; correlative of *master, mistress*, or *employer*. (2) One in a state of subjection; a menial; a domestic; a drudge; a slave."

These various definitions all suggest the class association of the terms *servant* and *slave*.

35. A curious illustration of the social position of servants in Europe is seen in their lack of political privileges.

The French Constitution of 1791 was preceded by a bill of rights declaring the equality and brotherhood of men, but a disqualification for the right of suffrage, indeed, the only one, was "to be in a menial capacity, *viz.*, that of a servant receiving wages." Title III., chap. 1, sec. 2. The Constitution of 1795, after a similar preamble, states that the citizenship is suspended "by being a domestic on wages, attending on the person or serving the house." Title II., 13, 3. The Constitution of 1799 has a similar disqualification. Title I. art. 5. It is probable that these provisions were intended to punish men who would consent to serve the nobility or the wealthy classes when it was expected that all persons would be democratic enough to serve themselves, not to cast discredit on domestic service per se. — L. Tripier, *Constitutions qui ont regi la France depuis 1789* (Paris, 1879), 20, 105, 168.

During the revolutionary movement in Austria, the Hungarian Diet at its session, in 1847–48, passed an act providing that the qualification for electors should be "to have attained the age of twenty years; Hungarians by birth or naturalized; not under guardianship, nor in domestic service, nor convicted of fraud, theft, murder, etc." Act 5, sec. 2. — William H. Stiles, *Austria in 1848–49*, 2 vols. (New York, 1852), 2:376.

The qualifications for suffrage in England also excluded domestic servants, but there was no discrimination against them as a class.

The Declaration of Independence, declaring all men free and equal in the presence of African slavery, thus has its counterpart in these free constitutions disfranchising domestic servants.

Possible Remedies: Specialization of Household Employments

1. Salmon, *Domestic Service*, chap. 2.

2. This does not refer to ordinary baker's bread, but to that made according to scientific principles, such as is sold at the New England Kitchen in Boston and by the Boston Health Food Company.

3. A beginning in this direction has already been made in the case of vegetables canned for winter use. In the canning factories of Western New York an ingenious pea huller is in use which does away with much of the laborious process hitherto necessary. In a trial of speed it was recently found that one machine could shell twenty-eight bushels of peas in twenty minutes. In some of the largest cities the principle has been applied, and this vegetable is delivered ready for use; but such preparation should be made universal and all other vegetables added to the list.

4. Cited by Albert S. Bolles, *Industrial History of the United States* (Norwich, Conn., 1879), 413.

5. Ibid., 130.

6. The Oriental Tea Company of Boston sends out coffee and guarantees it to maintain a temperature of 150° Fahrenheit for twenty-four hours. The experiment has been tried of sending it from Boston to St. Louis, with the result of maintaining a temperature of 148° at the end of three days.

7. The women connected with two churches in a city in Indiana have maintained for some time such sales, and they have proved very remunerative. In one city in New Jersey $1,200 was raised in a few weeks to pay a church mortgage. In a Long Island village several hundred dollars was raised for a similar purpose by the women of the church, who took orders for cooking and sewing. In an Iowa city funds were obtained in this way for missionary purposes. In a village of five hundred inhabitants, in Central New York, the women of one of the churches have sold, every Saturday afternoon for eight years, ices and ice-creams, and have cleared annually about seventy-five dollars. In another town, several women of limited incomes began paying their contributions to the church by baking bread and cake for other families, and finding it remunerative continued the work as a means of support. In one Western city an annual sale is held at Thanksgiving time, and about one hundred dollars netted for home missionary purposes.

8. The Woman's Exchange, *Forum*, May 1892.

9. Many illustrations of this can be given outside of those connected with the Exchange:

Mrs. A, in Central New York, has made a handsome living by making chicken salad to be sold in New York City.

Mrs. B, in a small Eastern village, has for several years baked bread, pies, and cake for her neighbors, and in this way has supported herself, three children, and a father. She has recently built a separate bakehouse, and bakes from thirty to one hundred loaves daily, according to the season, and other things in proportion. She says she always had a "knack" at baking, and that when she employs an assistant she has nearly every afternoon to herself.

Mrs. C, in a Western city, supports herself, three children, and an invalid husband by making cake.

Mrs. D makes a good living by selling Saratoga potatoes to grocers.

Mrs. E has cleared $400 a year by making preserves and jellies on private orders.

Mrs. F partially supports herself and family by making food for the sick.

Mrs. G supports a family of five by making jams and pickles.

Mrs. H has built up a large business, employing from three to five assistants, in making cake and salad.

Mrs. I, in a small Eastern city, began by borrowing a barrel of flour, and now has a salesroom where she sells daily from eighty to one hundred dozen Parker House rolls, in addition to bread made in every possible way, from every kind of grain.

Mrs. J, in a small Western city, sells salt-risings bread to the value of $30 a week; and Mrs. K, in the same place, Boston brown bread to the value of $75 a week.

Mrs. L, living on a farm near a Southern city, has built up "an exceedingly remunerative business" by selling to city grocers preserves, pickles, cakes, and pies. "One cause of her success has been the fact that she would allow no imperfect goods to be sold; everything has been of the best whether she has gained or lost on it."

Mrs. M supports herself by taking orders for fancy cooking.

Mrs. N, living in a large city, sells to grocers baked beans and rolls.

Mrs. O, in New York City, has netted $1,000 a year by preparing mince-meat and making pies of every description.

Mrs. P, in a small village on Lake Superior, has large orders from cities in Southern Michigan for strawberry and raspberry jam.

Mrs. Q, in a country village of five hundred inhabitants, sells thirty loaves of bread daily.

Mrs. R and two daughters last year netted $1,500 (above all expenses except house rent) in preparing fancy lunch dishes on shortest notice, and delicacies for invalids.

Mrs. S puts up pure fruit juices and shrubs.

Mrs. T prepares consommé in the form of jelly ready to melt and serve.

Mrs. U has made a fair income by preparing and selling fresh sweet herbs.

These illustrations can be multiplied indefinitely. They have come to notice in nearly every state in the Union, and in places varying in size from country villages without railroad stations to such cities as Chicago, Philadelphia, and New York.

10. Mrs. A has for several years gone from house to house at stated times sweeping and dusting rooms containing fine bric-a-brac.

Mr. B cares for all of the lawns of a large number of gentlemen, each of whom pays him a fixed sum for the season in proportion to the size of his grounds.

Mr. C cares for all of the furnaces and clears the walks in a city block.

Mrs. D earns a partial support by arranging tables for lunches and afternoon teas.

Mrs. E washes windows once in two weeks for a number of employers.

Mrs. F takes charge of all arrangements for afternoon teas.

Mrs. G earns $3 a day as a cook on special occasions.

Miss H waits on a table in a boarding house three hours a day.

Miss I distributes the clothes from the laundry in a large city school.

Mrs. J is kept busy as a cook, serving as a substitute in kitchens temporarily vacant.

Mrs. K derives a considerable income from the supervision of party suppers. "Her social position is quite unaffected by it."

Mrs. L "makes herself generally useful" at the rate of ten cents an hour if regularly employed and twenty cents when serving occasionally.

Mrs. M goes out as a waitress at lunches and dinners.

Mrs. N employs a young man working his way through school to keep wood-boxes and coal-hods filled.

Many college students in cities partially pay their expenses by table service.

Hotels and restaurants frequently send out waiters on special occasions.

One employer writes, "I think a central office in this city at which competent waitresses could be hired by the hour would be largely patronized."

The Syracuse, New York, Household Economic Club publishes a *Household Register*, giving the names and addresses of all persons in the city who do by the piece, hour, or day all forms of household work. Thirty-five different classes of work are enumerated.

11. See also article on the "Revival of Hand Spinning and Weaving in Westmoreland," by Albert Fleming, *Century Magazine*, February 1889.

12. One writes, "I find it much better to employ one servant and to hire work by the piece, and to purchase from the Exchange, rather than to employ an extra servant."

Another housekeeper writes: "I began housekeeping twelve years ago with three servants and had more than enough work for all. I now have two and have not enough work for them, although my family is larger than at first. The change has come from putting work out of the house and hiring much done by the piece."

A business man writes: "Our family is happier than it ever dared hope to be under the sway of Green Erin. We purchase all baked articles and all cooked meats as far as possible. A caterer is employed on special occasions, and work that cannot be done by the parents, three children, and two aunts, who compose the family, is hired by the hour. Since we signed our Declaration of Independence in 1886, peace has reigned."

Still another says: "I used to employ a laundress in the house at $4 per week and board. I was also at expense in furnishing soap, starch, bluing, and paid a large additional water tax. Now my laundress lives at home, and does my laundry there for $4 per week, and we are both better satisfied."

Several small families who do "light housekeeping" have found that they have in this way been able to live near the business of the men of the family, and thus have kept the family united and intact, as they could not have done had it been necessary to employ servants.

One employee writes, "If more housework were done by the day so that more women could be with their families in the evening, I think it would help matters."

Economics and Ethics in Domestic Service

1. *Works of Swift*, 11:365–441.

2. Cited from *Remarks on the Life and Writings of Swift*, 179, in *Works of Swift*, 11:365.

3. Frederic Burk, *Training of Teachers*, October 1897.

The Family Cook-Book

1. The single exception to this somewhat sweeping statement must be made in favor of the remarkable collection of cook-books made by Mrs. Elizabeth Robins Pennell and described by her in *My Cookery Books* (Boston: Houghton Mifflin, 1903).

Main Street

1. I am indebted to Miss M. L. Berkemeier for these suggestions.

The Record of Monuments

1. D. G. Hogarth, ed., *Authority and Archaeology, Sacred and Profane; Essays on the Relation of Monuments to Biblical and Classical Literature* (London, 1899), xiv.

2. The population of Frëjus has been thus computed by Charles Lenthéric in *The Riviera, Ancient and Modern* (London, 1895), 300–301.

3. Many interesting records are found in the difficulty of adapting changes in theological belief or in church ceremonial to a type of architecture preceding the change. In one of the oldest churches in New England the clergyman now wears a robe, but the church has no robing rooms; the architectural choir is often difficult to adapt to the older type of church in which the musical choir was seated in the rear gallery; it is difficult to adapt a church originally built exclusively as a place of worship to the present institutional church.

It is interesting to note the changes recorded when a new church building takes the place of an earlier one on the same site, as in the Madison Square Presbyterian Church, New York City. When a new site is selected, other factors besides change of purpose may enter in. *Cf. Review of Reviews*, 32 (December 1905): 689.

4. It is of interest to note how many external points of resemblance the modern social church bears to the monastic church of the Middle Ages. The session room or vestry room of the one has its counterpart in the chapter house of the other, — the refectory, the infirmary, the cloister, the garden, the rooms in which the industries of the monasteries were carried on, all suggest the architectural features of the social church. Yet the fundamental difference between the two is recorded in the difference in location, — the monastic foundation was in a secluded spot and implied isolation and self-sufficiency; the social church is in the heart of the city and its life goes outward rather than inward.

5. S. O. Addy, *The Evolution of the English House* (London, 1905), 169.

Miss Ruth Putnam gives an interesting illustration of a fortified Burgundian church of the fifteenth century— *Charles the Bold, Last Duke of Burgundy, 1433–1477* (New York, 1908), 382. H. Macmillan notes the frequency of fortified churches on the Riviera. — *The Riviera*, 7.

6. The cathedral of Halle is an interesting illustration.

7. "One Frier taught us at the church-porch of Wotton" —John Evelyn. — *Diary*, ed. William Bray, 4 vols. (London, 1907) 1:4.

8. In St. Clemente, Rome, one church of the twelfth century has been superimposed on one dating as early as the fourth century. St. Stephano, Bologna, consists of seven different edifices.

9. At first the monastery consisted only of cells and an oratory, but later developed every provision for life, including pillories for the punishment of the living and cemeteries for the burial of the dead. — C. A. Cummings, *History of Architecture in Italy from the Time of Constantine to the Dawn of the Renaissance*, 2 vols. (Boston, 1901), 2:133.

10. The church of Or San Michele in Florence was decorated with statues by the twelve guilds. The stained glass windows of the cathedral of Freiburg in Baden were given by different guilds, but although the subjects are religious nearly every window bears the emblem of the guild giving it, as — the pruning knife, the vine dressers; the mill wheel, the millers; a boot, the shoemakers; beer pitchers, the brewers; pretzels, the bakers; the forge and anvil, the blacksmiths; shears, the tailors. The cathedral of Chartres has nearly forty windows given by the guilds, each showing the service performed for the community by a particular trade. The church of La Madeleine, Troyes, has an interesting window given by the Jewellers' Guild.

11. The cathedral of Laon has its belfries adorned with figures of oxen, thus commemorating the services of oxen in drawing the stone for the cathedral from the plain to the summit of the hill that forms the site of the cathedral. On the exterior of Durham the sculptured figure of a cow commemorates the legend that the monks of Lindisfarne were led to the site of the cathedral by a dun cow. As the sculpture, however, is modern this can not strictly be considered an original record, but rather derived history. In many Roman Catholic churches, as in St. Severin, Paris, are hundreds of tablets expressing gratitude not only for the usual reasons of recovery from illness or accidents but for success in passing examinations, thus recording in enduring marble the important place that the examination has in the French educational system.

12. One curious misinterpretation has arisen in the case of churches where the choir is not in the same axis as the nave, as in the cathedral of Erfurt, the church of St. Jean in Troyes, and in numerous other places. The variation is locally explained as due to a desire to symbolize the drooping of the head of Christ on the cross. The real records are much more simple — the variation is due to practical reasons; a chapel was added not quite opposite across the street and therefore it had to slant, a street had to be pushed northward, the cramped nature of the site compelled a deflection, inferior workmanship led to miscalculation, addition of new parts (particularly a larger choir) made a variation necessary, the building of the church stretched over long periods of time and was the work of many hands. The whole subject is discussed by Francis Bond, *Dedications and Patron Saints of English Churches; Ecclesiastical Symbolism; Saints and Their Emblems* (London, 1914), 246–50.

13. Francis Bond in *Fonts and Font Covers* (London, 1908), discusses fully the whole subject of these records. Many representations of baptism are found in frescoes, on sarcophagi, tombstones, chairs, stalls, carved ivories, book covers, and capitals of columns. — Fonts and font covers were often utilized to represent through figure sculpture biblical scenes and religious history. "Its motif was no doubt more religious than artistic; it was an attempt to make intelligible and vivid to all the great realities of the Scriptures and of the histories of the saints and martyrs and doctors of the Church" (247). It is of interest to note that, as Bond has pointed out, "Some time elapsed before the religious changes (of the post-Reformation period) affected the font," 265.

P. M. C. Kermode notes a suggestion that the ancient well at Lonan may have been used for baptism in the transition from the use of living waters to the font. — *Manx Crosses; or, The Inscribed and Sculptured Monuments of the Isle of Man from About the End of the Fifth to the Beginning of the Thirteenth Century* (London, 1907), 104.

14. L. F. Day, *Windows: A Book About Stained and Painted Glass* (London, 1897), 110. The 300 illustrations in this work give opportunity for tracing the change in the subjects chosen from the early geometric and floral designs down to the modern period. — Philip Nelson, *Ancient Painted Glass in England, 1170–1500* (London, 1913), gives an exhaustive catalogue of all ancient painted glass in England and has 67 illustrations.

15. English ecclesiastical buildings show many interesting windows commemorat-

ing military and political events. Gloucester Cathedral has a window erected as a thank-offering for the victory of the English at Crécy. — C. Winston, *Memoirs Illustrative of the Art of Glass-Painting* (London, 1865), 304–6. The abbey church at Tewkesbury shows in the windows of the choir clerestory the knights who were victorious at Crécy.

16. Specially interesting illustrations of this are found in the windows of the Groote Kerk, Gouda. They include scenes from the Old and the New Testament, the Apocrypha, and also such remote scenes as the taking of Dalmatia in Egypt and the relief of Leiden, together with many heraldic emblems. — "In the sixteenth century windows were erected, not so much to the glory of God, as to the glorification of the Donor, who claimed a foremost if not the very central place for himself" — Day, 215. In the early windows the donor was very inconspicuous, sometimes being represented by his patron saint (chapel of Jacques Coeur, Bourges), but later, as in the windows of Ste. Gudule, Brussels, we find "the donor, with attendant angels, on a scale much larger than the rest of the world, competing in fact in importance with the figure of Our Lord in Majesty above." — Ibid., 216. The monarchs of Portugal, Hungary, France, and Austria with their queens are all represented in one chapel of this cathedral while other royal personages are represented in the glass of the high choir. The Church was ceasing to foster art as a means of inculcating its beliefs, and the State was recording through art its growing power and importance.

17. The Adoration of the Magi and the Day of Judgment are not infrequently found; many saints are represented; occasionally an episode from the New Testament is represented; more often scenes from the Old Testament are shown.

18. The caricatures of monks and clergy were apparently personal, not doctrinal. The list of subjects given by E. Phipson, *Choir Stalls and Their Carvings; Examples of Misericords from English Cathedrals and Churches* (London, 1896), 107–18, shows that apparently animals as well as monks were caricatured; combats between different animals are frequently carved; the story of Reineke Fuchs is a favorite one among the wood carvers; retributive justice among animals was a frequent subject — rats hang the cat, geese hang the fox, the hare stews the hound; similarly, women punish their husbands; fabulous creatures are frequent — the basilisk, centaur, griffin, harpy, mermaid, and unicorn; the devil and the whole range of demonology occupy much of the time of the carver. It is interesting to note that these carvings portray the ideas that were common in mediaeval literature, especially in the miracle and the morality plays, and that the same subjects were utilized by the carvers in stone who fashioned gargoyles, capitals of columns, spandrils, and other parts of the building. Whatever the medium employed, the range of subjects was the same throughout the same period.

The wood carver, like all other craftsmen, has represented the interior of his own workshop and shown the carver and his assistants at work.

19. This was executed in 1475 — more than a hundred years before Shakespeare gave us *As You Like It.*

20. R. H. H. Cust, *The Pavement Masters of Siena (1369–1562)* (London, 1901), 54.

21. Ibid., 60. The sack of Otranto, where 1,200 persons were massacred and most of the children sold as slaves, had taken place in 1480; the pavement is dated at 1481.

22. The pavement in Durham cathedral had a blue cross beyond which women were not to go. Slabs in the pavement of the entrance hall of St. Mark's, Venice, commemorate the reconciliation between Frederick Barbarossa and Pope Alexander III, brought about by the Doge of Venice.

23. Christian workmen are traced by their use of the Christian monogram and the symbol of the fish; Saracen patterns are used in Sicily. — M. D. Wyatt, *Specimens of the Geometrical Mosaics of the Middle Ages* (London, 1848), 8, 16.

24. See 18.

25. One illustration of this is found in the mosaic of Burne-Jones in the American Protestant Episcopal Church at Rome. See description in M. Bell's *Sir Edward Burne-Jones* (London, 1904), 83–87, and the artist's own account of his work, *Memorials of Edward Burne-Jones* (London, 1904), by Lady Burne-Jones, vol. 2.

26. B. Berenson, for example, says: "At the beginning of the Renaissance painting was almost wholly confined to the Church. . . . It was almost as cheap as printing has become since, and almost as much employed." — Bernard Berenson, *The Venetian Painters of the Renaissance* (New York, 1897), 26, 27.

27. The use of the cross and the development of the crucifix are important illustrations of the changes that come in religious belief and in its representation in material form. Oscar Montelius has published an elaborate study of the cross from its earliest use down to the present time and the numerous illustrations show the modifications it has undergone. "Solens Hjul och det Kristna Korset," in *Nordisk Tidskrift*, 1904, pts. 1–2. P. M. C. Kermode in *Manx Crosses* gives illustrations of crosses found on the Isle of Man covering a period of more than six centuries. Nearly all of the 171 found are sepulchral rather than architectural crosses. The inscriptions are in Ogam, Latin, and Runes; the art is Celtic and Scandinavian; the symbols are Christian; pagan myths are recorded. These myths are found in the Scandinavian mythology, especially in the older Edda and in the Sagas, and illustrate the stories of Odin, Gunnar, Loki, Thor, Sigurd, and other characters in Norse mythology. Scriptural subjects are few, especially in comparison with the number found on the high crosses of Ireland. The Calf of Man cross is of Byzantine type, Latin in form, with figure draped and without nimbus. It is apparently the only one on the Isle of Man showing the figure of Christ. W. W. Seymour in *The Cross in Tradition, History, and Art* (London 1898) gives 266 illustrations showing that the early representations of the figure on the crucifix show Christ young and beardless, with calm expression not denoting suffering; no nails and no wounds are represented, and the feet are free. Later, the feet are bound, and still later fastened with a nail. In the ninth century the wound appears, in the eleventh the robe becomes shorter and in the fourteenth has become a roll of linen. By the thirteenth century the figure represented a dead rather than a living man, hanging by the hands, with emaciated frame and haggard face, expressing extreme anguish. — The fullest development of the crucifix I have noted is in the Black Forest. C. E. Hughes describes one in the Prechthal that has some 20 different symbols. Roman soldiers on horseback, in the uniform of German cavalrymen, are sometimes found near the crucifix. — *A Book of the Black Forest* (London, 1910), 146, 147. An unusually interesting collection of mediaeval Scandinavian crucifixes is found in the National Museum, Stockholm.

28. Henry Osborn Taylor notes that in the Catacombs of Rome the representations of Noah and the Ark number 26; of Moses smiting the rock, 47; of Daniel among the lions, 32; of Jonas, 45; of Lazarus, 39; and of the Good Shepherd, 85. — *The Classical Heritage of the Middle Ages* (New York, 1911), 319. Painting at this time seemed a means of expressing religious ideas rather than an instrument of teaching religious truth as it was used by the mediaeval Church.

29. Favorite subjects were the martyrdom of St. Sebastian, of St. Lawrence, of St. Stephen, and of St. Peter; all the incidents in the life of Christ that during the mediaeval period expanded greatly the history of the Virgin Mary; the Last Judgment with special emphasis on the punishment of the bad and the rewards awaiting the good.

30. H. H. Cunynghame, *European Enamels* (London, 1906), 41; F. E. Hulme, *The History, Principles, and Practices of Symbolism* (London, 1910), 54–55.

31. It is of interest to note the reflection in architecture of nonparty government

in England. The county councils in their desire to separate local parties from national politics have not only adopted different party names but have provided an entirely different arrangement of seats.

32. It is interesting to note the incorporation in the city halls of France and of Italy of the *salle des mariages*, showing that the control of the institution of marriage has in these countries passed from the Church to the State.

33. S. O. Addy in *The Evolution of the English House* gives a connected account of the development of the house in one country.

Mrs. Valpey Trimple Fore, formerly of Memphis, Tenn., has suggested to me interesting records of the older and more modern southern plantation house. The older plantation house was large enough not only for the family but for relatives and travelling guests. Records of the presence of many slaves were seen in the spring house, the smoke house, the coal house in the yard (showing also lack of cellars), and the general lack of conveniences since abundance of slaves made them unnecessary. The separate detached kitchen led southerners to speak of going "into the house," even when at the north where the kitchen is attached. Houses were built with much room for storage, with high ceilings as a protection from summer heat, and with porches or galleries. The more modern houses are smaller, since better travelling means shorter visits, more attention is paid to conveniences since servants are fewer, there is less need of storeroom since general stores or commissaries provide supplies, and planters often live in town and have managers for their plantations.

34. Langeais, Blois, the Wartburg.

35. Chenonceaux.

36. Loches.

37. Amboise.

38. University of Durham.

39. The advertisements of sets of books frequently state the exact amount of space they occupy.

40. The beamed ceiling was once used in the kitchen because lumber was cheap; it is now used in the living-room, the library, or the dining-room of expensive houses because the cost of lumber makes its use a luxury.

41. The absence of large storeroom[s] and of large crocks and receptacles for both uncooked and cooked food records the small quantities of food kept on hand and the decline in the custom of paying visits unexpectedly; the elimination of washtubs and ironing boards records laundry done out of the house; the large oil can and the lantern have given place to electricity; the absence of large baskets means free delivery and of saws the cutting of all meats in markets. The kitchen has ceased to be the family living-room and dining-room and the center of general household activities, and its reduced size with its glass shelves, linoleum floor, small utensils of aluminum and granite, means compactness, efficiency, sanitation, and cheerfulness. Suggested by G. E. Hull.

One of the most interesting records concerns the kitchen sink. As late as 1901 the standard height was 30 inches; in 1916 it was 32 inches, in 1923 it is "yard high." The plumber as well as the director of athletics records the increasing height of women, and the historian might consider his evidence the more unimpeachable of the two, because unconsciously given.

42. The ground plan and guide book of a great department store show the great expanse of floor space with its record of the expense of elevator service, the dislike of customers of going up and down, and their greater readiness to purchase articles seen rather than those deliberately sought; broad aisles, many outside doors, and many stairways with their records of "safety first"; the luxurious rooms set apart for women customers with their provision for telegraphing, telephoning, posting let-

ters, writing, reading; tea rooms, restaurants, and grills; information bureau, check rooms, lost and found bureau; music rooms and art gallery; repair shops where gloves, shoes, umbrellas, and dresses are repaired "while you wait"; manicuring, hair-dressing, and rest rooms; — every conceivable desire is anticipated and provision made for meeting it, all indicating the great amount of time spent in shopping and the distances travelled to accomplish it. — The provisions made for employees seem quite as adequate, though less luxurious, and they are in the direction of interest in the personal welfare of each. — The ground plan gives a practically complete record of the business tendencies of the day, combining expansion with centralization, perfect system with convenience and efficiency, and the exemplification of the pos-sibility of "keeping the nimble dollar at work."

43. An examination of the plant of a modern city hotel shows that it is a self-contained community, barring the fact that it does not produce the raw materials of consumption, and that it numbers as many inhabitants as a village of 5000. The city hotel is thus comparable to the country village in much the same way that the city institutional church is comparable to the mediaeval monastic foundation.

44. *Third Olynthiac*, Sections 24–29.

45. R. S. Nichols, *English Pleasure Gardens* (New York, 1902), 42.

46. Illustrations of garden accessories suggested by D. Deming.

47. French seeds and cuttings were brought to America by the Huguenot settlers; at Port Royal is a species of willow brought from France and not found elsewhere in America; the Castilian rose is found in California gardens; the Lombardy poplar — the emblem of democracy — was introduced into America in 1798; the opening of Chinese ports in 1843 introduced the dielytra, forsythia, weigelia, and other shrubs; trade with Japan brought the deutzia and the spirea; thistles were taken to Tas-mania by the Scotch; Vancouver's Island is overrun with broom and wild roses taken from England; the ox-eye daisy was introduced into Iowa through freight cars that dropped the seed along railway tracks; "ballast" plants found near the Delaware River came from ballast heaps containing seeds of rare oriental plants; — scores of illustrations of similar exchanges could be given, all yielding records of trade routes.

An interesting illustration of the necessity of testing ocular evidence is given in connection with an artist who went to Greece for local color in painting scenes from the Homeric poems. He painted the cactus, not knowing that it was introduced into Europe after the discovery of America, and had so quickly adapted itself to its new habitat as to seem indigenous. The story is told of different artists in different coun-tries in southern Europe and, while it belongs to the class of "what might have been," it introduces a probable point in historical criticism.

48. Review of Barr Ferree, *American Estates and Gardens*, in *The Nation*, Feb. 23, 1905, 80: 160.

How Far Can the Past Be Reconstructed from the Press?

1. Edward Dicey, "The American Press," *Six Months in the Federal States* (London, 1863), 1:27–50.

2. H. F. Bussey, *Sixty Years of Journalism: Anecdotes and Reminiscences* (Bristol, 1906), preface.

3. "Newspapers as Historical Sources," *Atlantic Monthly*, May 1909, 650–57.

4. Two members of the *Punch* staff have shown the still more extensive use that may be made of *Punch* in reconstructing the past. See F. C. Burnand and A. à Beckett, "History in Punch," *Fortnightly Review*, July–December 1886, 49–67, 737–52, April 1887, 546–57.

5. The *Survey*, July 4, 1914, has an account of Michael Biro, the Hungarian car-

toonist of social unrest. With change of names, this form of illustration is well-nigh universal.

The *Liberator*, 1918–22, has many cartoons of this character.

6. The illustrations of fifty, or even of ten years ago probably show nothing comparable to the exploitation of a child of ten in the collection of money for a battleship.

7. Suggested by E. Coatsworth. — An incidental confirmation is seen in the names given dogs, — Rover, Fido, and Sport are no longer appropriate and such names disappear in favor of fancy names or those taken from popular personages.

8. The advertisements of beef extracts illustrate the bouillon cup; of teas, coffees, and of chocolate preparations the different varieties of cups used with each. Thus through the illustration every person may enter every social circle.

9. Suggested by A. Rogers.

10. Early magazines show initial and marginal decorations of dragons, sea serpents, griffins, and various grotesque animals. *Life* in 1901 shows a mermaid as a collector of water rents, the submarine is an octopus, the devil tortures the beef trust, while later the trusts are represented as a dragon about to devour liberty. In 1905 the devil in Hades caricatures modern society; by 1909 the fabulous animals disappear and the humorous devil appears; in 1915 the devil is apparently first represented in the character of a particular person. — Suggested by M. K. Brown.

11. *New York Times*, July 24, 1915.

12. Suggested by J. C. Coburn.

13. The extent to which social conditions can be reconstructed through the illustration is specially evident in the works of J. Grand-Carteret, *Les Mœurs et la Caricature en Allemagne en Autriche en Swisse* (Paris, 1885); *Les Mœurs et la Caricature en France* (Paris, 1888). It must be noted, however, that illustration tends naturally to humor and caricature, and that it is often more difficult to find material for a reconstruction of simple, normal life. — See also G. Paston, "The Illustrated Magazine of the Georgian Period," *Side-Lights on the Georgian Period* (London, 1902), 57–75.

14. A special make of shoes is advertised through an illustration of a man wearing them and sitting in an automobile.

15. Suggested by G. L. Price.

16. It was estimated that early in September 1914 the *Petit Parisien* was printing advertisements to the amount of $4000 per week that were used by families separated by the war to get into communication with each other. Cable from Paris to *New York Times*, September 25, 1914.

Many advertisements for news of relatives lost in the war appeared in American papers.

17. "Present Arms! Our soft cuff shirts fit them all," "Health and Safety at Mountain Lakes," "Sever relations with inefficient accounting," — the list could be indefinitely extended.

18. *New York Tribune*, November 10, 1918.

19. *New York Times*, October 29, 1918.

20. Recent birth announcements have included much information in regard to the ancestry of the child and the distinguished public services these ancestors rendered.

21. *Philadelphia Public Ledger*, November 1916.

22. Suggestive articles on advertising of an earlier day are found in H. Friedenwald, "Some Newspaper Advertisements of the Eighteenth Century," American Jewish Historical Society, *Publications* 6 (1897): 49–59; W. P. Trent, "Gleanings from an Old Southern Newspaper," *Atlantic Monthly*, September 1900, 356–64; A. B. Slauson, "Curious Customs of the Past as Gleaned from Early Issues of the Newspapers in the District of Columbia," *Records of the Columbia Historical Society* 9 (1906): 88–125.

23. "The Country Newspaper," *Harper's Magazine*, May 1916, 887–91.

See also E. A. Start, "The Country Newspaper," *New England Magazine*, November 1889, 329–35; C. M. Harger, "The Country Editor of To-day," *Atlantic Monthly*, January 1907, 89–96.

24. Suggested by M. H. Besser.

25. Hugh Chisholm, "The German Press," *Encyclopaedia Britannica*, 19:579.

26. Lawrence Lewis, *The Advertisements of the Spectator*; "The 'Spectator' as an Advertising Medium," *Atlantic Monthly*, May 1909, 605–15.

27. James Bonwich, *Early Struggles of the Australian Press* (London, 1890).

28. Léon van der Essen, *The Invasion and the War in Belgium from Liège to the Yser, with a Sketch of the Diplomatic Negotiations Preceding the Conflict* (London, 1917), 351.

29. Don Carlos Seitz, *Paul Jones: His Exploits in English Seas During 1778–1780* (New York, 1917).

30. *New York Tribune*, October 24, 1917.

31. An interesting advertisement illustrating this was that of thirty New York City Chinese restaurants that combined on a page advertisement in the city press, May 3, 1921.

On the College Professor

1. The article here quoted is "The Use of Print in the World of Affairs," by John Cotton Dana, librarian Free Public Library, Newark, N.J., December, 1910, 535–38.

Democracy in the Household

1. J. T. Dye, *Ideals of Democracy; Conversations in a Smoking Car* (Indianapolis, 1908), 77.

2. *Quarterly Review*, January 1878.

Monarchy and Democracy in Education

1. The only important exception to this statement is the University of Virginia. The feeling of college faculties evoked by its change from democratic to monarchical organization is probably expressed by a contemporaneous editorial. "The thirteenth of June is to be an important date in the history of the American college. On that day the democratic system of government by the entire body of professors, which has marked out the University of Virginia from almost all other institutions of learning in the country, is to come to an end. This system, in spite of all that can properly be said on the other side, has good features which it is a pity to see extinguished." — *Nation*, June 11, 1903.

It is evidently the college president who speaks in an editorial some weeks later in the same publication. "We believe that the president should be something of an autocrat in his proper domain and that faculty government would be bad government." — *Nation*, Sept. 24, 1903.

2. J. McKeen Cattell, *University Control* (New York and Garrison, N.Y., 1913).

3. *The Schoolmaster's Year Book*, 1904, 4.

4. Charles W. Eliot, "The University President in the American Commonwealth," *Educational Review*, December 1911.

Research for Women

1. Francis Parkman, "The Woman Question Again," *North American Review*, January 1880, 16–30.
2. Louis I. Dublin, "Home-making and Careers," *Atlantic Monthly*, September 1926, 335–43.
3. Callie Hull, com., "Funds Available in 1920 in the United States of America for the Encouragement of Scientific Research," *Bulletin of the National Research Council* 2 (March 1921): 1–81.
4. R. J. Usher, "Some Needs in Reference Work," *Library Journal*, September 15, 1926.
5. Bulletin no. 50, 1926.
6. Summary of the Bulletin under the title "Kettles and Shiners," *Survey* 66 (September 15, 1926): 637.

Many Claimants for an Honor — in America

1. Somewhat in the nature of an introduction to the work is an elaborate article by the editor under the title, "The Records of the Federal Convention," *American Historical Review*, 13 (October 1907): 44–65. The "Introduction" prefixed to volume 1 is apparently an epitome of the earlier article.
"Unless some inconsiderate person unearths some new scrap of authentic material, these volumes will remain the complete and be the definitive edition of the Convention's Records." — A. C. McLaughlin, *American Historical Review*, 16 (July 1911): 829.
The "inconsiderate person" was quickly in evidence. Gaillard Hunt describes two papers acquired by the Library of Congress, subsequent to the publication of the *Records*. They were a part of Madison's notes but had become separated from the body of his material and had passed to the auction room. They concerned the work of George Mason in the Convention, especially his views concerning the method of electing members of the upper house. — G. Hunt in *The Nation*, August 24, 1911, 162–63.
The discovery is cited as an encouraging indication that hope of finding additional material on the history of the Federal Convention need not yet be abandoned, though not as encouraging the hope that any new material will modify the conclusions reached by Mr. Farrand.
2. Other important works must be noted, especially that of W. M. Meigs. In *The Growth of the Constitution in the Federal Convention of 1787* (Philadelphia, 1900), he considers seriatim the discussion of every article, section, and clause as it passed through the Convention.
3. Why anyone should wish the office "of so short duration, and merely honorary" Mason at least did not understand; so he wrote prior to the Convention, but he adds that it is "*possibly* introductory to something more substantial." What this was seems evident from J. Q. Adams's *Memoirs*. When Adams began editing the papers of the Convention, he asked Jackson if he could explain their disorderly condition. Jackson apparently had no interest in the matter, though stating that he had taken extensive minutes of the debates but had promised Washington that they should not be published during his own life, "which he supposed had been a loss to him of many thousand dollars." — For the correspondence see Max Farrand, *The Records of the Federal Convention of 1787*, 3 vols. (New Haven, 1911), 3:24, 426.
4. An original copy of *The Debates and Proceedings of the Constitutional Convention of the*

State of New York Assembled at Poughkeepsie on 17th June, 1788, is in the Adriance Memorial Library, Poughkeepsie, New York, and a facsimile reprint was issued by Vassar Brothers Institute in 1905. From this it does not appear that Yates took part in the debates in the State Convention, but he consistently voted against ratification by New York. His colleague, John Lansing Jr., who also withdrew from the Philadelphia Convention, frequently took part in the State Convention and also voted against ratification.

5. E. G. Bourne, "The Use of History Made by the Framers of the Constitution," *Annual Report of the American Historical Association for the Year 1896*, 1:221–30.

Subsequent citations on Madison's library are from the same source.

Bibliography

The Lucy Maynard Salmon Papers at Vassar College

The Lucy Maynard Salmon Papers, comprising about 26 cubic feet or 48 linear feet of material, were given to Vassar College several years after the death of Lucy Salmon in 1927. They were originally arranged by Salmon's housemate and longtime friend, Adelaide Underhill, a librarian at Vassar, and are housed in the Department of Special Collections at Vassar College Libraries.

The collection ranges from 1818 to 1940, bulking between 1887 and 1927, the years that Lucy Salmon served on the history faculty at Vassar. A smaller collection of papers belonging to her mother, Maria Clara Maynard Salmon, are incorporated and account for the material from 1818 to 1861.

Types of materials found in this collection include Lucy Salmon's correspondence from and to family members, Vassar faculty, students, administration, and alumnae, as well as her friends and colleagues in the world at large; published and unpublished manuscripts; diaries and notebooks; photographs and daguerreotypes; genealogical material; clippings; and pamphlets, periodicals, and other printed matter. Maria Salmon's papers include correspondence, unpublished manuscripts, diaries and notebooks, and daguerreotypes.

Subjects included in the collection reflect Salmon's many interests: development of the history department at Vassar College; methods of teaching history and use of original source materials in students' research; establishment of standards for college entrance exams; the woman's suffrage movement; domestic service; civil service reform; civic welfare; and Salmon's involvement in various associations such as the Association of History Teachers of the Middle States and Maryland; Association of College and Preparatory Schools of the Middle States and Maryland; Association of Collegiate Alumnae; and the American Historical Association's Committee of Seven.

Books

Domestic Service. New York: Macmillan, 1897. 2d ed., with an additional chapter on domestic service in Europe. New York: Macmillan, 1901.
Historical Material. New York: Oxford University Press, 1933.
The Newspaper and Authority. New York: Oxford University Press, 1923. Reprint, New York: Octagon Books, 1976.
The Newspaper and the Historian. New York: Oxford University Press, 1923. Reprint, New York: Octagon Books, 1976.
Our Guests: Mary Ann and Her Predecessors. [Boston]: Privately printed, 1929.
Progress in the Household. Boston: Houghton Mifflin, 1906.
Why Is History Rewritten? New York: Oxford University Press, 1929.

Pamphlets

Attic Treasures. Poughkeepsie, N.Y.: Vassar College History Department, 1923. Reprinted in part from "What Is a College For?" *Vassar Quarterly* 5 (1920): 197.
Children's Books. Poughkeepsie, N.Y.: Vassar College History Department, 1925.
Dogs in Literature: A Collection for Vassar College Library. N.p., [1923].
The Dutch West India Company on the Hudson. Poughkeepsie, N.Y., 1915. Also in *Historical Material*. New York: Oxford University Press, 1933.
Ephemeral Material. Poughkeepsie, N.Y.: Vassar College History Department, 1923.
The Family Cook Book. Poughkeepsie, N.Y.: Vassar College History Department, 1923.
First Editions. Poughkeepsie, N.Y.: Vassar College History Department, 1923.
History in a Back Yard. Poughkeepsie, N.Y., 1912. Reprinted in *Historical Material*. New York: Oxford University Press, 1933.
Is This Vassar College? Poughkeepsie, N.Y., 1915.
The Justice Collection of Material Relating to the Periodical Press in Vassar College Library. Poughkeepsie, N.Y., 1925.
The Justice Collection of Works on the Periodical Press. Poughkeepsie, N.Y.: Vassar College History Department, 1924.
A List of References Bearing on the Restoration of Colonial Buildings in the Hudson Valley. Edited by Lucy M. Salmon from references compiled by Mary L. Berkemeier. Poughkeepsie, N.Y., 1913.
Main Street. Poughkeepsie, N.Y., 1915. Reprinted in *Historical Material*. New York: Oxford University Press, 1933.
Patronage in the Public Schools. Massachusetts Civil Service Reform Association, Women's Auxiliary Document no. 8. Boston: Women's Auxiliary of the Massachusetts Civil Service Reform Association, 1908.
The Relation of College Women to Domestic Science. Read Before the Western Association of Collegiate Alumnae, 9 December 1887, at Ann Arbor, Michigan. Portions reprinted in *Progress in the Household*. Boston: Houghton Mifflin, 1906.
The Ulster County Gazette, January 4, 1800. Poughkeepsie, N.Y.: Vassar College History Department, 1922. Rev. ed., [Poughkeepsie, N.Y.]: Vassar College History Department, 1924.
What Is Modern History? Poughkeepsie, N.Y., 1917. Reprinted in *Historical Material*. New York: Oxford University Press, 1933.

Articles and Book Reviews

"Address." *The College Evening of the Thirty-eighth Annual Convention of the National American Woman Suffrage Association* 1906: 8–10. Also in *Woman's Journal* 37 (1906): 33.

"Alcohol and Its Effects: Further Suggestion for a Fund to Acquire Information." (*New York*) *Evening Post*, September 23, 1908.

"American Education from the English Point of View." *Poughkeepsie Evening Star*, April 10, 1895, woman's ed.

"Assessing the Blame for the World War — A Symposium: Vassar College." [Comment.] *Current History* 20 (1924): 458.

"At a French University." (*New York*) *Evening Post*, October 14, 1899.

"The Bok Peace Plan." *Vassar Quarterly* 9 (1924): 116–17.

"The Causes of Household Troubles." *Outlook* 78 (1904): 297–99. Portions reprinted in *Progress in the Household*. Boston: Houghton Mifflin, 1906.

"Censorship in the United States." *Encyclopaedia Britannica*. 13th ed. 1926. Supplement, vol. 1: 562–63.

"Civil-Service Reform Principles in Education." *Educational Review* 25 (1903): 348–55. Also in *School Conditions: With and Without the Competitive System of Examinations*. Baltimore: Women's Auxiliary of the Maryland Civil Service Reform Association, 1903. Also in *Proceedings at the National Civil-Service Reform League* (1902): 128–35.

"The College Commencement." *Educational Review* 9 (1895): 427–47.

"The College Entrance Requirement in History: Discussion." *Monthly Report of the Schoolmasters' Association of New York and Vicinity* 14 (1907): 62–63.

"College Government." *Vassar Miscellany* 24 (1895): 149–60.

"The College Graduate in Fiction." *Vassarion* [Vassar College yearbook] 1905: 91–96.

"College Honors." *Educational Review* 13 (1897): 370–78.

"The College Library." *Libraries: A Monthly Review of Library Matters and Methods* 31 (1926): 322–25.

"The Curriculum." *Journal of the American Association of University Women* 15 (1922): 90–92.

"Democracy in the Household." *Sagamore Sociological Conference* 1911: 7–10. Later expanded and published in *American Journal of Sociology* 17 (1912): 437–57.

"The Development of the Newspaper." *Vassar Quarterly* 5 (1920): 244–52.

"Different Methods of Admission to College." *Educational Review* 6 (1893): 223–41.

"Discussion of Professor H. Morse Stephens' Paper, 'Shall Historical Studies Be a Necessary Part of College Entrance Requirements?' " *Proceedings of the Tenth Annual Convention of the Association of Colleges and Preparatory Schools of the Middle States and Maryland* 1896: 43–48. Also in *Journal of Pedagogy* 10 (1896): 19–22.

"Discussion of 'Some Aspects of the Influence of Social Problems and Ideas upon the Study and Writing of History.' " *Papers and Proceedings [of the] Seventh Annual Meeting [of the] American Sociological Society* 7 (1913): 109–11.

"Does the College Curriculum Promote Scholarship?" *Addresses and Proceedings of the National Education Association* 60 (1922): 737–45.

"Domestic Service." *Chatauquan* 27 (1898): 191–93, 308–10. Later expanded and published as "Economics and Ethics in Domestic Service" in *Progress in the Household* (Boston, 1906).

"Domestic Service and the World War." (*Philadelphia*) *Public Ledger*, October 15, 1916.

"Domestic Service from the Standpoint of the Employee." *Cosmopolitan* 15 (1893): 346–53.

"The Economics of Spending." *Publications of the Association of Collegiate Alumnae*, 3d ser., no. 18 (1908): 85–95. Reprinted in *Outlook* 91 (1909): 884–90.

"Education in Michigan During the Territorial Period." *Education: An International Magazine* 5 (1884): 12–33. Also published with *Federal Land Grants for Internal Improvements in Michigan*, by A. N. Bliss. Lansing, Mich.: W. S. George, 1885. Reprinted in *Pioneer Collections: Report of the Pioneer Society of the State of Michigan*, vol. 7. Lansing: Thorp and Godfrey, 1886.

"Education in the Household." *Journal of Industrial Education* 8 (1894): 5–10. Also in *New England Magazine: An Illustrated Monthly*, n. s., 11 (1894): 185–88. Portions published in *Progress in the Household*. Boston: Houghton Mifflin, 1906.

"The Election at Versailles." *American Monthly Review of Reviews* 19 (1899): 427–31.

"The Encroachments of the Secondary Schools on the College Curriculum." *Proceedings of the Twentieth Annual Convention of the Association of Colleges and Preparatory Schools of the Middle States and Maryland* 1906: 56–63.

"Entrance Examinations for Admission to College." [Discussion.] *Academy: A Journal of Secondary Education* 3 (1888): 252–53.

"The Environment of Vassar College: History." *Vassar Miscellany* 36 (1907): 385–90.

"Errors Creep into Print to Bother the Researchers." *New York Times*, May 16, 1926, sec. 9.

"The Evolution of the Teacher." *History Teacher's Magazine* 3 (1912): 23–25.

"Examinations, in Theory and Practice." *Library Journal* 30 (1905): 15–18.

"The Family Cook-book." *Vassar Quarterly* 11 (1926): 101–11.

"Fellowships." *Inlander* 3 (1893): 245–49.

"Fellowships." *Michigan Alumnus* 10 (1904): 389–92.

"Fulton Female Seminary, November 1836–January 1842." In *History and Reunion of Falley Seminary*. Fulton, N.Y.: Morrill Brothers, 1890.

"The Garden City Cheap Cottages Exhibition." *Craftsman* 9 (1905): 166–79.

"Going to College." *Vassar Miscellany*, September 25, 1914.

"The Historical Museum." *Educational Review* 41 (1911): 144–60.

"History in Elementary Schools." *Educational Review* 1 (1891): 438–52.

"History in the German Gymnasia." *Annual Report of the American Historical Association* 1897: 73–89. Reprinted in *Annual Report of the American Historical Association* 1898: 519–32. Reprinted in *Educational Review* 15 (1898): 167–82. Reprinted in *The Study of History in Schools: Report to the American Historical Association by the Committee of Seven*. New York: Macmillan, 1899.

"History of the Appointing Power of the President." *Papers of the American Historical Association* 1 (1885): 291–419. Reprint, New York: G. P. Putnam's Sons, 1886.

"How Should the Entrance Examination Paper in History Be Constructed?" *Proceedings of the Sixteenth Annual Convention of the Association of Colleges and Preparatory Schools of the Middle States and Maryland* 1902: 101–21. Reprinted in *Educational Review* 26 (1903): 22–35.

"The Impractical College Girl Speaks." *Vassar Quarterly* 1 (1916): 194–96.

"Instruction in the Use of a College Library." *Bulletin of the American Library Association* 7 (1913): 301–9. Also in *Papers and Proceedings of the Thirty-fifth Annual Meeting of the American Library Association* 1913: 301–9.

"The Justice Collection of Material Relating to the Periodical Press." *Special Libraries* 16 (1925): 310–15.

"A List of Some American Libraries Containing Special Collections of Historical Material Serviceable to Teachers of History." Prepared by L. M. Salmon and Adelaide Underhill. In *A History Syllabus for Secondary Schools*. Boston: Heath, 1904.

"Lydia Booth." *Vassar Miscellany* 25 (1896): 156–60.

"Mary Pemberton Nourse Research Fund." [*Vassar College*] *1944 Class Register: A Quarterly Bulletin* 2 (1917): 1–2.

"The Middle States Convention of History Teachers." *Nation* 78 (1904): 227–28. Also in (*New York*) *Evening Post*, March 26, 1904.

"Monarchy and Democracy in Education." *Unpopular Review* 2 (1914): 356–71.

"Mrs. Richards and Our Debt to Her." *Journal of Home Economics* 7 (1915): 27–28. Also as foreword to the *Report of the Household Aid Company of a Two Years' Experiment in Social Economics, Boston, 1903–5*. [Baltimore: American Home Economics Association, Ellen Richards Memorial Fund Committee], 1915.

"A Museum of Vassar College." *Vassar Miscellany* 41 (1911): 43–46.

" 'My Motto Is Progress.' " *Vassar Quarterly* 6 (1921): 266–70.

"The New American History." *New York State Teacher* 2 (1904): 31–32. Reprinted in *New York State Teacher* 2 (1905): 49–50.

"New Ties with Greece." *Vassar Quarterly* 10 (1925): 96–97.

"The Newspaper and Research." *American Journal of Sociology* 32 (1926): 217–26.

"The Next College President." By a Near-Professor. *Popular Science Monthly* 83 (1913): 265–85.

"On a Certain Indefiniteness in History." *Eighth Annual Convention of the Association of History Teachers of the Middle States and Maryland* 1910: 6–12.

"On Beds and Bedding." *Good Housekeeping* 52 (1911): 781–82.

"On Economy." *Good Housekeeping* 52 (1911): 98–101, 251–53.

"On the College Professor." *Library Journal* 36 (1911): 51–54.

"One of the Woman Questions: An Attempt to Solve the Problem of Domestic Service in an Industrial School for Girls." (*Indianapolis*) *Journal*, April 10, 1887.

"The Opportunities for Vassar Graduates in History." *Vassar Miscellany* 42 (1913): 375–77.

"Our American Cities: Opinions and Piquant Points on American Politics and People." *McGregor* (*Iowa*) *News*, March 2, 1887.

"Our Correspondents: [Schedules for Statistics of Domestic Service]." *Good Housekeeping* 10 (1889): 88–89.

"Philosophy, Art, and Sense for the Kitchen." *Craftsman* 10 (1906): 811–17. Later published as "Our Kitchen" in *Progress in the Household*. Boston: Houghton Mifflin, 1906.

"A Pilgrimage to Boston." *Club Worker* 11 (1910): 65–66.

"Place-names and Personal Names as Records of History." *American Speech* 2 (1927): 228–32.

"Points of View." *Vassar Miscellany* 22 (1893): 439–41.

"Points of View: 'Women in European Universities.' " *Vassar Miscellany* 24 (1895): 174. Review of an article in *Educational Review* (Dec. 1894), by Louis Frank, "University Opportunities for Women."

"Political Parties: Their Uses and Abuses." *Vassar Miscellany* 18 (1888): 29–42.

"Progress in Education at Vassar College." *Vassar Quarterly* 5 (1919): 1–10.

[Question on Historical Syllabus in Elementary Schools.] 2 vols. Washington, D.C.: *Annual Report of the American Historical Association for the Year 1906*, 1908, 1:101.

"Quizzing Our Sea-Goers." (*New York*) *Evening Post*, June 1, 1908.

"Quotation from a Paper of Miss Salmon's, 'Some Principles in the Teaching of History.' " *Journal of Geography*, September 1902.

"Recent Progress in the Study of Domestic Service." *Atlantic Monthly* 96 (1905): 628–35. Reprinted in *Progress in the Household*. Boston: Houghton Mifflin, 1906.

"Reflections of a Prospective Pensioner." By a Near Pensioner. *School and Society* 9 (1919): 429–36.

[Remarks on Study and Teaching of History.] 2 vols. Washington, D.C.: *Annual Report of the American Historical Association for the Year 1908*, 1909, 1:78–80. Reprinted in *Proceedings of the Conference on History in Secondary Schools* (1910): 78–80.

"Remember the Library." *Vassar Quarterly* 8 (1922): 55.

"Report of the Conference on the First Year of College Work in History: IV. Use of

Sources." 2 vols. Washington, D.C.: *Annual Report of the American Historical Association for the Year 1905*, 1906, 1:154–58.

"Research for Women." *Vassar Quarterly* 12 (1926): 1–15.

Review of *The Civil Service and the Patronage*, by Carl Russell Fish. *American Historical Review* 11 (1905): 172–74.

Review of *The Dawn of Italian Independence*, by William Roscoe Thayer. *Vassar Miscellany* 22 (1893): 403–8.

Review of *The Good Neighbor*, by Mary E. Richmond. *Vassar Miscellany* 37 (1908): 328–29.

Review of *History of Mississippi*, by Dunbar Rowland. *Saturday Review* 3 (1926): 104.

Review of *"The Holy Experiment," a Message to the World from Pennsylvania*, by Violet Oakley. *Vassar Quarterly* 8 (1923): 101–3.

Review of *John Wyclif*, by Lewis Sergeant. *Vassar Miscellany* 22 (1893): 350–51.

Review of *Life and Letters of Dean Stanley*, by Roland E. Prothero. *Vassar Miscellany* 24 (1895): 235–40.

Review of *The Nature and Elements of Poetry*, by Edmund Clarence Steadman. *Vassar Miscellany* 22 (1892): 160–62.

Review of *Ninth Annual Report of the Bureau of Labor and Industrial Statistics*, by Henry A. Robinson. *Quarterly Publications of the American Statistical Association*, n.s., no. 20 (1892): 235–38.

Review of *Principles of Journalism*, by Casper S. Yost. *Political Science Quarterly* 39 (1924): 719.

Review of *Social Forces in American History*, by A. M. Simons. *American Journal of Sociology* 17 (1912): 687–88.

Review of *Studies in the Teaching of History*, by M. W. Keatinge. *American Historical Review* 15 (1910): 924–25.

Review of *William the Silent, Prince of Orange: The Moderate Man of the Sixteenth Century*, by Ruth Putnam. *American Historical Review* 1 (1896): 329–31.

Review of *Women in Industry: A Study in American Economic History*, by Edith Abbott. *American Journal of Sociology* 15 (1910): 698–702.

Review of *Women's Wages*, by William Smart. *Journal of Political Economy* 1 (1893): 608–10.

"Sairy [*sic*] Gamp and Dora Copperfield." *Boston Cooking-School Magazine* 3 (1898): 1–3. Reprinted in *Progress in the Household*. Boston: Houghton Mifflin, 1906.

" 'Servant,' 'Menial,' 'Drudgery' Are Words to Be Tabooed." (*Philadelphia*) *Public Ledger*, October 15, 1916.

"Some Aspects of Education in England." *Educational Review* 31 (1906): 67–91.

"Some Historical Aspects of Domestic Service." *New England Magazine: An Illustrated Monthly*, n.s., 8 (1893): 175–84.

"Some Political Principles Applied to Education." *Educational Review* 11 (1896): 220–32.

"Some Principles in the Teaching of History." *First Yearbook of the National Society for the Scientific Study of Education* 1902: pt. 1, 11–61. Reprinted in *Publications of the National Society for the Scientific Study of Education, 1902–1906*. Chicago: University of Chicago Press, 1908.

"The Sources of Robinson's *History of Western Europe*: A Suggestive Explanation of the Accompanying Chart." *Text-Book Bulletin for Schools and Colleges* 4 (1904): 1–4.

"A Statistical Inquiry Concerning Domestic Service." *Publications of the American Statistical Association* 3 (1892): 89–119.

"Study of History Below the Secondary School." *Annual Report of the American Historical Association* 1898: 511–18. Reprinted in *The Study of History in Schools: Report to the American Historical Association by the Committee of Seven*. New York: Macmillan, 1899.

"The Study of History in Schools, Being the Report to the American Historical Association by the Committee of Seven." *Annual Report of the American Historical Association* 1898: 427–98. Later published separately. New York: Macmillan, 1899.

"Syllabus for the Study of the History of Civil Service Reform." *Club Woman* 10 (1903): 170–75. Also published separately by the Massachusetts State Federation of Women's Clubs, 1903.

"The Teaching of History in Academies and Colleges." *Academy: A Journal of Secondary Education* 5 (1890): 283–92. Also in *Proceedings of [the] Convocation of [the] University of the State of New York*, 1890. Reprinted in *Woman and the Higher Education*. New York: Harper and Brothers, 1893.

"Training Teachers in France." *Educational Review* 20 (1900): 383–404.

"Types of State Education." *New England Magazine: An Illustrated Monthly*, n.s., 15 (1897): 601–8.

"The Union of Utrecht." *Annual Report of the American Historical Association* 1893: 137–48. Reprint, Washington, D.C.: Government Printing Office, 1894.

"Unity in College Entrance History." *Educational Review* 12 (1896): 151–68.

"Unity of Standard for College Entrance Examinations." *Academy: A Journal of Secondary Education* 3 (1888): 222–31.

"The University of Michigan." *Vassar Miscellany* 21 (1892): 242–49.

"The University of Michigan at Vassar College." *Michigan Alumnus* 20 (1913): 140–41.

"The Vacation Conferences: American Historical Association." *Vassar Miscellany* 38 (1909): 207–8.

"Vacation Reading." *Public Libraries* 19 (1914): 233–38.

"Vassar College Introductory Course in History." *History Teacher's Magazine* 1 (1910): 145–48.

"What Can Be Done to Stimulate Interest in History?" [Discussion.] *Report of the Fifth Annual Convention of the Association of History Teachers of the Middle States and Maryland* 1907: 38–39.

" 'What Influence in College Life Has Proved of Most Force in My Later Life?' Opinions of Michigan Alumni." *Michigan Alumnus* 8 (1902): 408–9.

"What Is a College For?" *Vassar Quarterly* 5 (1920): 196–97. Reprint, Poughkeepsie, N.Y.: Vassar College History Department, n.d.

"What Is Patriotism?" *Teachers College Bulletin*, no. 8 (1896): 9–16.

"Why Is History Rewritten?" *North American Review* 195 (1912): 225–37.

"The Woman's Exchange: Charity or Business." *Forum* 13 (1892): 394–406. Reprinted in *Progress in the Household*. Boston: Houghton Mifflin, 1906.

"Woodrow Wilson: The President's Policies Analyzed in the Light of His Natural Inhibitions and His Past Record." By a Neutral. *Nation* 103 (1916): 256–58.

"The Work of the Association." *Report of the Second Annual Convention of the Association of History Teachers of the Middle States and Maryland* 1904: 3–10.

Syllabi

Suggestions for the Year's Study: History 1. [Poughkeepsie, N.Y.]: Vassar College, 1905. 4th ed., rev. Poughkeepsie, N.Y., 1913.

Suggestions for the Year's Study: History 1–2. 5th ed., rev. Poughkeepsie, N.Y.: Vassar College, 1921.

Suggestions for the Year's Study: History A, AA. [Poughkeepsie, N.Y.]: Vassar College, 1905. 3d ed., rev. Poughkeepsie, N.Y., 1912.

Suggestions for the Year's Study: History D. 2d ed., rev. Poughkeepsie, N.Y.: Vassar College, 1913.

Suggestions for the Year's Study: History D, DD. [Poughkeepsie, N.Y.]: Vassar College, 1908.

Suggestions for the Year's Study: History R, S., Pt. 1. [Poughkeepsie, N.Y.]: Vassar College, 1905.

Suggestive Lists for Reading in History. 2d ed., rev. and enl. Poughkeepsie, N.Y.: Vassar College History Department, 1913.

Suggestive Lists for Summer Reading in History. [Poughkeepsie, N.Y.]: Vassar College History Department, 1905.

Letters to the Editor

No attempt was made to gather all of Salmon's letters to editors, especially those that she did not sign or signed with a pen name.

"Autobiography and History." *Nation* 94 (1912): 183.

" 'Back to the Home' in Aid of Housewives." *(Philadelphia) Public Ledger*, November 12, 1916.

"Certain Hindrances to Progress." *School and College* 1 (1892): 180–81.

"Coeducation Again." *Nation* 46 (1888): 116.

"Coeducation at Chicago." *(New York) Evening Post*, July 18, 1902.

"The Common Law." *Vassar Miscellany Weekly*, December 15, 1916.

"Cruelty to Women." *(New York) Evening Post*, May 10, 1913.

"An Early Plea." *Vassar Quarterly* 9 (1924): 116.

"English and American Examinations." *New York Times*, September 8, 1919.

"Forgotten Plan." *(New York) Evening Post*, March 17, 1919.

"Historical Museum Needed: Record of a Nation's Growth Should Be Preserved for All to See as Well as Read." *New York Times*, June 6, 1926, sec. 8.

"History in the Cook-book." *New York Times*, April 12, 1926.

"Our Greatest Historian." *New York Times*, March 7, 1926, sec. 8.

"Property in Letters." *Nation* 75 (1902): 206.

"Reading on Ocean Liners." *(New York) Evening Post*, August 5, 1911.

"To the Class of 1905." [Vassar College] *Class of 1905 Bulletin* 1 (1915): 1.

"Women and Their Work: Coeducation at the University of Chicago." *(New York) Evening Post*, March 26, 1902.

Index

Acknowledgments

This collaboration is the happy fruit of scholarly happenstance.

Bonnie G. Smith began research Lucy Maynard Salmon early in the 1980s while her son Patrick was a student at Vassar College. She thanks the Vassar College History Department for inviting her to speak on Salmon at the conference in honor of Evalyn Clark in 1985, where the presence of such towering figures as Beatrice Berle and Caroline Ware further whetted her appetite for understanding Miss Salmon. She belatedly thanks Daniel Sherman for sharing his historical expertise on many occasions and for arranging an introduction to the late J. B. Ross, another of Salmon's students and a distinguished historian.

Nicholas Adams discovered Salmon after he came to teach at Vassar College in 1988 when he overheard the occupant of the Lucy Maynard Salmon Chair, Clyde Griffin, talk about this extraordinary Vassar professor. Visits to the library unearthed her many books and resulted in an editorial about Salmon for the *Journal of the Society of Architectural Historians*. While working on the editorial he met Bonnie Smith, whose lecture on Salmon at Vassar College in 1985 stirred in the memory of his partner, Laurie Nussdorfer. Just as generations of young Vassar historians were directed to "go to the sources," so he was directed to "go to Bonnie Smith."

Both authors wish to thank the president of Vassar College, Frances Fergusson, for generous financial support for this publication and encouragement of the project, and Nancy MacKechnie, curator of special collections in the Vassar College Library, for her bibliographic contribution to this book and for her generous management of the Salmon Collection. Thanks are also due to Gita Nádas, assistant curator of special collections, who cheerfully supplied materials to the authors and oversaw the study room during their many visits. At Vassar College we have benefited from two acute readings. The first, from Vassar College historian Elizabeth A. Daniels, helped us to understand the context of Salmon's experience. The second, from James Merrell, the current distinguished occupant of the Lucy Maynard Salmon Chair in the History Department, gave invaluable comments which we have tried to incorporate.

This book is dedicated to Evalyn Clark and to the late Mildred Campbell, professors of history at Vassar College. Miss Clark graciously encouraged our work and was our link to the world of Lucy Maynard Salmon. When we asked whether we might dedicate this book to her, she asked us also to remember Miss Campbell. "She was the real connection," she said, eyes twinkling, making sure that we clearly understood the source of her knowledge. Our request for permission to dedicate a book to her taught us a lesson in history: so it must have been under Miss Salmon.